Other People's Dilemmas

Other People's Dilemmas.

BOOKS BY THE SAME AUTHOR

Shards

❊

Life in The Raw Lane: Nepal

❊

Loose Cargo

❊

Careening thru Cambodia

❊

Episodes from a Twenty Year Vacation

❊

Höttlland, Part II: A Life after Deaths

❊

Höttlland

Contents

OTHER PEOPLE'S DILEMMAS

Without a doubt, 1979 was a remarkable year; remarkable in the sense that it was during those twelve months that Conor Pearson became involved with five different women. 'Involved', now there's an apt word, basically a euphemism for shared carnal knowledge without the forced unlawful element. But despite having been the common denominator in the equation, Conor was hard pressed to explain just what those five women had seen in him that year. After all, in the opinion of others, not to mention his own, he'd been anything but a ladies' man.

Marla

There were ten of them who came sauntering through the arrivals door that hot July afternoon. Six men and four women, walking in pairs, gazing around with curious and exhausted eyes at the unfamiliar surroundings. But it was Marla who'd caught Conor's attention. Tall, lithesome, with long ash-blonde hair, and clad in a loose-fitting blouse and flowing skirt, she was as close to stunning as Conor had ever seen, moving with the air of practiced aloofness of someone used to having her way, above all with men. In the few seconds it took her to cross the arrival hall of the airport, he envisioned her as some sophisticated socialite attending a gala in a slinky, floor-length, satin gown, seductively posed with a foot long cigarette holder, as a phalanx of servile male admirers flittered around her.

"How many people can you jam into your van?" Conor's work colleague, Susan, had asked several days prior, when the two of them were having coffee in the basement cafeteria of the government office where they worked.

"I've never really counted," he answered. "Eight or nine, I suppose… including me. Why do you want to know?"

"There's a group of exchange students flying in this Saturday and it's my job to make sure they're transported to their billeted accommodations. Rather than renting a fleet of taxis, I thought of you. I should be able to squeak a few dollars loose for your time and gas. Do you think we could fit all ten of them in on one trip?"

"Unless they all happen to be seven feet tall, I think so," Conor told her, turning to accept their bill from the waitress.

Having just spent nine hours stuffed into a crowded plane, the idea of now piling into Conor's van for the "delivery" tour did not go over well with certain members of the group. But despite a round of multi-lingual grumbling, pile in they did, with their substantial private belongings stacked behind the rear seat or on various laps.

Right from the moment Conor pulled out of the airport parking garage, the rear-view mirror provided a series of stolen glances at the mysterious woman who had captivated his attention so easily. Occasionally caught in the act, he was often rewarded in return with a friendly smile. Luck had been with him that day, for as the group slowly whittled down, it was clear that Marla and Olive, a husky, almost muscular woman from Poland, who was Marla's designated partner, would be the last to be dropped off. Even more fateful was the fact that when the van pulled up in front of the address Susan had given him, their accommodation was not ready.

"So what are we gonna do?" Conor asked when Susan had returned to the van with the unexpected news.

"The flat won't be ready until tomorrow," she explained, with an air of exasperation. "I don't know why it isn't ready. They had over a month's notice. A hotel is not in the budget, so we'll have to see if we can put them up at the YWCA for the night," she added, as she flipped through a pile of papers. "I'm really sorry about this 'ladies'," Susan apologized, turning to face the two remaining passengers, both of whom were starting to show the effects of jetlag. "Why don't we go someplace for coffee first, so I can give the 'Y' a call and make sure they have space."

"I'm almost afraid to ask," Conor said, once perfunctory small talk at the cafe had fizzled out and conversation turned to Marla's academic status. "I understand that you're here for a couple of months to see how the Canadian medical system operates. But how does someone become so interested in slime mould... at least enough to want to get a doctor's title?"

"Slime mould is more interesting than most people think," Marla replied, tilting her head and blowing a plume of smoke upwards in a classic "Garboesque" pose.

"Obviously," Conor muttered.

"Really," she told him, cupping her right elbow in her left palm, waving her freshly lit cigarette back and forth as she spoke.

"It's the name given to several kinds of unrelated eukaryotic organisms with a life cycle that includes a free-living single-celled stage and the formation of spores. That's one of the reasons I chose to study it."

"Wow... nobody could ever accuse *you* of not being a scintillating conversationalist."

"I think you are trying to make fun of me," Marla told him. "But I do not mind. Slime mould was only one of my interests. My second doctor's title was in psychology."

"Hang on...you have two Dr. titles?" Conor exclaimed, nearly spilling his coke. "So like, are degrees a dime a dozen in Holland? You said you're from Rotterdam right?"

"I lived there for awhile."

"How can someone manage to have two degrees at your age? When did you start university, at twelve? And why does someone want, or need two Dr. titles?" Conor continued, not waiting for an answer. "Makes for a rather lengthy business card, or?"

"I do not know why you try to mock me," Marla repeated, visibly miffed, as she leaned forward to take a sip of her coffee.

"What is it the English say about 'glass houses? You are not exactly on solid ground when it comes to mocking someone else."

"How so?" Conor replied.

"Your clothes for example. At the airport I thought, 'why are we being picked up a by a hippie dressed like an ice-cream salesman?"

"An ice-cream salesman?" Conor chuckled, a frown forming as he absent-mindedly stroked his beard.

"Long hair, loose shirt and baggy pants... you don't exactly look like a government employee."

"Who said I was?"

"I heard Susan speak about your office, so I assumed you work together."

"But why an ice-cream salesman? Besides, I'm not English."

Mildly irritated by the tone of the discussion, Marla made a point of ignoring Conor's query, and for the remainder of their stay at the cafe, pointedly directed any comments solely to Susan. A short while later, as the pair were being dropped off at the YWCA, Conor attempted to make amends, sensing his flippancy had greatly reduced his chances of getting to know Marla better.

"If you need any help moving to the flat tomorrow, let Susan know," he called out, as Marla and Olive struggled up the walk with their luggage. But Marla was not to be easily swayed, leaving Olive to answer "thank you" before they both disappeared into the building.

But they didn't call the next day and as the week went by, Conor's repeatedly queried Susan as to how the new arrivals were making out.

"I'm not in touch with them on a daily basis, you know," Susan answered sharply. "My job was to see they got settled, and be there in case they run into any problems. Why are you so interested anyways?"

"Just curious," Conor lied, discouraged by the fact there seemed to be little opportunity to re-contact Marla, without appearing too obvious. It was only after several weeks of striving to find a way to enter the maze that held Marla at its centre, that Conor came up with the idea of inviting her and Olive out to a friend's cabin at the lake for the weekend. Able to gain Marla's phone number from Susan, he was elated when they agreed. Early on Saturday morning, the two women were waiting curbside in front of their house when Conor pulled up.

"So you're ready to see another part of Canada?" he asked as the two clambered in, Olive taking the empty front seat. Aware that he was on thin ice with Marla, Conor made little attempt to engage her in small talk on the drive, limiting his remarks to factual descriptions of the passing landscape.

"I guess you must be used to flat land like this," he questioned, glancing in the rear-view mirror.

"Our fields are not as big as they are here," was the sum total of Marla's response.

After a round of introductions at the cottage with Sandra, the cabin's owner, it was suggested the foursome take advantage of the ideal weather and spend the afternoon on the main beach. Much like it had been in the van, conversation on the beach was sparse. It was only when Olive and Sandra decided to take a leisurely stroll along the town's omnipresent boardwalk, that Conor seized the chance to engage Marla alone.

"So, I take it you've had time to settle in a bit. What do you think of Canada so far? At least the part you've seen. I meant to ask you at the cafe whether this is the first time you've been here."

"I haven't seen very much of it and it is my first time. I've gone for a walk in the neighbourhood where we're staying but I don't know how representative that is of life in Canada. I tend to prefer small towns to big cities, but I've always thought I could live just about anywhere," Marla said, brushing a fleck of sand from her shoulder.

"Anywhere?"

"I've been in many countries in Europe, and I quickly sense whether I could live somewhere or not," she said, stretching out on the blanket and propping herself up on her elbows. "But I'm not sure about Canada yet," she added with a smile.

"You say you could live anywhere," Conor began. "But you don't strike me as someone who could do without certain amenities."

"What do you mean?" she answered.

"Things like an electrical outlet for a hair dryer or curling iron. Not too many tents in the desert have such necessities."

"You are making fun of me again. I am not like this," Marla told him firmly.

Realizing he had brushed up against another red line, Conor quickly diverted to a more neutral subject.

"Which countries have you travelled to in Europe? Do you have a favourite?"

"I like Austria and Switzerland," she answered. "Probably because they are not as flat as Holland."

"I don't think I could ever live in a place like Switzerland," Conor told her. "Have you ever seen their television programs?"

"I don't judge a place by its television," she said, scrunching up her face.

"You would if you'd seen any of it," Conor retorted.

The conversation remained light for the next hour or so, and it was only when Marla happened to mention her boyfriend that Conor's concentration deepened.

"Martin will arrive at the end of August. We've planned to travel out to the west coast by train to see more of the country."

"How long will you be traveling before you go back to Holland?" Conor asked, half-suspecting that reference to Martin had been made to ward off any wayward intentions.

"About a month," she answered, turning over to lay on her stomach, with her head resting on folded arms, a less than subtle indication she had no desire to continue the conversation.

The subsequent silence ended with the return of Sandra and Olive a short while later.

"So are you two all talked out?" Sandra inquired, having picked up on the somewhat icy atmosphere between them.

"Pretty much," Conor admitted.

"Then what say we all head back to the cottage? I'd like to get an early start on cooking supper."

"Sandra," Olive interrupted. "Do you know if there is a store that sells souvenirs?"

"What sort of souvenirs?" Sandra asked.

"My niece likes collecting fridge magnets and my nephew likes post cards, especially from places they will probably never get to see."

"You should have told me earlier. We walked right past the drugstore. They have things like that. If you like we can stop off there on the way back to the cabin."

"I'm not in the market for any fridge magnets," Marla grumbled into her blanket. "Silly, pointless things if you ask me... but I'll come with you," she added, casting a scowl in Conor's direction as she got up and collected her belongings.

Walking back to the cabin on his own, disheartened by his failure to develop a comfortable rapport with Marla, Conor was at pains to ignore some of the less than admirable traits Marla had displayed during their stay on the beach. That was especially true in comments she'd made about Olive while she was off on the walk with Sandra.

"I have no idea what those responsible for pairing me with her were thinking," she'd hissed. "I mean we have absolutely nothing in common."

But despite her rather tasteless expression of displeasure at having been saddled with Olive as a roommate, Conor still held out hopes of getting to know her better over the course of the weekend. Those hopes, however, were about to suffer a setback, when he arrived back at the cottage to discover they had unexpected company.

Donna

"I hope you don't mind us showing up like this. I know I should have called ahead," Evie, a mutual friend of both Sandra and Conor, apologized, as Sandra unlocked the door and ushered everyone onto the screened veranda. "Unannounced and uninvited," Evie added. "It was just so hot in the city, we just had to get out… This is Donna, by the way."

"Pleased to meet you," the frail looking woman said sheepishly, extending a hand to each member of the group. With Marla and Olive retreating to their room to change out of their bathing suits, Sandra excused herself and headed off to the kitchen to start preparing dinner.

"Let me know if you need any help," Evie called, before turning her attention to Conor. "So what's all this then? Down here with three women? Must be nice," she joked. "I've been dying to meet this woman Sandra said you've been talking so much about lately," she added, handing Conor a bottle of beer from the cooler she'd brought in from her car.

"I haven't been talking so much about her," Conor protested, glancing at Donna. "I don't know what tales Sandra has been spreading. Marla's just an acquaintance."

"Quite a good-looking acquaintance, I would say. Anyway… it seems like you've got yourself quite the little harem this weekend. I guess you won't mind two more though, eh?" she added, looking to Donna and offering a mock toast. "Safety in numbers."

It was just after seven that evening when the group sat down for a communal meal.

"Wine all around?" Donna inquired, holding up an open bottle in expectation.

"Whew... I shouldn't have started with beers," Conor complained. "But what the heck, I'm not driving anywhere tonight, so why not?" he said, nodding towards an empty glass.

As so often happens when people don't know each other, the dinner conversation remained somewhat stilted for the first while. It was only once sufficient wine had been consumed and Marla and Evie discovered their mutual medical interests, that it became more animated. Although his preference would have been to talk to Marla alone, Conor used the new group dynamic to observe her more closely. It was in the midst of one of these observation sessions, that Sandra issued an invitation for Evie and Donna to stay the night.

"You don't want to drive back to the city tonight, especially now that you've been drinking. You're more than welcome to stay... Of course that's if Conor doesn't mind giving up his room, and you two are okay with sharing a bed. Would that be okay with you?" she asked Conor directly. "The living room couch is pretty comfortable."

"Not a problem," Conor answered with a tightened smile, aware he had little choice in the matter.

"That's very generous Sandra," Evie said. "I didn't want to assume we could stay the night. We just wanted to drive out for dinner. But... thank you. I agree that it's best we do stay. I'm already feeling the effects of the wine."

A short time later, as Marla and Olive were helping to clear the table and Donna had excused herself to the outhouse, Evie approached Conor and Sandra in the kitchen.

"There's something I should warn you about," she said, glancing around to make sure no one else was in earshot. "You may have already noticed that Donna likes her drink," she told them. "I mean she *really* likes her drink. Personally, I don't know how she can handle so much alcohol. It's quite disturbing. I've talked with her about it before, but it hasn't helped much. Somebody who drinks as much as she does must have a lot of unresolved issues."

"Why are you telling us this?" Conor asked.

"Just so you know," Evie explained. "She's gotten into some pretty embarrassing situations in the past."

"Such as?" Conor asked.

"I don't want to get into all that. I just don't want her to cause any trouble here. Besides, now that we're going to stay, you may see for yourself. But hopefully she'll behave."

"Oh this is just what I need," Sandra moaned.

"I'm sorry," Evie said. "She's not a bad person and I promise I'll keep an eye on her," Evie added, turning to fill the sink with water and detergent. "Let me do the dishes... you did the cooking. Go and take care of your other guests. I'll get Donna to help me when she comes back."

Despite several nuanced admonishments from Evie during the course of the evening, Donna proceeded to live up her reputation. It was well into the wee hours, long after the others had trundled off to bed, that she and Conor found themselves alone on the back porch. In spite of their respective intake of wine, their conversation up to that point had remained remarkably coherent.

"So how is it that you know Evie?" Conor asked.

"Through work," Donna answered, with a slight slur.

"So you're a nurse too?"

"No."

"I don't understand."

"Evie is the nurse... remember. Anyways, it's not so important," Donna replied, dismissing the issue with a wave of her hand. "If you must know," she corrected seconds later. "I work at a shoe store. Evie came in one day looking for a new pair of shoes and we struck up a conversation."

"And you became friends?"

"Is that so peculiar to you?" Donna asked, somewhat perturbed.

"I know that look," she added. "You're wondering, is Evie so hard up for friends that she befriends a saleswoman in a shoe store?"

"Whoa... wait a minute. I never inferred that," Conor argued, irked by the insinuation. "I was just curious how you know her... that's all."

"Look..." Donna said abruptly. "I don't mind playing the resumé game, but let's get it over with. I'm 34, a single Mom with one daughter, the result of spending a few hours with a Saturday night special. And my work? Well my job may not be Utopian but it pays the bills. It doesn't exactly call for a PhD, but you need to be well informed... and friendly. The customer may be king, but he or she can also sometimes be a royal pain in the butt. The job will have to do until my prince comes along...Satisfied? What can I tell you? Evie and I just hit it off."

"Hey, I didn't mean to pry, I was just..."

"And what is it that *you* do that makes your life so meaningful?" she asked, cutting him off in mid-sentence.

"I write for an internal magazine that I doubt anybody reads."

"Sounds enthralling," Donna asked with a smirk, as she refilled her glass. "So why do you do it?"

"Probably for much the same reason as you. It currently pays the bills while waiting for something better to come along."

After a brief pause, during which time the alcohol continued to loosen her tongue, Donna decided to delve more deeply.

"I'm not particularly proud of where my life is at right now. It seems fraught with dead ends," she told him before pausing to take another sip of wine. "Do you ever wonder where you might have ended up if you'd had a different childhood?" she asked in a tone noticeably less confrontational.

"Different in what sense?" he asked.

"Different parents for example. My parents never really saw me for me," she said with a snort. "They only saw who I wasn't. I think I was a disappointment for them, a specimen far afield from what they'd envisioned. I wasn't the wonder child in a textbook family,"

Donna growled, straightening up and holding her glass in a mock toast. "Actually I shouldn't be saying parents, because my father was virtually never around. He was always on the road and when he did come home, he tried to make up for his absence by bringing gifts. I came to associate his love with a dollar sign."

"Samsonite," Conor said.

"Samsonite? What are you talking about?" Donna asked with a frown.

"Recommended for all excess baggage."

"Smart ass..." Donna sneered. "Are you this flippant in every normal conversation?"

For a moment Conor considered answering, but in the end chose to remain silent.

"You know, normally I don't get off on being ridiculed," Donna told him. "But for some strange reason I like talking with you. It's nice... just the two of us out here. I don't like crowds," she added, shaking off a sudden chill.

"Five people is a crowd?"

"It is for me. It always amazes me how in a one on one, people can come across as intelligent, caring... well spoken. But put them together in a group and they morph into a band of braying donkeys."

"Wow..." Conor replied. "For someone who's downed as much wine as you tonight, you're incredibly articulate. You crush that old theory that 'the more the wine, the more the whine'."

"What do you mean 'as much wine'?" Donna jeered. "What's it to you how much I drink?"

"Well you do seem to enjoy it," Conor replied. "No thanks," he said, placing his hand over his glass as she attempted to top it up. "I plan on waking up alive tomorrow morning. Do you realize we've almost polished off a third bottle?"

"Whatever… Man, what a party pooper," Donna shrugged, filling her own glass to the brim, before setting the bottle back down. "But speaking of waking up… Do you sometimes get up in the morning and think 'what is this?'"

"This?"

"This," she answered, waving an outstretched arm. "This so- called life. I can't tell you how many times I've felt like I've lived most of mine in 3 D."

"Three D?"

"Deluded, Deranged or Depressed."

"Yow… Now who's being the party pooper."

"But it's true."

"Maybe so…But who wants to live like that? You need to try and stop being a victim."

"What I *don't* need is simplistic advice like that. You think I have a choice?"

"But there's ways of getting help. You have to have the courage to confront their demons and seek help rather than merely being one of the walking wounded."

"Spare me your… I'm not one of the walking wounded," Donna shot back. "I'm more like a walking wound."

"Have you never *tried* to see anyone?"

"Of course I have," she said dismissively. "But there are so many quacks out there. It's not easy finding someone you feel you can trust and be comfortable with."

"Hey Donna… look, I'm not trying to be flippant, but life is a risky business. Everyone goes through bad phases. I mean the state of the world alone is enough to bring you down. A friend of mine once said, that 'anyone who isn't bitter and cynical by the time they're 50, hasn't been paying attention.'"

"I don't think being bitter and cynical is the same as being depressed. Depressed is when you find yourself at the bottom of a deep, dark well, staring up at the blue sky, convinced you'll never be able to get out."

"But if you haven't been able to find help, how do you deal

with the dark days?" Conor asked.

Donna hesitated, reflecting on the question, prompting Conor to continue. "I don't remember who said this... that depression is the sand that makes the pearl."

"Pffuuiii...that's a laugh. I'm far from being a pearl. There's been times when I've even felt ready to call it a day, but I wouldn't do that to my daughter. Believe me, I've been through the mill, up the creek, around the bend, under the carpet etc., etc. It's only rarely that I've been over the moon."

"Like tonight right?" Conor said jokingly.

"Yeah, you bet sonny boy," Donna answered before taking a healthy gulp from her glass.

"Is that why you drink?" he suddenly asked, his own judgement marred enough to not have him realize the question risked incurring her wrath.

"I don't know if I drink that much more than anyone else. I just don't hide it," she answered, surprisingly calm. "There's numerous reasons. Taking the bitter edge off reality is probably the main one... at least my reality."

"Hey, you guys," a voice suddenly broke in. Conor looked up over his shoulder to see Sandra standing behind the porch screen door. "You guys should hear yourselves... Talk about the blind leading the blind. All of us in the cabin and probably half the street can hear every bloody word you're saying. Nobody's able to sleep with you two yakking at each other, so can you please move this Foolosophy 101 class somewhere else. It's almost 3 o' clock. Either put a zipper on it or shove off somewhere else."

"Sorry about that," Conor mumbled.

Chastened by Sandra's remarks, he was about to call it a night when Donna abruptly suggested they go for a walk.

"That's a great idea," Sandra said. "As far away as possible. Preferably Brazil. Anything to put an end to this non-stop babbling."

"You really wanna go for a walk at this time of night?" Conor asked, once Sandra had closed the door and returned to her room.

"It'll help to wear off a potential hangover," she told him.

"How does that work?"

"It'll get your blood running so the alcohol will pass through your system more quickly."

"Where did you dig up that piece of wisdom?"

"Believe me, I know what works and what doesn't."

"I guess it's worth a try," Conor answered, struggling to pull himself up and still retain his equilibrium.

With the cabin only two blocks from the lake, the pair were at the water's edge within minutes. Neither of them had any intention of going in, so they simply stood there, propping each other up, while staring at the moon's reflection on the rippling waves.

"This is the first time I've been to this place," Donna confided.

"It's so peaceful."

"Yeah, you can't even hear people yakking on the back porch somewhere," Conor said with a smirk. "But really, you've never been here before? The lake is so close to the city."

"I don't have a car and forget about taking the bus. Besides, I couldn't afford to stay in a hotel, and I don't know anyone with a cottage. Anyway, what's the big thrill 'escaping' to the lake when the place is laid out like the grid of a city. All the cabins are so close to each other. I mean what's the sense in that?"

"You do have a point. People rush to get away from all the household chores in the city and come down here every weekend and basically do the same things."

Temporarily marooned under the light of a single streetlamp, they slowly drifted off towards a row of tall hedges that separated the sandy beach from the front yards of lakefront cottages.

"Do you wanna sit down for awhile?" Donna asked, grabbing Conor's hand and pulling him towards the bushes.

"I thought it was walking that was going to help."

"Just for a minute or two," she said playfully.

The next thing he knew, Donna had dropped to the ground pulling him down with her. Dispensing with preliminaries, they were soon tearing at each other's clothes, fortunately out of sight of any other late-night wanderers. In the midst of the hazy, albeit heated passion, it dawned on Conor that Donna likely had no idea which member of the male species she was currently with, and probably didn't really care. At that same instant, having noticed Conor's hesitation, Donna blurted out "If you're having trouble thinking of someone else... make me anyone you want me to be."

With his confidence collapsing, Conor inhaled deeply and rolled over on to his back. Gazing up at the cloudless night sky, he was suddenly engulfed by a wave of sadness. Given the condition of his addled brain, it was impossible to tell whether it was for Donna, himself or both.

"What's the matter?" Donna asked, raising herself up on both elbows.

"I think I drank myself sober," Conor replied.

"So?"

"So, I suddenly feel different. I mean what are we doing here? We're not friggin' rabbits. We barely know each other. Doesn't this seem a little demeaning?"

"Oh God... a late-night lecture on morals. Just what I need," Donna fumed. "Hey look, it's my body. I can do what I want with it, with anyone I choose to."

"It would be nicer to be wanted for who you are rather than what you are," Conor retorted.

"What's that supposed to mean?"

"Like I said, we barely know each other."

"So, I take it we're like the dinosaurs," she told him, struggling to her feet.

"Dinosaurs?" Conor replied.

"We're done," she told him, re-buttoning her blouse and

brushing sand from the seat of her slacks.

"In more ways than one," Conor answered as he joined her in the vertical world.

"What was the point of them anyways?" Donna asked.

"Point of what?"

"The dinosaurs."

"Beats me," he said as they left the beach, maintaining an awkward silence on the way back to the cabin. It was only when they had turned the corner on to their street that the stillness was broken. "What are you doing?" Conor asked, as he watched Donna plugging her nostrils with the nail side of two fingers and humming a deep resonant tone.

"Watch this," she said, resuming the hum. Within seconds, she convulsed into a brief series of sneezes.

"What was that all about," he asked as they continued to walk.

"Haven't you ever noticed that a sneeze is like a nasal orgasm?" she said with a grin. "I take what I can get."

No sooner had she offered this brief explanation, Donna blurted out, "You do know that behind every successful man, there stands a great woman, don't you?"

"*Where is this coming from?*" Conor thought to himself.

"Except for maybe Hitler," he answered, surprised by his own spontaneity. "Who fails on both counts. And Stalin, and Idi Amin and a few thousand others."

Either startled or confused by his response, Donna remained silent for a moment.

"Do you suppose Adolf was really poking Eva?" she suddenly said." I mean he reputedly had only one ball, didn't he? Not that that had anything to do with … Were they even married?"

"Hitler always claimed he was married to Germany. God knows he certainly screwed *her*. Hard to say whether he was doing the same with Eva. If he was, the world can be grateful they didn't produce any offspring. I only know that a few hours after they got married in the Bunker, they committed suicide."

"Saved on a honeymoon that way," Donna chortled.

"Why are we talking about this?" Conor asked, just as they arrived at the sidewalk leading to the cabin, at which point he reached out and gently took hold of Donna's arm. "I hope our little beach-front coupling is going to remain a secret," he said.

"Why are you making such a big deal out of this?" Donna wanted to know. "God, men can be such buffoons. Just so you know, I have no desire to broadcast this from the rooftops."

"I'm just sorry that it happened."

"Why? I'm not. Just let it go. I already have."

Despite the previous night's conviction he had drunk himself sober, the next morning Conor awoke feeling as if Goldfinger's trusted henchman had thrown his steel-rimmed hat across the room, slicing off the top section of his aching head. As a result he passed on breakfast and spent the bulk of the morning on a spinning couch.

"God, Conor... you look terrible," was Sandra's greeting when he dragged himself to the beach several hours later.

"That's seems fitting given that's how I feel," he groaned, plopping down on a blanket beside Olive.

"I don't want to say 'serves you right' but," Sandra added with a grin.

As various members of the group chatted aimlessly amongst themselves over the next hour, Conor watched as Donna did an admirable job of maintaining her nocturnal promise, completely avoiding any conversation or even eye contact with him.

"*Well she's either a great actress or doesn't remember a thing about last night,*" he mused before glancing at Marla, convinced in his sorry state, that she was giving him a look of 'I know what you were up to last night.'

Conor managed to live up to his end of the bargain of keeping the beachfront episode to himself, not only the next day but well beyond. It was only years later, long after the memory of the nighttime escapade had faded, that the truth finally slipped out.

"Conor… you big, dumb nut," Evie told him, after he had sputtered out his 'revelation.' "Your reputation as a chivalrous prince has been in the gutter for years. Donna spilled her guts on all the dirty details the very next morning at breakfast," she added with a laugh. "If there's any truth to the old adage that one day you'll be able to look back on this and laugh, you're going to have a hilarious old age."

Bemused by his own naivety, all Conor could do was smile.

Marla redux

Although discouraged by the lack of opportunities to converse privately with Marla on the weekend, once back in the city Conor's thoughts nevertheless continued to revolve around her. The "lake" invitation, however, had set a precedent, paving the way for a number of subsequent casual visits to the second floor flat where Marla and Olive were housed. As a result of these random visits Conor had slowly begun to sense that beneath the aloofness and 'savoir faire' image' Marla maintained, lay a deep-rooted arrogance. Although his attraction still overrode his better judgement, the accuracy of his growing suspicions were driven home one Saturday afternoon, when he dropped by to find Marla was not at home.

"She's gone shopping for groceries," Olive told him, inviting him into the apartment. "She's been gone an hour so she should be home soon if you want to wait. Would you like something to drink?"

"Water would be fine," Conor told her.

As the two of them settled into the sparsely furnished living room, searching for a comfortable level of discourse, Conor happened to ask how she and Marla were getting along.

"It must be kind of weird sharing a place with someone you hardly know," he said. "Especially given you come from different backgrounds and cultures. At least you both speak English."

"Mine is not so good," Olive admitted. "But we can understand each other... Sometimes I wish we couldn't."

"What do mean?" Conor asked, his curiosity piqued.

"Marla is sometimes... I do not know how you say this in English... snooty?"

"Snooty?... You mean arrogant?"

"Yes."

"Really?" Conor answered, not altogether surprised at the accusation.

"What is it she does?" Conor asked, sensing Olive was eager to unload.

"Oh many things... She criticizes how I dress. She has told me I have no manners. She even makes fun of my accent."

"What do you say in return?" Conor asked.

"I say nothing. I do not want to fight. We are roommates for the next few months."

"She *can* come across as domineering at times, but you have to stand up for yourself," Conor told her. "You know what you could say is she keeps this up?"

"No," Olive answered.

"Ask her if she's not worried about going cross-eyed."

"I don't understand," Olive said.

"It's a way of confronting her arrogance. You'd get cross-eyed from looking down your nose at somebody so much. On second thought, it might just make things worse. Perhaps it's better to just ignore her comments."

With Olive's complaints still ringing in his ears, several days later, Conor placed a call to Marla, ostensibly to arrange to meet. What he had not yet decided, was whether he would bring up the subject of her behaviour towards Olive.

"We do not need to make a date," Marla told him,

brusquely.

"You don't want to get together?"

"No. It is not that. You misunderstand me. I plan to have a small party here at the flat so I can show people how we entertain in Holland," she explained. "Of course you are invited."

"Wow," William gushed, handing back a photo to Conor, as the two of them sat in a booth at a diner. "And you're dating this beauty?"

"I wouldn't exactly call what we've been doing, dating," Conor said. "I've seen her a few times but nothing's happened, so to speak."

"So to speak?"

"You know what I mean. I don't know if I should be..." he said, breaking off his train of thought. "She's only here for three months, so there's nothing long term in the cards. Plus she's mentioned that she has a boyfriend... that's a less than subtle hint."

"Who says it has to be long term?" William replied.

"Nobody... but I'm not really interested in an extended one-night stand either."

"A part of me can understand your reluctance. I mean the way she looks, she's probably a ruthless heartbreaker. But if you both know the ground rules... Why don't you try arranging to be alone with her somewhere? Like for a weekend at that new resort up at Black Island Cove?"

"That's pretty presumptuous don't you think? Inviting her for the weekend... alone."

"The worst that can happen is that she'll say no."

"I suppose it's worth a try," Conor mused.

An hour before Marla's party was set to begin, Olive was standing in the living room, silently observing her roommate meticulously laying out an assortment of smoked meats, cheeses and raw vegetables, taking special care to arrange buns she had discovered at a Dutch bakery.

"You're not coming dressed like that are you?" Marla asked, nudging Olive aside to place some napkins on the table.

"Like what?" asked Olive.

"Like a farm girl."

"But I am a farm girl."

"Yes, I know that," Marla grumbled. "But you don't have to advertise it."

Billed as an afternoon function, it was just past five when Conor arrived, walking into an already crowded living room.

"Hmmmppf..." he said to Susan, after spotting her huddled in one corner of the flat. "Any idea who all these people are?"

"Me? I thought you would know more of them than me. From what I hear you're the one who's become a regular guest."

"I wouldn't call it regular," Conor argued. "But I've never met any of these people before."

"I presume they're colleagues from the clinic where she works," Susan said, stifling a yawn. "Why not just ask?"

"I don't want to bother her. She's too busy immersing herself in the role of hostess."

"And from the looks of it, thoroughly enjoying it," Susan added.

It was well past nine when the last of the guests departed. With Olive in the kitchen starting in on the dishes, Conor made his move, intending to start off with innocuous subjects before easing into his invitation.

"So... are you satisfied?" he asked Marla. "With how the party went," he added, when she appeared not to understand the question.

"People hardly touched any of the food," she complained, gazing at an undisturbed tray of food. And look how much wine is left."

"I wouldn't get too upset. People here aren't used to having a party start in the afternoon, unless it's a barbecue. If it's any consolation, the guests *looked* like they were having a good time. Why don't you leave everything for now. I can help you clean up later. We can sit down and get rid of some of that leftover wine.

You told me your family is from Rotterdam, right?" Conor asked, once the two of them had settled on the couch. "But you studied or are studying in Amsterdam?"

"Why do you want to know such things?" Marla said, with a suspicious look, as she extracted a cigarette from a pack lying on the table. "This is not so interesting."

"I'm just curious. Do you have any brothers or sisters?"

"I don't know why you must know about my family," she told him, waving her hand to keep the smoke from drifting in his direction. "I'm actually not from Rotterdam. I'm from a small village that most people would have never heard of, so I just say Rotterdam. I have two older brothers. I am the only daughter, 'the little princess.' At least that's what my father called me when I came along."

"What does your father do?"

"He works for the Dutch railway," she said. "I suppose one could say our family was quite well off. My brothers and I went to private schools. My parents even sent me to a specialist in Switzerland to have my face 'sanded', when I developed a bad case of acne."

"Your face sanded?" Conor repeated, scrunching his forehead. "The way you say that, I'm not sure if you are bragging or complaining?"

"It was torture. I hated them for that at the time. I didn't know why they put me through that."

"Well it seems to have worked. I would never have guessed you had a bad case of acne. How old were you when you had it done?"

"Fourteen."

"Didn't you have any say in the matter?"

"I told them I didn't want to go but they insisted. They said they didn't want their daughter to grow up with a scarred face. It didn't fit with their idea of a perfect Dutch family."

"And what constitutes a perfect Dutch family?"

"You'd have to ask them. They were a strange lot. My father was often away attending meetings at various clubs and my mother, hmmpphh… when she wasn't busy being the perfect housewife, she was either at her fitness studio or off visiting a beauty salon, desperately trying to hold on to her youth."

"You make it sound like you had a privileged and underprivileged childhood at the same time."

"Privileged but traumatic," Marla replied.

"Traumatic?"

"I have talked too much," she said abruptly, stubbing out her cigarette and reaching for her glass of wine. "We must talk about something else. You now know much about me, but I know little about you, other than that you are a man who seems to have a lot of female friends," she said with a sly grin.

"I don't know if that's true," Conor answered, briefly recalling Marla's insinuating glance on the beach. "Well you know that I work with Susan."

"Yes, of course. But I don't really know what it is you do besides drive people around and invite them to the lake."

"That's not exactly part of my job description, but at least it allowed me to meet you… and Olive," he added quickly, thinking the compliment too overt. "Normally, I'm stuck in the office, writing articles for an internal periodical I doubt anyone actually reads."

"Sounds fulfilling," she mocked. "Why do you do this?"

"It probably sounds crass to say 'for the money', but at the moment, that's true," he said. "I'm hoping things will change by the end of the year… that I'll be given different responsibilities. But before I forget, I have a question about those degrees of yours. Where does someone find a job with a degree in slime mould?"

"Slime mould was my first doctoral thesis," she corrected. "My other PhD is in psychology. Martin has the same degree.

In fact that is how we met."

Realizing the conversation was heading in a direction that would make it harder to issue, much less accept an invitation, Conor shifted tactics. "I know it wasn't exactly nature pure, but you seemed to enjoy yourself at the lake a couple weeks ago."

"It was pleasant, yes."

"There's a place further up the lake that is quite remote in contrast to where we were. You can walk along a deserted beach and not see another soul. When the wind is howling, and the waves are crashing against the shoreline, it almost feels like you're at the ocean."

"Sounds interesting," Marla replied, in such a neutral tone it was impossible to tell if she truly found it so.

"I was wondering if you might be interested in going up there for the weekend."

"It sounds more appealing than the place where the cabin was," Marla said. "But if it is so remote, where would we stay?"

"There's a hotel or we could book one of the cabins. They're all separate from each other in the woods. It's very private."

Despite the inherent implications of the invitation, Marla did not hesitate to agree. "I've been hoping to see more of Canada's so-called wilderness. There's not much wilderness in Holland, unless you count sleazier parts of Amsterdam."

A single phone call the next day confirmed a reservation for the following weekend. For much of the ensuing week, Conor struggled to keep his anticipation and enthusiasm within some semblance of reality. Only once was his self-imposed pledge to secrecy put to the test, when one day at lunch, Susan asked how things were with Marla.

"Why are you asking me?" he replied, feigning disinterest.

"I don't keep daily tabs on her."

"Aww, come on Conor. It's not exactly a secret you have a thing for her," Susan goaded.

"A thing?"

"You know what I mean," Susan said. "Play dumb if you like, but it's pretty obvious. But if you want my advice, I think you're barking up the wrong tree. I don't think you're her type."

"And what type is that?" he asked, tempted to reveal plans for the upcoming weekend.

"The way she carries herself, not to mention talks, she obviously comes from a wealthy and cultured background."

"So what am I? Some sort of hillbilly?" Conor protested.

"Make fun if you want... Even if things were to click between you, which I don't think they will, there's a ticking clock. You know she's only here till September."

"I'll keep that 'sound advice' in mind, should I develop an interest in her," Conor said with a dismissive guffaw.

"Yeah, right," Susan replied, with further comments diverted by the arrival of their meals.

"I see what you meant about this place being remote," Marla said, staring out the window as they drove north. "I haven't seen any sign of civilization for the last half hour. What do people do if their car breaks down?"

"Get eaten by bears."

"Seriously, isn't that a problem?" Marla repeated.

"It's not *that* isolated," Conor said. "I'm sure someone would pass by in a week or two." he added with a smile, before returning his attention to the empty highway.

As it turned out, the place was not quite as remote as Conor might have hoped. Despite having gone to great lengths to keep the weekend rendezvous a secret, within minutes of arriving at a parking lot not far from the resort, Conor had no sooner gotten out of the car to show Marla a scenic view of the lake, when he spotted an old school friend emerging from the nearby woods.

"You didn't see me," were Conor's first words to Carl, when he walked over to greet him, out of earshot from Marla.

"Yeah... hello... nice to see you too," Carl answered,

somewhat peeved by the brusque greeting. "What are you doing here?"

"You didn't see me here, okay?" Conor repeated.

"Hey... okay. You made your point," Carl told him, now clearly irked. "I have no idea what's going on," he added, glancing to where Marla was still standing by the car. "But okay already. I didn't see you... or her."

"I'll explain it to you some other time," Conor told him, clapping Carl on the shoulder before walking back to join Marla.

"What was that all about?" Marla wanted to know, as they watched Carl walk off and get into a car at the other end of the lot. "I thought you said this place was remote."

"Just somebody I know from the city," Conor explained. "Go figure... I haven't seen that guy in years. Anyways, I stopped here because I wanted to show you the beach I was telling you about. But why don't we go check in first. We'll have plenty of time to come back here later."

"You're the guide," Marla remarked, as she got back in the car.

Once they'd registered and dropped off their luggage at the cabin, Conor suggested they go for a walk along the shore fronting the hotel, rather than returning to the remote beach. Since their unexpected meeting at the parking lot, the winds had picked up considerably, turning the lake's placid surface into a frothy, swirl of pounding waves.

"This is what I meant about looking like the ocean," Conor told her, feeling confident enough to put his arm around her shoulder as they strolled along the sand.

"It's impressive," Marla answered. It reminds me a bit of the North Sea beaches in Holland."

"I guess I should take that as a compliment," Conor said.

"A compliment?" Marla said, stopping in mid-stride.

"That I've managed to show you something that impressed you," Conor explained. "I don't have two degrees, so I have to try any way I can."

"Do you feel like watching a movie?" he asked, retrieving a bottle of wine he'd purchased at the hotel store, following dinner at the hotel restaurant. "There's a bunch of DVD's on the bookcase," he added, fumbling through a drawer in search of a corkscrew.

"I'm fine with just wine," Marla answered, as she sprawled her lengthy figure out on the couch. "I don't need a movie... and definitely no television. I don't know what it's like in Canada because there's no TV in our flat, but I loathe television in Holland. The shows are so infantile... even in prime time. You wonder who is watching that stuff. Besides, we didn't come to such a romantic setting just to watch a movie."

"You're right," Conor answered, setting her glass down on the coffee table, before kneeling on the floor.

"Let me make room for you," Marla said, sitting up and swinging her legs off to one side.

"So here we are," he continued once next to her on the sofa, raising his glass in a toast. "Ensconced in a warm, cozy cabin in the woods, armed with a good bottle of wine... it seems the perfect time to tell me where someone with a degree in slime mould finds a job."

"Are all Canadian men so flippant in such situations?" Marla asked.

"You're asking the wrong person. I've never been with any Canadian men in 'such a situation.'"

Ignoring Conor's second attempt at humour, Marla raised her glass to match Conor's toast. "Here's to a nice weekend... if that's possible with a hopeless jokester. And as I told you, slime mould is not my only interest. If you must know I plan to use my degree in psychology to go into the field of psychosomatic illnesses."

"You mean as a therapist?"

"Possibly... I haven't decided yet."

"Psychosomatic? That's where people only think they

have something wrong with them? Like a hypochondriac?"

"They're not the same thing," Marla explained, "But why are we talking about this? It hardly seems the time or place to be discussing psychosomatic illnesses."

"It interests me," Conor said.

"If you must know," Marla began, with a sense of resignation. "A psychosomatic disorder is a psychological condition that involves physical symptoms. It usually lacks a medical explanation."

"But isn't that how you define a hypochondriac?"

"A hypochondriac constantly worries about their health, although there is basically nothing wrong with them."

"So how do you differentiate between the two if neither have clear symptoms?"

"Really Conor," Marla said. "I feel like I'm giving a lecture."

"Please... humour me for a minute," Conor pleaded. "This stuff genuinely interests me. Maybe I can put it another way. What brings on a psychosomatic disorder?"

"It can be any number of things... a crazy lifestyle, a personality disorder, depression, neglect, sexual abuse and on and on."

"And how can you recognize it?"

"People feel tired all the time, have trouble sleeping, suffer muscle pain, indigestion, migraines."

"A lot of people suffer from those things. They can't all be psychosomatic can they?"

"It would be part of my job to find out. A psychosomatic illness is an actual physical illness that is the outcome of extended periods of emotional stress... Is that clear enough?" she said, leaning forward to playfully pinch Conor's cheek. "Please, enough about illnesses, real or imagined."

As innocent as Marla's gesture was, it was enough to dissipate Conor's nervousness. With his own built-up passion now set free, within minutes they had made their way to the bedroom. Fantasies however, rarely live up to the glare of reality, and it should have come as no surprise to Conor, that his long sought after intimacy with Marla, would turn out to be a disappointment. Initiating the downward trend was her minor counsel, "Not so fast, we're in no hurry," uttered shortly after they'd climbed into bed. As potentially off putting as that statement might have been, Conor did not take it as a personal insult and the passion continued unhindered until both lay back exhausted. Oddly enough, in the post-coital silence, instead of reflecting on the memorable moments such intimacy can create, Conor found himself fixated on the inch-long strand of black hair he'd seen protruding from Marla's right breast.

"Two more draft please... when you have a chance," William called out to a passing waiter, trying not to sound too presumptuous.

"So," he began, his attention returned to Conor. "How was the weekend with the woman who's managed to get you so bent out of shape? Was it a success?"

"Depends on what you call a success," Conor answered glumly. "We talked a lot and I got to know her a little better."

"That's it? You expect me to believe you spent the whole weekend with a goddess and all you did was talk?"

"I'm not gonna go into any detail, if that's what you're hinting at."

"So you did sleep with her."

"We had a pleasant evening together."

"If that's all you've got to say, I don't know why I bothered coming."

"Let's just say the weekend wasn't all wine and whatever," Conor added. "It was pretty hard not to notice a couple of negative things about her."

"Goes with the territory, lad," William said with a grin before finishing off his beer. "Maybe your expectations were just too high."

"Maybe."

"But that picture you showed me, the one of the group on the beach. She looks like such a classy lady. What negative aspects could she possibly have?"

"I'm not talking just about the weekend. I've noticed some things about her ever since we met."

"Elaborate," William said, as he nodded appreciation to the waiter who'd just delivered his draft.

"Well for one thing she can be pretty nasty to her roommate. I've never seen her do it myself, but there's no reason Olive would lie about something like that."

"Olive being the roommate?

"Right. Marla can come across as arrogant at times."

"Was she like that on the weekend?"

"Not really, but there were other things that nerved me."

"Such as?"

"Her incessant smoking for one. It made kissing her seem the equivalent of licking an ashtray."

"Ughhh. That would be a turn off... Was that it?"

"I'm not gonna sit here and give her a rating from one to ten. Let's just say the weekend was not what I expected."

"Which was?"

"That's part of the problem... I don't know."

"Look, before the band starts up again and we have to yell at each other," William warned. "You need to do some serious thinking about what it is you want from this gorgeous woman."

"Tell me about it," Conor moaned, shrugging his shoulders as he reached for his beer.

As Conor had tried to explain to William that evening at the pub, the illicit weekend had produced a batch of mixed emotions. Uncertain whether he wished to continue pursuing the relationship, if it could even be called as such, he thought the best way to deal with it was to lay low for awhile in the hope that time and distance would help clarify things. Once the self-imposed exile was implemented, it did not escape Conor's attention that Marla made no attempt to get in touch with him. The cycle of silence might have lasted even longer had it not been for a request for his attendance, and that of "the two foreign girls" at a party Evie intended to throw.

"You remember Evie don't you?" Conor asked Marla in a phone call the next day. "You met her at the lake."

"She was the one with the friend who liked to drink?" Marla asked.

"That's the one. You noticed that too, eh?" Conor answered, wondering what else Marla may have noticed.

"It was pretty hard not to. The whole cabin could hear you and that woman babbling. Then it suddenly stopped."

"Yeah, Sandra came out and read us the riot act, so we went for a walk," Conor explained. "Anyways, Evie is throwing a party on the weekend and wants you and Olive to come."

"I'd love to," Marla said. "I liked Evie and didn't really have the chance to talk with her as much as I would have wanted."

"Is Olive home?" Conor asked abruptly.

"She's in her room. Probably sulking. We had a bit of a row this morning at breakfast."

"Well I told Evie I'd get back to her as soon as I could about who would be coming," Conor said, purposely not asking what had been behind the argument. "Can you go and ask her?"

"I'd rather not." Marla told him. "I'll just slip a note under her door and get back to you tomorrow. You said this Saturday?"

"Right. Evie said something about 8:00 o' clock."

"That woman can be such a boor sometimes," was Marla's curt description when she called the next day to pass on news of Olive's refusal. "After she read the note about the party, she told me she has a date with one of her co-workers from the clinic and walked out of the room without another word. Frankly, I'm glad she's not coming."

Agreeing that he would pick her up at eight, Conor hung up, wondering whether Olive's real reason for declining was her wish to spend as little time as possible in Marla's vicinity.

As evidenced by the loud music wafting out over the 11th floor balcony, the party was in full swing as Conor and Marla walked across the parking lot of Evie's apartment block.

"Do you like to dance?" Marla asked with a surprisingly girlish giggle, while they rode up in the elevator.

"Depends on the music," he answered. "And I usually prefer dancing without a gas mask. Evie smokes more than you do, so I suspect I might need one tonight."

"Well you may not want to dance... but I certainly do." she added, as the elevator doors opened and they made their way down the hall in the direction of the booming music.

"Hopefully you'll be able to dance to your heart's content tonight," Conor told her as they reached the door. "That is if they can hear the bell and let us in. "

Despite the loud music, Evie was sitting on the couch in what appeared to be a deep discussion with a group of friends. Conor waved hello before taking Marla's jacket and tossing it on a pile in the bedroom. By the time he returned to the living room. Marla was already out amidst the dancers in the smoke-filled room. A short while later, Conor was helping himself to a drink in the kitchen, when he was joined by the somewhat inebriated hostess.

"She's quite something isn't she," Evie cooed, watching from the doorway, as Marla swayed seductively, her figure accentuated by a tight-fitting dress.

"You can say that again," Conor answered, filling his glass with a healthy portion of red wine.

"I don't think there's anyone who hasn't been eyeing her since you guys got here. And that includes the women."

"And she knows it," Conor said

"Do I detect a trace of jealousy?" Evie probed. "Straight arrow Conor, is there something going on between you two or are you going to cop out and tell me you're just 'friends?'"

"Depends what you mean by 'something'," Conor answered, all too aware of Evie's tendency not to keep secrets.

"You know what I mean," she said, leaning on the counter for support.

"Let's just say it's a work in progress," was all Conor was prepared to offer.

"I knew it, you old rascal," Evie said with a note of glee.

"But judging from the number of men who've been ogling her on the dance floor, you may have your work cut out for you. Good luck is all I can say."

Enjoying herself immensely, Marla made no attempt to vacate the dance floor for over an hour, switching partners at will and content to gyrate on her own when none seemed available. Her dance marathon may have continued even longer had it not been for a neighbour, who in her rush to complain about the noise, had forgotten to remove dried patches of Clearasil from her face, pounded at the door and requested the music be turned down.

"Have you seen Evie anywhere?" Marla asked, as she slumped down on the couch beside Conor, taking the glass from his hand and helping herself to a hearty slurp. "It's her party but she seems to have disappeared."

"It's a wonder you can see anything in this smoke," Conor answered, before retrieving his glass. "Besides, you've been on the dance floor for days."

"I told you I like to dance," she answered.

Just at that moment, the door to the bedroom opened and out walked Evie with a ruddy-faced man, who another guest had previously referred to as 'Steve the Club'.

"Been out for a little stroll have we?" Conor said with a feigned snarl, that prompted Evie to stick out her tongue as she and Steve made for the kitchen.

It was just after three when the party finally wound to a close. Knowing he had no right to criticize what he felt had been Marla's flaunting behaviour on the dance floor, an icy silence reigned supreme on the drive back to Marla's flat. Having had nothing to say herself, Marla simply leaned over and kissed Conor on the cheek as they pulled to a stop in front of the house.

"I'd invite you in, but I have to get up early for work," she told him, the already half-opened door a sign she did not wish to embark on a lengthy conversation. "Why don't you call me later in the week? And thanks for tonight. I had fun."

But he didn't call, either that week or the next. And as the days with no contact drifted past, he slowly came to realize that what had started off as a bad case of infatuation, had now shifted shift into the realm of rational thinking. It was a phase that may have continued indefinitely had he not happened to glance at the calendar one morning at the office and realize that Marla's stay was rapidly approaching its end. Sensing he would regret it if he didn't see her alone one more time, he called to issue an invitation for dinner. When the crowded restaurant proved to be less than an ideal location to discuss the sensitive subject of what had gone on between them over the last months, Conor suggested they retire to his house for drinks.

There was a noticeable awkwardness between them as Conor showed Marla into the living room and retreated to the kitchen for the promised drinks. Returning to the living room with two glasses of red wine, he settled into a chair on the opposite side of the coffee table, hoping to ease the tension by bringing up a familiar subject.

"I know you didn't think my timing was very astute that night at the cabin, when I asked what prompted you to get into the field of psychosomatic medicine."

"Oh... so we are off on this tangent again, are we?" Marla asked with a frown. "And here I was thinking you invited me over to talk about slime mould again."

"Touché."

"I suppose you can blame my mother for my decision," she said, raising her glass without suggesting a toast.

"You mean the beauty salon patron?"

"One and the same," Marla answered. "I had just turned seventeen when she was diagnosed with the early onset of

Alzheimer's. She was only in her late forties, very young to have contracted the disease. It was terrible to watch her deteriorate. It felt as if we were losing a piece of her every day. During that time, the whole family, especially my father, felt like our lives were on hold. But she was lucky, if you can call it that. Sometimes it can take years, sometimes decades for the disease to progress but she passed away only three years later."

"But Alzheimer's doesn't qualify as a psychosomatic disorder."

"No, but that's what steered me towards wanting to study medicine. Over time I just gravitated towards psychosomatic illnesses."

Despite Conor's honourable, if somewhat tenuous intentions of not attempting to rekindle any embers between them, the more the wine flowed, the more the two of them relaxed, eventually ending up spooning together on the carpet. Even if a part of Conor had been interested in taking matters further, Marla's comments quickly ruled out anything beyond cuddling.

"You know I cannot do this again," she told him, as they turned to face each other. "Martin will arrive in two days' time. I don't regret what has happened between us, especially the weekend at the resort, I found it special, but we cannot repeat it.

"I understand," Conor said.

The next morning, Conor had just returned from his coffee break when he noticed an incoming call from Evie.

"Hi Conor. I know you're busy doing nothing at work, so I won't keep you. I just wanted to ask you something. At the party a few weeks ago, Marla happened to mention that she and her boyfriend… what's his name again?"

"Martin."

"That she and Martin are planning to travel out to the West Coast when he gets here. This morning I realized they'll be leaving this Friday. Did you know that?"

"I know that," Conor said, feeling a shudder pass through him.

"I don't know if you were planning anything special as a farewell gesture, but what do you think about you and I taking her and Olive out for a "goodbye dinner" on Friday evening?"

"What about Martin?"

"Obviously we'd include him, silly boy. Anyway, I wanted to talk it over with you before giving Marla a call."

"I'm okay with it," Conor told her, although a part of him knew he wasn't.

With only five hours left before the couple were scheduled to catch a late-night train west, Conor, Evie, Marla and Martin found themselves at an upscale restaurant several blocks from the main station. Perhaps having had enough of Marla's critiques over the past few months, Olive had politely declined the invitation to join them. Seated directly across the table from Martin, Conor tried his best to act relaxed. As one might expect, with a newcomer in their midst, conversation remained somewhat stilted in the beginning. It was only after several drinks that everybody began to loosen up.

"I know you were only here for a few months Marla," Evie said. "But how does life here compare to your life at home... or in other parts of Europe for that matter? Could you ever imagine living here?"

"I've travelled a great deal, but I haven't lived anywhere else other than Holland," Marla admitted. "As far as life here," she continued, glancing quickly at Conor. "One of the things I've noticed is that there doesn't seem to be as much street life. It seems a bit sterile at times, at least in the suburbs. Everybody has a house that they stay cooped up in. Oh and the food is really different... especially the bread," she added with a chuckle." It's like a marshmallow. Terrible. I hate it."

"Okay... nix the bread," Evie said with a smile. "What about other countries you've been to in Europe? Do you have a favourite?"

"I love Ireland," Marla said, looking at Martin, who seemed to be content in that he didn't have to make conversation. "The intense green of the hills, the cliffs, the sea. The one thing I disliked about Ireland was that nearly all the pubs offered 'authentic Irish music.' That gets boring after awhile. How many versions of 'The Wild Rover' can you listen to? But the people are great though and so is the beer."

With attention focused on Marla recanting her travel tales, Conor was able to discreetly observe Martin. One thing he couldn't help noticing was that since their arrival at the restaurant, neither he nor Marla had shown any overt signs of affection for each other. He also sensed that Martin was slightly bored by the conversation, perhaps having heard portions of it numerous times previously.

Conversation fell off with the arrival of the meal, but shortly after dessert had been ordered, Martin raised his wine glass, cleared his throat, and signalled that he wished to say something.

"I know we have just met," he began, looking at Conor and Evie. "But I want to make a toast to my two new friends and thank them for taking care of my Marla over these months," he announced, resting his free hand on Marla's shoulder, who looked slightly embarrassed. "It is unfortunate we will not have more time to get to know each other better, but I am sure I will learn more about you from Marla, while we are travelling. Both of us are looking forward to seeing more of your country," he added with a broad smile. "As you probably know by now," he said, pausing to set his glass down. "Marla is someone who enjoys new experiences. That's one of the things I love about her. She likes bringing new things and new people into her life," he said, before picking up his glass again and turning to face Conor directly. "But only for a short while."

Conor showed no reaction, choosing to simply smile meekly and raise his glass in return. A short while later, as dessert arrived, Conor excused himself to go to the washroom. Before returning to the table, he approached the waiter out of sight from the group and paid the bill.

As the dessert dishes were being cleared away, Martin signalled the waiter that he'd like to pay, only to be told the matter had already been taken care of. The news was not well received.

"This I do not like," Martin said firmly, addressing his remarks to Conor. "You should have at least told us beforehand, so we could have objected or split the bill."

"Consider it a bon voyage gift," Conor told him.

"Martin," Evie interrupted, having sensed the rising tension. "I think there's something you should know."

Conor felt himself freeze.

"Conor doesn't particularly like how he earns his money. Let him at least enjoy how he spends it."

The remark seemed to diffuse matters, and once a final round of drinks were finished, the foursome departed for the train station. After picking up their luggage at a storage locker Martin had visited earlier in the day, they made their way through the cavernous rotunda and on to the platform. Given that the train's journey commenced there, a conductor informed them that Conor and Evie could accompany Martin and Marla on to the train until they had found their quarters.

"Just make sure you get off when you hear the whistle," he told them, touching his cap as a sign of respect. "That is unless that is you want to wake up in Regina."

Once their compartment had been found, the awkward silence made it clear there wasn't anything left to be said. A round of perfunctory embraces followed, Conor making sure that his with Marla did not last too long.

Walking back through the subterranean passage that led to the station's main hall, Evie noticed that Conor was tearing up.

"I had the feeling that something was going on between you two," she said, wrapping her arm around his shoulder.

"Somebody who was just a friend wouldn't get so upset at seeing her leave. But you must have known it would come to this. Anything long term was doomed from the start... plus she has a boyfriend."

"You noticed that too, eh?" Conor replied, forcing a grin. "Did you catch his drift? The bit about, "only for a short time?"

"I did. Do you think he suspected something? "

"No idea."

"As painful as it might feel right now, it's probably a good thing they're leaving. But maybe she'll stay in touch," Evie told him. "Then again," she added as they walked out into the cool evening air. "I'm not so sure that would be such a good thing. It might just prolong the agony. One way or the other, I guess you'll just have to learn how not to miss someone."

*

Author's Note: As none of these five encounters took place immediately after one another, readers are advised to follow Conor and take a pause before moving to the next one. Not that it did him a lot of good.

Alice

The heat in the crowded hall had been unpleasant but tolerable, with music from the DJ's speakers loud enough to annihilate all but the most strenuous of conversations. Vision, not to mention breathing, was hampered by the lingering smoke of a hundred or more cigarettes, interlaced with stale perfume, body odour, and the pungent smell of cheese and cold cuts laying largely untouched on the nearby buffet table. What better way to spend a Saturday night?

"So how do you know the prospective bride and groom?" Conor asked the couple who'd just returned from the dance floor after a break in the aural festivities.

"We actually don't," a husky, blonde-haired woman answered, introducing herself as Sheila, as she settled into the seat directly across the table from Conor. "This hunk here is my husband, Terry."

"Conor," he told them, half rising to shake Sheila's hand before switching to do the same with her husband.

"It's nice to meet you Conor," Sheila said, somewhat out of breath. "Is that a Scottish name?"

"Irish."

"I can never tell the difference... And as I said, no, we don't know Miriam and... what's his name?" she asked, turning to Terry.

"Ron... I think."

"A mutual friend sold us tickets. She knows how much we like coming to these events to dance."

"And drink," Terry added with a grin, hoisting his plastic cup of beer as evidence.

"Since when did you need a social for that?" Sheila jibed.

"And you?" she said, turning back to Conor. "How do you know the happy couple?"

"I don't. A friend sold me a ticket and then got sick so I'm flying solo tonight."

"Same thing with Alice," Terry interjected. "Except her partner is permanently sick if you ask me. That's one of the reasons they just got divorced."

"Terry," Sheila said with annoyance. "I'm sure Alice wouldn't appreciate your blabbering about her marital status. Just so you know," she said, returning to Conor. "Alice is the friend who sold us the tickets."

"I was just explaining," Terry sputtered.

"I know what you were just doing," Sheila said. "You know as well as I do this is Alice's first outing since the divorce. She's already feeling a little gun shy, so please put a lid on it."

"Where is she anyways?" Terry asked, finishing his drink and getting up to signal he was heading off to join the long line at the bar. "Anybody else want anything?"

"I think she's gone to talk with Miriam," Sheila answered. "I'm sure she won't be long. I'll have another rum and coke since you're going."

"Strange," Conor thought to himself a short while later, as he stood up to greet the woman introducing herself as Alice. "How it is a name can conjure up an image literally miles off the mark?"

Alice did not bother to extend a hand, simply nodding hello, before occupying Terry's empty chair and immediately falling into conversation with Sheila. Her apparent disinterest, however, provided Conor the opportunity to discreetly compare how much his imagined version differed from reality. Rather than the tall, thin blonde he'd somehow pictured, Alice was in fact a striking brunette several inches shorter than himself, dressed in a loose-fitting sweater and jeans, with glasses that he felt did little to compliment her.

The two women were still busy gabbing, the content rendered inaudible amidst the general din of the crowd, when Terry returned with the drinks. With Terry showing no interest in engaging in any further small talk, Conor's gaze shifted to the front of the hall where the first strains of Jumpin' Jack Flash were sending people flocking back to the dance floor.

"Excuse me," Conor said, interrupting the women's conversation. "I really like this song. Do you feel like dancing?" he asked Alice. Caught off guard, she offered no response, and for a moment simply stared blankly, as if he had committed some sort of faux pas.

"Sure why not," she said finally, as if it was an act of charity.

Once on the floor, however, it didn't take long for them to discover they shared an enjoyable, mutual sense of rhythm. As the evening wore on, when not dancing up a storm, the two of them could be found huddled in a corner furthest from the speakers, exchanging the obligatory comparative tastes in music, books and movies, before venturing into deeper subjects. What surprised them both that evening was that no matter what subjects discussed, be it work, travel, future goals or past relationships, none of the rapport seemed forced.

It was just after midnight, when Terry and Sheila interrupted the latest confab to announce their departure. Aware that Alice had come with them, rather than offering to drive her home, which he sensed might seem a little bold, he asked for her number, a clear admission that he'd like to see her again.

"Especially some place where we don't have to yell at each other over the music," he told her, as he helped her on with her coat. Now somewhat used to her awkward pauses, Conor watched in silence as Alice mentally ran through her options before agreeing to supply him with her number.

The pair saw each other regularly over the next few weeks, walking away on each occasion, pleased at how comfortable things seemed to be between them. The mental intimacy that had been apparent from their first meeting, had quickly developed into a physical one, and despite having known about Alice's divorce before she broached the subject herself, Conor did not sense he might be serving as some sort of rebound replacement. It was well into their second month together, that Conor began to notice what he would later come to call "warning signs." One of the hardest to ignore were the telltale symptoms of a helper syndrome, that often bordered on the obsequious.

"Alice," Conor said one morning in exasperation, as they sat over breakfast in the tiny kitchen of the apartment she'd moved into after the divorce. "Believe it or not, I can butter my own toast."

"I'm sorry. It's just an old habit," she apologized, slightly embarrassed. "I used to do it for Arthur all the time."

"Well in case you haven't noticed, I'm not Arthur," he replied, wondering whether this aspect of her personality could be linked to her being a nurse. A more worrisome trait however, was to surface one evening after an intense round of passion.

"Promise me you won't ever leave me," Alice had whispered in his ear as they lay in bed.

At a loss how to respond, Conor had remained silent.

"Did you hear what I said," she repeated.

"Why would you say something like that?" Conor asked. "I can't promise you a future. You might be the one to leave one day."

"Never," she insisted, propping herself up on one elbow.

"How can you be so sure?"

"I just know."

"But..." Conor began, then hesitated.

"But what?" Alice asked. "What were you going to say?"

"You probably thought you and Arthur would never split up. Maybe he even promised he would never leave you."

"You're not at all like Arthur... thank God," she told him, flopping back down on the pillow. "You've never been married."

"No."

"How come?"

"I guess I never felt the need or the urge," Conor admitted.

"But you've had long term relationships?"

"I don't know what you would call long term."

"At least a year," she said.

"I've had one or two that long."

"And why did they end?"

"Hey... What's with the cross examination?"

"I'm just curious. I've told you about Arthur."

"Not really."

"Well, you don't *want* to know," Alice said, in a tone indicating she did not wish to elaborate. "Why did these two relationships end?"

"There's rarely just one reason. But with Jill... it was mainly that her work took top priority. We ended up spending so much time apart, we just grew apart. Nothing unique."

"So the split was mutual?

"More or less," Conor answered.

"And the other one?" Alice persisted.

"Totally different. She met someone else."

"Did you try and win her back?"

"Win her back?... You make her sound like some sort of kewpie doll."

"Okay... did you at least fight for her?"

"No. I was actually relieved when she met someone else because I'd already felt myself pulling away. She just made it easier to split."

"Maybe she felt you distancing yourself and that's why she went looking for someone else."

"No idea."

"Didn't you talk about problems with each other?"

"Not as much as we could or should have been, I suppose."

"*We* don't seem to have trouble discussing things," Alice pointed out.

"So maybe I learned something," Conor replied.

"You never gave any thought of getting married to Jill, or the one who left... before problems arose?"

"Birgit... No."

"And if the right one comes along?" Alice said, trying to sound jocular.

"You sound like a song lyric. Hard to say... I don't think so. What about you and Arthur? You've never talked about how things went south with him."

As she lay there in silence, Conor watched Alice, as recollections of her former husband bounced across her face like a flat stone skipping across a calm lake.

"It was the classic version," Alice said, with a sneer. "Man leaves wife for a younger woman. But for Christ's sake he was only 35 and I was 33. We'd only been married for three years . Since when is thirty-three old? The guy was... and no doubt still is, an 'A-1' jerk. You wanna hear something even more off the wall?" Alice continued, without waiting for an answer. "Whenever we were having problems, which I can tell you was often near the end, he would claim it was because I was adopted."

"You never mentioned you were adopted."

"What did you expect? That when we first met I'd say, 'Hi, I'm Alice, I was adopted'."

"Why are you getting so hostile? It may not be something you bring up in dinner conversation, but it's nothing to be ashamed of."

"I'm not getting hostile," she fumed. "And who said I was ashamed?"

"Hey look, it's no big deal. I'm just curious why you never mentioned it before. So, why did Arthur see a connection between the problems you were having and being adopted?"

"In his tiny little brain, he figured I was hypersensitive to feeling rejected because I was adopted."

"And you didn't see a connection?"

"Of course not. I was adopted very young, and my foster parents were very caring people. They were very open with me about the circumstances of my adoption and my biological parents. They told me that my 'real Mom'... God I hate that phrase... was only 17 when she had me, and my Dad, just 19. Basically kids. They gave me up because they were too young to be parents. It was a different story with my sister."

"You never mentioned anything about having a sister."

"Half-sister," Alice corrected. "Another delightful phrase. Her name is Angela. I didn't learn about her until I was in my mid 20's, after I'd tried tracking down my biological mother."

"I've never heard any of this before."

"I guess I didn't think it was that important. Especially in light of Arthur's cockamamie theory about adoption. At any rate, she refused the agency's request to reveal her identity to me. If there ever was any sense of rejection, then that was it."

"Did your foster parents know who she was or where she was?"

"They knew the reasons behind the adoption, but they didn't have any information about my mother's identity or whereabouts. I'm sure they would have told me if they'd known."

"Why did you want to track her down?"

"Nature versus nurture, I guess. Obviously I'd been influenced by my foster parents while growing up. I wanted to find out what I might have inherited from my biological parents. I thought it might help to find out why I am the way I am sometimes."

"So what did you do when you found out she wasn't interested in having any contact?"

"I had a good cry... for about three seconds. Then I told myself it was her loss and moved on."

Apparently in no need of any further coaxing, after a short uneasy silence, Alice went on.

"Adoption agencies are normally pretty closed-mouthed when it comes to revealing details of an adoption. But as it turned out, my 'real mother' was more amenable to having contact with Angela than she had been with me. Angela tracked her down, met with her, and in the process, discovered she had two other siblings, me and a brother. She pressed 'Mom' for our names and was somehow able to track me down, I presume through the agency. Together we managed to contact Roger, our missing brother. What makes this saga even more incredible is that none of us have the same father. Apparently 'Mom' was a bit of a slow learner," Alice added derisively.

"So she gave all of you up for adoption?"

"You got it."

"So when you learned Angela knew where your Mom was, did you ever try and contact her yourself?"

"I saw no point. She'd made it clear that she didn't want anything to do with me."

"But maybe she'd changed her mind after meeting with Angela."

"If she had she could have easily gotten in touch with me through Angela. But she didn't."

"How do you know she won't someday?"

"Could prove difficult given that she died last year."

"Did Angela learn anything about your mother's own childhood or background? By any chance was she adopted?"

"What is it with this adoption kick? You're starting to sound like Arthur."

"Why are you getting so hostile again?"

"What do you expect? Talking about this woman gets me riled up. It's pretty clear that responsibility was not part of her vocabulary and she didn't care about anyone but herself. Enough of this."

"Do you still have contact with Angela or Roger?" Conor asked.

"Don't push me Conor," she warned.

"I'm just interested in hearing about your past."

After another moment of silence and a few deep sighs, Alice's flash of anger receded as quickly as it had arisen, allowing her to continue. "Angela and I were close in the beginning, but it was different with Roger. He had his own family by then and didn't seem overly interested in getting to know us. I respected his decision. In the first year, Angela and I talked all the time, mostly about our mutual lives before we'd known of each other's existence. The more we talked, the more I realized how lucky I'd been with my foster parents. I think she was a little jealous, or maybe even resentful, hearing about my life, so after awhile I had to be careful what I told her. It wasn't my fault her childhood had been less than enchanted. She'd had a series of bad foster parents, one worse than the other. Frankly, it's disgusting how little effort some agencies make to monitor foster parents once an adoption has been arranged. There are some real weirdos out there, and anyone can put on a good front. I know of one couple who took in a young boy of five. They already had two children of their own, but did not formally adopt the child because it mean they would lose the allowance provided to foster parents. That poor child was made to feel like a second-class citizen until he was 18 and could get out from under their grip. Maybe if you were talking to Angela right now instead of me, this silly rejection theory might hold water. She certainly felt that."

"You didn't say whether you still have contact."

"Not so much. Once we'd exhausted talking about the past, we realized we didn't have much in common. We just drifted away from each other. What contact we still do have is limited to birthdays and Xmas. It didn't help when she moved to another city. It's sad, but it's reality."

"Whew…" Conor muttered. "That's quite the story."

"I didn't intend for it to come out like this but I'm glad it did."

"So am I."

"So, to bring this epic story to a conclusion, if you can't promise me that you'll never leave me, at least promise that you'll never lie to me," she said, turning to snuggle up beside him.

"That I can promise."

Approximately two months after that bedtime conversation, Conor was sitting in his living room, basking in the warm rays streaming through the window, when he heard the doorbell ring. Reluctantly pulling himself out of the chair, he made his way through the kitchen and descended the three steps to the side-door landing. There on the opposite side of the outer screen door, swivelling from side to side with a sheepish grin on her face, stood Alice.

"Well…" Conor said, with a degree of caution. "This is an unexpected surprise."

"Aren't most?" Alice said, reaching for the handle before Conor had shown any sign of wanting to invite her in.

"Most what?" he replied.

"Surprises. Most are unexpected. Aren't you going to let me in?"

"Sorry," he answered, unhooking the latch.

"I see you haven't gotten round to staining this yet," Alice remarked, as she took a seat at the kitchen table.

"I'm sure you didn't traipse halfway across town to critique my carpentry skills, Alice. What's up? To what do I owe the honour?"

"I needed to talk to you," she said.

"That much I figured," Conor said. "You could have called."

"I needed to see you in person… to talk about what's been going on."

"Alice," Conor replied, struggling to restrain his frustration. "Why do you want to do this? I thought that after the problems we'd been having we'd agreed to give each other some space to sort things out."

"But it's been over a month, and I haven't heard a word from you."

"I didn't realize we set a time limit," Conor answered, his shoulders sagging as he spoke.

"How much time does it take to figure out what you're feeling?" Alice asked, leaning forward with both elbows on the table.

"I've felt a lot of things in the past month."

"You haven't shared anything with me."

"That's probably because there's been a lot of conflicting messages. I've needed time to see which sentiment was the strongest."

"And?"

"You may not want to hear this, but I've come to the conclusion that what happened between us was a mistake."

"A mistake?" Alice harrumphed, straightening up. "It sure didn't seem like it at the time."

"It wasn't in the beginning," Conor answered. "But I shouldn't have let it go on for as long as I did."

"There must have been a reason you did."

"Alice, we've covered all this before."

"No.. that's just it. We haven't covered 'all this' before.

I'm hearing this 'mistake business' for the first time."

"Well you knew things weren't going well. That's why I asked for some space."

"I did notice that something had changed, but why all of a sudden do you want to call it a mistake? You have to admit we got along well together," she said. "And I don't mean just in bed."

"I get along with a lot of people, Alice... many of whom are women."

"But you don't sleep with all of them... do you?" she asked.

"Of course not."

"So what made it different with me?"

"That's a pretty silly question. You expressed as much interest as me."

"So, you were just an innocent bystander?"

"No, but..."

"Does it really matter who started something?" Alice cut in.

"I felt we were developing a deep bond. I just don't understand where that all went and why I was banished to oblivion."

"That's a bit of an exaggeration, don't you think?" Conor asked.

"Well what would you call it? You certainly haven't made any attempt to contact me over the past month."

"I wasn't trying to banish you. We agreed to give each other some space and in the past month I've come to recognize it for what it was."

"It?"

"Our... time together, for lack of a better word. It was enjoyable but at some point I started to feel there wasn't any basis for a longer relationship."

"And just when did you have this epiphany?" she asked snidely. "If you felt that way, why didn't you say something about it at the time? You said you'd learned to be more open.

If you were so unsure, why did you continue to sleep with me?"

"Hold on, Alice," Conor countered. "If you remember, it was me who put a stop to it."

"Yeah, after we'd slept together I don't know how many times."

"I wasn't counting. But I wanted us to stop before we decided to take a break."

"You decided."

"You agreed."

"What choice did I have?"

"Alice," Conor broke in. "I told you that I'd sensed there were problems. That maybe we wanted different things and that I needed some time out to see if things had run their course."

"Run their course?" Alice fumed.

"Okay... bad choice of words. But I've tried to explain..."

"Yeah, yeah... so you've said... no basis for a long-term relationship. What makes you so certain? Hold that thought," she said, raising her hand. "Before you answer, I need to use the bathroom," she announced, scraping her chair on the floor as she pushed away from the table. "That will give you a few more minutes to think about how you came to that conclusion."

Left to his own devices, Conor's thoughts briefly turned to the conversation they'd shared about adoption that night in bed.

"I'm back," Alice announced jauntily upon her return, jarring Conor back to the present.

"You know Alice," he began tentatively, before she had a chance to retake centre stage. "Just now...while you were upstairs, I was thinking about what Arthur had said about adoption and rejection."

"Oh God... why are you drudging that up? I cringe every time I think about that," Alice answered.

"I was wondering whether or not …"

"You're not seriously going to try and suggest that's why I can't accept your decision, are you?" she cut in. "Jesus Conor… can't you come up with anything better than that?"

"I'm not implying anything," Conor protested. "Just listen for a moment," Conor told her. "I'm not hopping on Arthur's bandwagon, so don't jump down my throat. I read an article recently about how adoption can influence how people feel about rejection in general."

"Oh Christ," Alice countered, slamming her fist on the armchair. "That is such mumbo-jumbo. It's completely ridiculous. Where did they come up with such an inane theory? No wait," she'd added, holding up both hands. "Let me guess… the Internet. Hey… why are we even talking about this? I didn't come here to talk about this ridiculous theory."

"I know that, but…"

"Ahhh yes… Now I know… That would make it all so much easier for you wouldn't it? 'Poor old Alice can't accept being told there's no basis for a longer relationship because she was adopted and therefore can't deal with rejection. I would have expected more from you Conor."

"Please… just hear me out. This article was written by a doctor well respected in his field," he explained as he watched Alice crossly fold her arms on her chest and lean back in her chair. "According to him, children who are adopted, especially at a later age, often have difficulties dealing with rejection, loss, grief, shame, intimacy and even struggle with their sense of identity."

"You honestly believe that only adoptees struggle with such things?" Alice grunted with disdain. "I'm sorry to disappoint you and quash your hypothesis, but if you recall, I was a baby when I was adopted. Much too young to feel rejected."

"Would you at least agree that for some people being adopted is a traumatic experience?"

"Of course it is. I've told you about Angela's experiences.

There's no escaping a sense of rejection," Alice said. "But insinuating that I can't deal with rejection by you simply because I was adopted is insane."

"You don't think there might be a connection?" he asked.

"No, I don't… One has nothing to do with the other and I really don't see the point of arguing over such a stupid theory," she sneered.

A lengthy silence between them lingered for awhile, the only sound being the ticking of the kitchen clock.

"I think I may owe you an apology," Conor finally said, threading his fingers together as he rested his chin on his hands.

"For what… banishing me?" Alice goaded. "Or merely for dredging up this crazy adoption theory?"

"For not having made more effort to explain why I didn't…errr, why I don't feel," he quickly corrected, "we have enough of a basis for a long-term relationship."

"You can add for toying with my emotions to that apology."

"I don't know if that's a fair accusation. I didn't go into this relationship with any pre-conceived notions. When doubts started to seep in, I should have been more up front with you. But I just wasn't sure what I was feeling. That's why I decided we should stop sleeping with each other. I didn't want to continue under false pretences."

"False pretences?"

"Once I felt uncertain whether we were destined for anything long term, it would have been dishonest not to put a stop to it."

"You know one thing that's still missing in all this, is what made you have these doubts?"

"I didn't make a mental list," Conor answered, knowing that he in fact had. "At some point I just sensed we felt differently about certain things."

"What things?"

"Well for one, when you brought up this subject of my

'never leaving you' or how I felt about marriage. It made me realize that you seemed more eager or interested in something long term than I did. I felt that imbalance and suggested we take a break."

"But why didn't you talk about it at the time if that's the way you felt?"

"I needed to make sure what I did and didn't want. This may be hard to accept, but I think it was the right conclusion."

"So in other words... you haven't missed me."

"Less than I thought I would ... to be honest,."

Alice sat in silence for a minute. "You know it makes me sad to admit this, but if I'm going to be totally honest as well, I knew things were shifting between us before you asked for a break."

"You never said anything."

"It felt sad to recognize that. A part of me hoped that if we spent more time together, things would get better. I mean every relationship has its ups and downs. We enjoyed doing a lot of things together. It wasn't all bad was it?"

"For sure not. But after awhile there was just something missing."

"What was missing?"

"It's not so easy to put into words," Conor told her. "It was just a feeling I had."

"That isn't much help," Alice complained. "I never felt something was 'missing'. I enjoyed our times together. I found it fulfilling to talk with you and you had such a calming effect on me."

Conor could offer no response.

"Just for the record, I'm not exactly sure what impressions you have of me, but whatever they are or wherever they came from, you should know that I'm not someone who's easily susceptible to delusions or flights of fancy. In fact, I'm probably one of the most rational people I know. I say that because I really felt there was potential for us. I wanted to explore that. Is that so terrible?"

"No."

"I still don't know why you feel the way you do. You make it all sound so obscure. But if you really feel we don't have enough in common to be partners," Alice said. "I hope we can at least still be friends."

"I've never closed the door on that, Alice," Conor said.

"This isn't exactly the result I'd hoped to achieve by coming here today, but maybe it hasn't been a total loss," she mused. "It's shown me something I didn't want to see before."

"And that is?" Conor asked.

"My own passivity. That I need to stand up more for my own views and feelings."

"Isn't that what you've been doing here today?"

"To a certain extent," Alice said, letting out a big sigh. "At least we know where each other stands and there's something to be said for that."

"That alone increases the chances we can still be friends… without rancour, or even worse, false hopes."

"Then I'd like to leave on that note," Alice said, rising from her chair and moving towards the landing. "So," she said turning to face him. "Thanks for making my life a little easier, even if it was just for awhile."

"Are you being sarcastic?"

"Not at all, and I'm sorry you see it as such."

After a lengthy, heartfelt embrace and the promise to keep in touch, Alice departed. But as it turned out, they didn't live up to their vows. Two months later, having had no contact in the interim, Conor learned from a mutual friend that Alice had quit her job, and left the city, leaving no forwarding address. For several days he mulled over the idea of trying to discover her whereabouts, but in the end realized her message couldn't have been any clearer.

*

Pause Two.

Rachel

In 1948, the British poet, T.S. Eliot, published "The Cocktail Party", a three-act drama in which one of the characters speculated on whether one could only love what is created by the imagination. Given that Mr. Eliot is no longer around to ask, it's difficult to know if that statement emerged as a result of personal experience, or was merely something he had lifted from another gifted writer. Looking back at the aftermath of his brief but intense encounter with Rachel in 1979, Conor couldn't help but recall Eliot's character, and how applicable his comment might have been to his own situation.

The curling season had gotten off to a late start that year, largely because the league's secretary had somehow failed to register in time to guarantee available ice time. Set up three years prior by Conor's work colleagues, the league's late start had prompted a number of the old stalwarts - ones who tended to take the game more seriously - to seek other venues. Hoping to flesh out the roster, the remaining members appealed to friends and acquaintances to join, many of whom had never cured before. Conor had initially not paid much attention to the new recruits, choosing to stoke his competitive streak by focusing entirely on winning, a gambit that had paid off with three wins in the first four games. It wasn't until the fifth week, when his team happened to play on the sheet directly adjacent to a foursome of new players, that he first took any notice of an attractive short-haired blonde. With no subtle way of introducing himself, all he could do was discreetly observe her various gestures and expressions, a process that only heightened his unharnessed fascination.

It was to Conor's good fortune, however, that part of the league's weekly tradition involved a post-game retreat to the upstairs restaurant. There, players could eat, drink and rant about their own recent wins or losses, while watching and commenting on the current games underway on the sheets below. For several weeks, during these post-match rendezvous, Conor continued to keep the woman, whose name he'd learned was Rachel, in his line of vision, noting how she would always sit with the same group, but rarely take part in what appeared to be their lively discussions. Whether real or imagined, such a confident silence made her seem even more mysterious. As not everyone knew each other, the various groups tended not to mingle, making it difficult for Conor to establish direct contact with Rachel without appearing too obvious. Fortunately, other league members had recognized the 'segregation' problem and decided to hold a "get to know you" party. Having hoped to use the gathering to casually introduce himself, Conor had been deeply disappointed when Rachel didn't show up. Able to talk with other members of her team, he learned that her absence was due to having driven her boyfriend to the airport, news that initially only added to his disappointment. Through luck or serendipity, the following week's game turned out to be against Rachel's team, offering up the long-sought opportunity to engage her in small talk. During the game, comments exchanged between them largely revolved around the game itself. Conor was about to venture into more personal subjects when his skip glided past on his way to deliver his final shot of the end, and casually remarked, only half in jest, "stop consorting with the enemy, Conor, and concentrate on winning this end."

After the game, which Rachel's team won 8 to 5, Conor made a point of joining her table upstairs.

"You guys played amazingly well tonight," he told her. "Either that or we played amazingly lousy."

"I think we were just lucky," Rachel answered.

"You know you missed a really good party last week," he continued. "We all had the chance to get to know each other a little better. Someone said you couldn't come because you had to drive your boyfriend to the airport."

"Former boyfriend," she corrected.

"Oh," Conor said, trying not to sound too pleased. "Where was he going?" he asked.

"He's off to a new job in Toronto."

"What does he do?" Conor asked, knowing he didn't really care.

"He's in public relations," Rachel told him.

"Okay... And if you don't mind my asking, what is it you do?"

"Kindergarten teacher."

"Really?" Conor replied, feeling somewhat tongue-tied, which immediately thrust him into jokester modus. "At least you didn't say hairdresser."

"What do you have against hairdressers?" Rachel asked matter-of-factly.

"Nothing," he answered, raising his hands in mock defence. "But it's pretty hard to extend the conversation if someone tells you that's what they do. I mean, what are you going to say? 'What's your favourite shampoo?'" he added, watching in dismay as the comment produced a frown.

Despite getting off to a rough start, with the ice having been broken, Conor continued his attempt to get more acquainted at the post-game encounters. Although he felt they were gradually becoming more relaxed with each other, he couldn't help noticing how scanty Rachel's remarks often were. Uncertain if such brevity was rooted in shyness or disinterest, it wasn't until late-February that he asked if she'd like to go out to dinner 'sometime.' The invitation seemed to startle her, but she ultimately agreed.

"That maître d' can forget about a tip," Conor mumbled after they had accepted the menus from their waiter.

"Hmmmm," Rachel said, nodding slightly.

"I can see the place is crowded, but when I made the

reservation, I specifically requested 'a quiet table'. So where does he sit us? Right next to the door to the noisy kitchen."

The remarks were met with another simple nod, with Rachel more interested in perusing her menu.

Unable to endure the silence that ensued after they'd ordered, Conor bluntly asked, "Is it shyness or am I boring you? It feels as if we're in a French movie."

The puzzled look on Rachel's face prompted him to explain. "People don't say much, and nothing ever happens."

"I take it that was meant to be funny," Rachel replied, somewhat tersely.

"I guess that was the intent..." he said, inwardly abandoning any further attempts at humour. As a result, an uncomfortable quiet reigned over the meal. It was only when Rachel had finished pointing to her dessert choice on the menu, that Conor stumbled upon what he hoped would be a more workable subject.

"A few weeks ago, you mentioned that your boyfriend had moved to Toronto," he said.

"Former boyfriend," she reminded him, granting him a slight smile.

"He was a member of your team at the beginning of the season, wasn't he?"

"He was."

"Wasn't that a bit awkward curling on the same team with a former boyfriend?"

"It didn't bother me," Rachel told him. "Fortunately, he quickly realized he didn't like curling. Said he found it boring and quit after the second week."

Sensing he'd hit on a topic she was willing to discuss, Conor pressed on.

"So how come you guys split, if I'm not being too nosey?"

"We weren't really getting along anymore. We'd been living together in a Co-op for a long time, and I think he was just tired of having so little privacy... and obviously tired of me. His frustration was making him increasingly condescending… downright mean sometimes… always sniping at me and other people in the Co-op. He needed a change, so it's a good thing that he left when he did."

"Why didn't you tell him to take a taxi?"

"A taxi?"

"To the airport."

"There were no hard feelings between us, so when he asked me, I said 'sure'."

Having felt there'd been enough discussion of the former boyfriend, Conor was pleased when their conversation was interrupted by the waiter's return. After ordering coffee, Conor used the brief disruption to change the subject.

"I'm curious about something," he began. "Before our two teams played each other, did you notice I'd been observing you?"

"Of course," Rachel answered.

"Really?" Conor said. "So much for being discreet."

"I'm surprised you didn't pick up on *my* observing you. I also made a few inquiries about you."

"From who?"

"I'm not going to betray my sources."

"So you were spying on me while I was spying on you?"

"One could say that."

"And what sort of information did you manage to gather?" Conor asked.

"For one thing, you didn't seem to possess similar traits to my former boyfriend," Rachel told him.

"How could you tell that from merely observing me or listening to tales from a potentially unreliable source? For all you knew, I could have been just as mean or condescending."

"I can take care of myself, Conor," Rachel said.

Shortly after leaving the restaurant, rather than retreating to a local bar on what was essentially still their 'first date,' they ended up at Rachel's apartment.

"Would you care for some wine?" she asked, urging Conor to make himself comfortable in the living room.

"Wine would be great."

"Red, or white, sweet or dry?"

"Red and dry, please," he told her, taking a seat on the couch.

With Rachel in the kitchen, Conor conducted an impromptu survey, skimming over the sparsely but tastefully decorated room, before landing on a shelf crammed with books.

"Are you a big reader?" he asked, getting up to inspect the titles. "Or are these books just meant to impress visitors?"

"I hate to disappoint you, but I do read a lot," she assured him, her voice muffled by the half-closed door.

"Favourite authors?" Conor asked, as he returned to the couch.

"Depends…" she answered, pushing the door open with her hip as she entered with two glasses of red wine. "On my mood. I like all genres," she explained, setting the glasses down on the coffee table. "And you? What kind of books do you read?"

"I've taken a pause from reading lately."

"Why that?"

"I came across a pile of books I'd read recently and realized I didn't remember what half of them were about."

"Nobody's asking for book reports are they?" Rachel said, picking up her glass and gesturing Conor to do the same. "I read for the enjoyment of the moment… although some books *are* worth forgetting."

The exchange of literary preferences lasted for several more minutes until Rachel set her glass down and moved across from the chair where she'd been sitting, to join Conor on the couch. Curling her legs up beneath her, she casually stretched out her arm, letting it rest on the back of the couch, directly behind Conor's head.

"You didn't specify any favourite authors," Conor repeated, suddenly conscious of a pang of nervousness.

"I'm not really interested in talking about books," she

said, moving a bit closer. "Are you?"

"We can talk about other things," he said, before taking a sip of wine.

Without another word, Rachel simply leaned over and kissed him. Emotions that had been bubbling just below the surface, wasted no time heating up, with neither of them making the attempt to move to the comfort of the bedroom. Instead they rid themselves of their cumbersome clothing right then and there, before falling down on the thick carpet.

"Don't come inside me," Rachel whispered a short while later.

"*But I am inside you,*" Conor thought, having misunderstood the intent of her request. "Too late," he said.

"What!" Rachel cried out, pushing on Conor's chest and twisting herself out from beneath him. "You didn't really, did you?"

"Didn't what?"

"Come inside me... I'm not on the pill."

"I thought you were asking me not to come inside you, which felt kind of demeaning seeing that I already was... inside you."

"How could you misunderstand something like that?" she asked, stifling back a laugh.

With the mood seriously bent if not broken by the misinterpretation, Conor clumsily rolled over on to his back. Not knowing what to say or do, the two of them lay there for what seemed a long time.

"Sorry," Conor said, finally breaking the stoney silence, as he pulled himself up and leaned against the couch. "I just didn't realize what you meant."

"It's okay," Rachel said. "It was stupid of me to not use my diaphragm or ask you to use a condom."

"I didn't have one. I..."

"Never mind. You did but you didn't, so there's nothing to worry about," Rachel told him. "You may not believe this," she said after another long pause. "But I don't normally sleep with someone on a first date."

"I'm not sure what just happened could be described as sleeping together," he replied. "More like dozing or a quick nap."

An even lengthier silence followed this last comment, prompting Conor to slowly get up and retrieve his scattered clothing. Rachel chose to remain naked, sitting with her arms wrapped around her scrunched-up knees, as she silently watched Conor getting dressed.

"Aren't you going to get dressed?" he asked, glancing around for his shoes.

"There's no point," she told him. "I'll just go to bed after you leave."

"That bad eh?... I really don't know what to say."

"You don't have to say anything," Rachel told him, pulling a blanket from the couch and bundling herself in it.

"Why don't I call you later in the week," he said, bending down to place a hand on her shoulder, as she gave him a blank stare. "Okay then... I guess I'll be going," he told her, aware that any further delay might lead to another awkward comment.

"*What the hell just happened?*" he asked himself, as he made his way down the icy sidewalk to his car. Seemingly immune to the winter chill, he sat there for several minutes, wincing as feelings of guilt and bewilderment rattled through him, until a sudden shiver convinced him to start the motor. Glancing in the rear-view mirror as a billowing plume of exhaust spewed out into the frigid night air, he waited for a gap in the steady line of traffic before pulling out for the twenty-minute drive home, plagued by the recurring question of '*how did all this go so wrong?.*"

Still unsettled by the course events had taken that night, Conor did not call later that week, nor did he attend curling the following week, measures taken in the hope of clarifying what he wanted to do. What he failed to take into account was that Rachel would eventually reach out to him.

"Hello?"

"Hello… it's me," Rachel said, in almost a whisper.

"Oh hi,"

"Why weren't you at curling last week?" she asked.

"Didn't feel up to it," he lied. "Too many things going on."

"You didn't try calling either, like you said you would," she pointed out.

Fully expecting her to continue, Conor was surprised when the line suddenly went dead.

"Hello? Are you still there?" he asked.

"Yes."

"You were saying?"

"I didn't have anything else to say."

Although he too was at a loss for words, Conor nonetheless felt obliged to make conversation, plowing through a variety of benign subjects, hoping to spark a reaction. But no matter what the topic, Rachel's input remained curt and concise. Realizing nothing was likely to prompt her to engage, he finally told her there was a pressing matter he had to attend to and hung up.

The pattern of calls continued over the next week or two, each time quickly descending into a deadening silence.

"Nobody is ever going to believe me when I tell them she becomes a mute on the phone," Conor thought. After much reflection, he decided he would simply time the length of dead air, preparing for the next encounter by retrieving a stopwatch from his office desk and placing it next to the hallway phone. He didn't have to wait long to put his plan into action. A mere two days after their last "non-exchange," a call came in just after dinner.

"Hello?"

"Hi, it's me."

"Hello Rachel," Conor answered, trying to sound nonchalant as he picked up the stopwatch and clicked it on. By the time the minute hand had swept past zero for the first time, not a single peep had emerged from Rachel. Struggling with the option of either breaking his vow or simply hanging up, Conor finally caved in just as the watch was approaching the two-minute warning.

"Rachel, do you realize you haven't said anything for almost two minutes?" he told her. "That's crazy, don't you think?"

"You know I'm not big on small talk," she answered. "I only talk when I have something to say."

"Then I can only assume you have nothing to say. So why call? I mean there's nothing wrong with being concise, but you don't instigate *any* conversation. Do you have any idea how frustrating that is? You're taking Emerson's quote 'be sincere or be silent' to the extreme."

"Sometimes I'm afraid you'll find me boring."

"I thought it was me who was boring you. But either way, silence doesn't exactly make for a satisfying dialogue."

Much to Conor's frustration, even these brief comments failed to provoke a lengthier response.

"Rachel... We need to talk. I mean really talk," he declared.

"But not on the phone, face to face. I promise I will call you in a day or two and we can arrange something." And with that, Conor said goodbye and placed the handset back in its cradle.

Feeling somewhat desperate after numerous bouts of reflection produced nothing more than a series of dead-end doubts, Conor called up his friend, William, hoping for a little barroom consultation.

"How did I manage to misjudge her so badly?" he asked, once their first round had been delivered.

"So let me get this straight," William replied. "You observed this woman for several weeks, finally got around to talking with her and then on your first date, she sleeps with you. So where's the problem?"

"Napped." Conor said, reaching for his glass.

"Napped?"

"Inside joke, forget it," Conor told him.

"Seriously, what's the problem?"

"Well for one thing, it's a struggle to get her to communicate."

"But she slept... or napped with you on the first date, so the woman's obviously interested in you. What more communication do you need?"

"What I don't need are cutting remarks. If I wanted clichés I'd buy myself a self-help book," Conor retorted. "I don't understand why my interest in her has all but evaporated."

"Lad, what's to understand? I get the lack of communication bit, especially the phone calls. That would bug the hell out of me too. I think this is just a classic case of that old, 'what looks good from afar, is often far from good.' Who doesn't judge a book by its cover once in awhile? It seems pretty simple to me. If your interest has really flamed out, it's time to put this bout of infatuation out to pasture."

The discussion with William had not been of much help and the day after their meeting, Conor placed a call to Rachel.

"Whatever you want to say, why can't you just say it over the phone?" was her initial response.

"I've seen what happens between us on the phone. I'd prefer to talk in person," Conor explained. Receiving no reply, he went on. "Okay... if this is the way it has to be," he told her with an air of resignation. "I've done a lot of thinking about us over the last week."

"As have I," Rachel told him.

"I'm interested in hearing what conclusions you've come to, but let me go first," he urged, grateful that Alice's ghost was not hovering overhead, able to hear what he was about to say. "The simple truth is I don't see a future for us...as partners.

"Rachel? Are you still there?" Conor asked, when there was no response.

"I'm here," was the subdued reply.

"Did you hear what I just said?"

"Yes."

"Don't you have anything to say? "

"I'm disappointed," she began hesitantly. "And at the same time angry, which makes for a strange brew. I'm disappointed because you seem to be closing the door before really seeing who's behind it."

"And angry?"

"I don't know if I have the right to be angry because you're being honest. Maybe it's more being humiliated than angry. It feels like I was nothing more than a passing fancy for you."

"A passing fancy?" Conor echoed, affronted by the accusation.

"Well, we did sleep together."

"I don't see what that has to do with this."

Met with more silence, Conor continued.

"I don't know if this will help put things in perspective, but when I first saw you at curling, I was intrigued. The way you seemed to stay above the fray. That fascinated me and I wanted to know who was behind that aloofness. So I made some inquiries, took the step of talking with you and..."

"So what are you saying?" Rachel interrupted. "You enjoyed the chase but not the catch?"

"Not at all. But I've been struggling to put my finger on why I started to feel different. For sure the one-sided phone calls haven't helped."

"I've told you... I don't talk when I don't have anything to say."

"But don't you see," Conor said.

"No, wait," she broke in. "You have to admit we don't really know each other. Yet after a single 'date', you're telling me you feel there's no basis for anything further."

This time it was Conor who fell silent.

"Conor?"

"Yeah... I'm here. I don't know what to tell you. It's just something I felt and ..."

"What did I do?" Rachel asked, her tone softening slightly.

"It's more what you don't do," he answered. "You know I could have handled this differently. Fed you excuses why I couldn't talk or meet, like I had to cut the grass, wash the car or whatever. But I wanted to be up front with you," Conor told her. "But you know what's terribly ironic about all this?" he added.

"I'm listening," Rachel answered.

"I've long believed that when two people can maintain a lengthy silence with each other and not feel awkward about it, it's a sign of a deep friendship. Neither feels the need to constantly be talking. And now here I am saying that I find it disturbing that you are silent so often … especially on the phone. You rarely share what you're thinking."

"Aren't you just re-enforcing my point?" she told him, her impatience noticeable in her tome. "To only speak when there's something to say. And right now I have nothing further to say."

And with that, Rachel abruptly ended the call.

There were no further calls in the following few weeks, leading Conor to think Rachel had accepted his decision to part ways. Coincidental or not, she did not show up for any of the remaining curling games and for his part, Conor felt no need to inquire about her absence. Two months passed without any communication. Emboldened by the lack of contact between them, Conor made a point of seeing that Rachel was included on the guest list for an 'end of season' party he'd decided to hold. On the evening of the party, Rachel arrived with Katie, one of the members of her curling team. Beyond an initial greeting and perfunctory hug in the hallway, she and Conor did not exchange more than a few words amidst the tumult of the party. It was only later, when Conor had gone upstairs to collect something from his den, that further contact took place. Seated at his office desk, he was flipping through a notebook for an address, when he suddenly felt a pair of hands on his shoulders. Cringing involuntarily at the unexpected touch, Conor turned to see Rachel staring down at him.

"Have you been trying to avoid me?" she asked.

"God, you scared me," he told her. "I didn't hear you," he added, as he closed the notebook and placed it back in the drawer. "And no I haven't been avoiding you."

"It sure feels like it. You haven't said more than two words to me since I got here. If you didn't want to talk to me, why did you bother inviting me?"

"I haven't had the chance to talk to a lot of people tonight," he said. "And to answer your question, I made sure you were invited because you're a member of the league."

"That was your only reason? I was hoping I meant a little more to you than that," she said. "

"Rachel, you know how parties are sometimes. As the so-called host, I've been trying to mingle as much as I can."

"I don't seem to have made that list."

"There's been no devious plot to ignore you," Conor told her, standing up and edging towards the doorway. "You know I should really be getting back downstairs."

"Well, don't let me keep you," Rachel snarled. "But before you go, there's something you should know, Conor. I didn't come here tonight harbouring any illusions about us. I admit it took me some time to accept your decision, but I've come to see that you were probably right. We don't have enough in common for a long-lasting relationship. But up until tonight I thought maybe we could at least still be friends."

"I really don't know."

"Well if it's something you have to think about, we probably can't. But I'm okay with that. And I'll tell you something else. Friends or no friends, one way or the other, you'll never be rid of me."

"What's that supposed to mean?" Conor asked, pausing in the doorway.

"It's just my way of saying you won't forget me even after

I'm long dead and gone."

Convinced there was no sense in pouring fuel on a remark he felt was highly flammable, Conor chose to say nothing, as the two of them went back downstairs and melted separately into the crowd.

To no one's surprise, they did not remain friends. Word of each other's whereabouts and exploits was occasionally passed on through a mutual friend, but neither Conor nor Rachel made any attempt at contacting each other. Despite having lost touch with her for several years, Conor was nevertheless saddened to hear that Rachel had died unexpectedly at the age of 42, the result of a brain haemorrhage detected too late. Recalling the prediction she'd made in his den that night, he was spurred to search for her obituary, only to discover that it contained a quote, from T.S. Eliot, of all people. *"Only those who risk going too far, can possibly find out how far one can go."*

*

Pause Three.

Cheryl

"It would only be for two days, I promise," Jessica explained in a late-night phone call. "I've wanted you to meet Cheryl for ages and this seems like the perfect opportunity. She's going to be in town for a conference next month and I thought it would be nice if she could stay with you rather than some dingy hotel. I think the two of you would hit it off. Tell me it's okay," Jessica pleaded. "Please, pretty please."

"I guess it would be alright," Conor replied, his uncertainty clearly noticeable. "Although the idea of spending an entire weekend with a complete stranger doesn't exactly thrill me," he added. "What's she like? And please don't just say 'interesting.'"

"I don't want to create any false impressions or expectations. You'll have the chance to discover that yourself if you agree to let her stay. All I'll say is that Cheryl is one of the nicest people I know. She's been a good friend ever since we were kids. We've stayed in touch all these years even though she moved out to the West coast right after graduating. But there's no reason to worry. She'll be at the conference all day, both days, so you'll only have to show her a good time in the evenings."

"If this Cheryl has been such a good friend, how come I've never heard of her before?"

"I'm sure I've mentioned her."

"Not that I can recall."

"Well then this is your chance to finally meet her."

"What kind of conference is it?" Conor asked.

"To be honest, I'm not exactly sure. It has something to do with her job. She's a geriatric nurse at a hospital in Victoria. I'd really be grateful if you'd say 'yes'."

"And this 'nice' Cheryl is okay spending two days with someone she doesn't know from a hole in the ground?"

"For sure. Cheryl is really easy-going. Besides, like I said, it won't be two days, only two evenings. I think she's probably a little curious after all I've said about you."

"Oh great," Conor snorted. "I can just imagine the kind of stories you've passed on. So she knows about me, but I know nothing about her, other than that she's 'nice'. Just what *did* you tell her about *me*?"

"Don't be so paranoid, Conor," Jessica scolded. "I told her you were an 'interesting' guy, easy to talk to, and as far as I knew, not an ax murderer. She trusts my judgement. She's looking forward to meeting you… assuming you agree."

Despite his reservations, Conor consented. In the three weeks that followed, he all but forgot about his promise. It was only when Jessica called the night before his imminent houseguest was scheduled to arrive, that his memory was jogged.

"So, I take it the red carpet is all rolled out?" Jessica asked.

"Yeah, I rolled it out last night," Conor replied. "But it's probably covered in snow by now."

"I'm sure Cheryl won't mind. I was talking to her last night, and she sounded pretty excited. I'm not sure if it was because of the conference or the chance to meet you. Maybe a bit of both. Let's see if you can live up to her expectations. I'm expecting a full report, so you better behave yourself."

"Behave myself? What sort of friend have you made me out to be?"

"Oh Jeez, Conor... Lighten up, will ya? I'm just ribbing you. I have no doubt the two of you will enjoy each other's company. By the way, she told me to tell you that she insists on taking a taxi from the airport."

"Why that?"

"She's already grateful you're letting her stay there. She doesn't want to put you out further by collecting her at the airport. Besides, she can put it on her expense account. So have fun."

With that wish extended, Jessica rung off.

It was bad weather out west that caused Cheryl's plane to be late. As a result it was just after ten when the taxi dropped her off at Conor's house.

"It's nice to meet you, Cheryl," he said, ushering her into the hallway.

"Same for me," she replied, rubbing her hands to shake off a chill. "Jessie's told me so much about you."

"Yeah, so I've heard," he said, taking her coat and luggage and inviting her to make herself at home in the living room. "I'm just going to take your suitcase up to the spare room," he told her, easing back into the hallway. "Won't be a minute. When I'm back, would you care for some wine?"

"Oh... I'm not sure that's a good idea," she said. "I've got a long day ahead of me tomorrow, and what with all the running around today and then the delay with the flight … I'm feeling kind of pooped."

"Okay, if you'd prefer not. It's your call." he said.

"Maybe just one glass," she said. "But don't fill it to the brim."

"Red or white?"

"Red please, preferably dry."

"*Seems nice enough,*" Conor thought as he climbed the stairs, and pushed open the door to the spare room. *"Maybe it won't be so awkward after all."*

A short while later, Conor returned to the living room with two glasses and a bottle of Chianti, setting all three down on the coffee table as he proceeded to fumble with the corkscrew.

"Jessica told me that you've been friends since you were juvenile delinquents."

"It's been much longer than that," Cheryl answered. "We've known each other since grade school. So we're talking many years. Before I forget, I really appreciate your letting me stay here."

"It's my pleasure," Conor replied, as the cork popped. "At least I hope it will be," he added jokingly. "Say when," he added, holding the bottle above her glass. "I have to admit I'm a bit curious why we've never met before. I've known Jessica for ages and visited a number of times since she moved back home, but I can't recall her having ever mentioned your name."

"I've been gone from the hometown since '75. I rarely get back and when I do, there's often not enough time to get together with Jessie. Yet we've managed to stay in touch by phone and letters."

"You call her Jessie?" Conor asked, handing her her glass.

"Always have, always will."

"Must be a hometown thing," Conor said, raising his own glass in a toast. "I've always called her Jessica. At any rate, here's to our mutual friend who's responsible for our finally meeting."

"Cheers," Cheryl answered, leaning forward to clink glasses. "Did she ever tell you her nickname?"

"No… What sort of nickname?"

"A lot of us call her, 'Thrasher'."

"Why that?"

"Well if you've known her that long, you must have noticed how quickly she can separate the wheat from the chaff on virtually every subject known to mankind."

"Thrasher, eh?" Conor repeated, leaning back in his chair. "It does kind of fit. Anyway… on another subject… What drew you to Victoria? That place always conjures up the image of blue-haired ladies with cat-eye glasses having tea and dainties at the Empress Hotel."

"That's not far off the mark," Cheryl chuckled. "It is a pretty conservative town, and the mild weather attracts a lot of retirees."

"Hence your being a geriatric nurse?" he prodded. "Jessica told me."

"There's never a shortage of patients," she said with a smile.

"So what's life like out there amongst the ancients?"

"It took some getting used to at first, but I've come to really like it. I managed to buy a house before prices went through the roof, so I have my own little shelter from the storm. I could never move back to Jamestown, even if it's not the best of times on the coast right now."

"You mean work wise? If I'm not being too nosey," Conor asked.

"It's not so much work… although that is pretty stressful at times. Let's just say there's trouble in Paradise at the moment," she said. "But I don't want to bore you with all that. I'd rather hear about you and Jessie. How did you guys meet?"

"If she's told you so much about me, I'm surprised she's never mentioned anything about our initial encounter because it's a funny story.

"I'm all ears."

"We'd both been invited separately to a party thrown by a mutual friend. I was told it was going to be a costume party with a Mexican theme, so a friend and I dressed up in sombreros and serapes. But when we got there, we found out that Jill, the mutual friend, had only told us that and nobody else."

"So nobody else came dressed as Mexicans?" Cheryl asked.

"No. We were the only two amongst twenty or so others who were all in normal clothes. That was Jill's idea of fun."

"And Jessie?"

"She was there with her then husband. I don't remember his name."

"Christopher," Cheryl told him.

"Okay… Anyway, I don't know if it was a case of her being nervous or what, but that night she was really loud and boisterous. If I had based my opinion of her solely on that first night, I doubt we would have ever become friends."

"Then how did you become friends?"

"About three months after that party, I dropped in on Jill one evening, and Jessica, or Jessie, happened to be there. She and her husband had just broken up and she was not in the best of shape. I had the feeling I'd interrupted an intense discussion, and I was about to leave when out of the blue, Jessica - sorry it just feels weird to start calling her Jessie - she asked me what I was doing the following weekend. I told her 'Nothing as far as I know,' and that's when she asked me if I would accompany her to her office Xmas party."

"At that point you had only met her once before? At the party?" Cheryl asked.

"Right… But then I did something that I still feel embarrassed about. When she asked me that, I simply told her, 'do I look like the kind of guy who would go to an office Xmas party?' From the stunned look on her face, it wasn't the response she 'd been expecting or hoping for."

"Ouch…" Cheryl said, hunching up her shoulders. "Splits

from her husband and then is jilted by a perfect stranger. And she still managed to be your friend?"

"That only came later. A month or so after my faux pas, we ended up at a social together with Jill. In between dances, Jessica and I got into a deep conversation, mostly about relationships. I guess that was really the start of it all."

"One of the things Jessie's mentioned about you was how much she values being able to talk to you about almost anything."

"It's been the same for me. We used to tell each other that whenever either of us got into another relationship, we wouldn't settle for anything less in a partner than the rapport we had as friends."

"Sounds like a noble goal… Feeling like you can talk to someone about almost anything is something special… especially if it's someone of the opposite sex… But we don't want to go there, do we Cheryl," she said, lifting her glass. "One question though. If you and Jessie have been such good friends for so long, wasn't there ever a time when either of you thought you might become a 'couple'?"

"There was never a strong urge to take it further… at least from my side. I think we valued the friendship too much to risk possibly damaging it."

"Fair enough I suppose," Cheryl said, setting down her glass. "You know I'd really like to talk more, but I think I should head off to bed. There's a breakfast planned at the conference, so I'll be up early. I'll try and be quiet so I don't wake you. Hopefully we'll have some time tomorrow night to continue the conversation and get to know each other a little better."

"I hope so," Conor told her. "I put out an extra towel and face cloth for you in the bathroom. If you need anything else, just holler. This is a pretty quiet neighbourhood, so you should get a good night's sleep."

Household chores and yard work kept Conor busy for most

of the following day. Having forgotten to ask Cheryl when she might be back from the conference, he had not made any definite plans for dinner. As it turned out, the conference ran longer than anticipated, and Cheryl did not return until just after nine.

"Have you had dinner?" was the first question posed, as he let her in. "If you want I can order us in a couple of pizzas."

"I have actually," she said, handing him her coat. "That's one of the reasons I'm late. A group of us decided to go out for dinner on the spur of the moment. I'm sorry... I should have called. Why don't you order something for yourself. In the meantime, if it's okay, I'd like to take a quick shower."

"Fine," he told her. "I had a late lunch so maybe I'll just grab something to snack on while you're in the shower. Would you like some wine when you're done?"

"More of what we were drinking last night would be great, even though I had some wine at dinner."

Approximately half an hour later, Conor was cleaning up in the kitchen when Cheryl joined him, having changed from her business suit into jeans and a flannel shirt.

"God... I feel almost human again," she confessed, nodding as Conor pointed to the wine bottle on the counter. "Say when," he urged, as he started to fill her glass. "So how *was* the conference today?" he asked, as the two of them moved to the living room and sat across from each other."

"Long," she answered, rubbing the back of her neck. "And intense. There's usually way too much information to absorb at these conferences, and I often get a stiff neck from staring at the power point presentations the whole day."

"I could get you a warm towel or hot water bottle if you think it would help," he said.

"Thanks, but no thanks. The shower helped loosen me up but what I could really use is a massage."

Although unsure if the request had been directly aimed at him, Conor nonetheless flinched, as the comment hung in the air for a moment. "I'm not what you could call a profi, but maybe I can be of some help," he said with some hesitation.

"Ohhh, that would be soooo… great," Cheryl answered. "Maybe later. I'm enjoying this wine right now."

"Whatever you prefer."

"You know, in the taxi this evening," Cheryl began, switching subjects. "I was thinking again about what Jessie had said about how you guys talk about everything."

"We do. Some of our most intense discussions happen when one of us is troubled about something. Small talk has never been a forté for either one of us, so we don't tend to 'chat' much."

"I'm the same. But you seemed to do okay last night," she goaded playfully.

"I persevered," he replied with a smile. "But I probably exhausted my capacity last night, so tonight I may just bore you to tears."

"I'm sure we can find something of interest to talk about. If not I'll just go for the massage."

"Fair enough," Conor said, raising his glass. "So here's to an enjoyable evening."

"Politics, religion, or death?" Cheryl asked, after they had clinked glasses.

"If it's only those three, I'll take death."

"Interesting," she mused aloud. "That's a subject that's always fascinated me. Not many people are comfortable talking about it. Jessie for example."

"Really?" Conor said. "So much for our talking about everything."

"Don't get me wrong. It's not something I bring up every time we call or see each other. But I clearly recall her reaction when one time I told her I believed dead people become a part of our conscience."

"Uhh hhuh." Conor murmured. "Explain please."

"You have to imagine a scenario where dead relatives or friends are able to observe everything you do: that they have access to your innermost thoughts."

"I'm not sure my imagination would stretch that far, but it's an interesting concept," Conor replied. "If it were true, it might make people behave differently."

"Maybe in a perfect world, but I think it is true," Cheryl answered, emphatically nodding her head. "I've found that after someone close to me has died, I've often sensed their presence very strongly. Sometimes it's only for a few days, but other times longer. It's as if they're looking over my shoulder. Have you never felt that?"

"For sure. I think that's pretty normal if you were close to someone. But don't you think this 'presence' you feel is just old memories coming to the surface?"

"It's more than that. At least for me. I feel myself wondering if they would approve of what I'm doing … or not doing."

"I don't mean to be flippant, but that almost sounds like something a member of a religious sect would say."

"God no...me a member of a sect? No way," she told him. "Actually, I shouldn't use that word, seeing I consider myself to be a pagan."

"Pagans believe in gods," Conor pointed out.

"True.. just not *That* one. But no, I'm not a member of a sect and never have been."

"So when you feel this person's presence hovering, do they ever say anything to you?"

"Not directly. I don't hear voices if that's what you mean. I just feel they're urging me to ask myself, 'should you be doing this?' Like a part of your conscience."

"Hmmm," Conor said with a sigh. "I think it would make me crazy to have some dead relative second guessing me all the time."

"You make it sound almost spooky. It's not so dramatic," Cheryl assured him, unsure if she was being mocked. "Boy, Jessie was right," she said, pausing to take a sip of wine. "You *are* easy to talk to and you actually listen. Most guys I know don't know how to do that. But one other thing about death...

don't you feel that the death of a good friend or relative trivializes everything? That it takes awhile to get back to feeling there's a point again?"

"That's something I can agree with you on. But I'm starting to feel we've just about covered death to death," Conor kidded.. "What else are we gonna talk about?"

"To be honest... I'd rather take you up on the massage before I get too loaded to enjoy it," Cheryl answered, immediately setting her glass down and reaching for the top buttons of her shirt. "Do you happen to have a blanket?" she asked, as she loosened the shirt at her shoulders. "I feel a little chilly. I can just sit here on the rug with you behind me on the couch. That way you'll have easy access to my neck."

"I guess that would work," Conor replied, setting down his own glass before retrieving a blanket from the sun room. After lowering her shirt to leave her shoulders bare, Cheryl wrapped herself in the blanket, and sat down with her back against the couch, gesturing Conor to take his place behind her.

"Is this helping at all?" he inquired after several minutes of kneading.

"Ohhhh, yes it is," Cheryl cooed, briefly halting the massage to arch her head slowly from side to side. "My neck feels a lot better but now it's my upper back that feels kind of stiff. I must have been overcompensating for my neck in my shoulders. Would it be asking too much to massage my back a bit as well?" she asked. Without waiting for an answer, Cheryl undid the remaining buttons on her shirt, slipped out of it and tossed it on the couch.

"You sure you're not gonna be too cold?" Conor asked, watching as Cheryl spread the blanket on the floor and lay face down.

"Right now I'm okay, but I'll tell you if I do," she answered, reaching back to undo her bra, leaving the expanse of her upper back free. "I'm not sure how this will work best. You can either try kneeling beside me or just straddle me. Whichever is better," she told him before resting her head on her folded arms."

Having found a comfortable position at her side, Conor continued softly massaging the muscles around her neck and shoulders, before moving down to her upper back.

"How come your hands are so warm?" she asked.

"Blame the wine," he answered with a snicker.

"What you're doing feels really good, but you can apply more pressure. I'm not made of glass."

Duly following her instructions, Conor continued the massage for several more minutes, until he started to feel a pain in his own back.

"I hope this is helping you," he said. "But squatting in this position is starting to give me a kink in *my* back."

"Then just try straddling me," Cheryl casually suggested.

Clearing his throat, Conor did as he was told, shifting to a position where both of them could enjoy the treatment.

"For someone who said they didn't know what they were doing, you're doing a pretty good job," Cheryl told him.

"I didn't say I didn't know what I was doing. I just said I wasn't a profi."

"Well I've been to various so-called profis before, and very often you feel like you're nothing more than a slab of meat. I can tell you, none of them had such a sensual touch."

Once again, Conor felt a flinch pass through him, sensing that a subtle line had been intentionally crossed.

"I guess I should take that as a compliment," he told her.

Not having received a more overt response, Cheryl seemed reluctant to make any additional comments, and for the next twenty minutes or so, the pair refrained from further conversation, content to simply engage in the pleasurable benefits of skin on skin.

Suddenly without warning, Cheryl rose up slightly on one elbow, her free hand holding her loose bra in place.

"Do you want to go upstairs?" she asked, softly but firmly.

"That would be nice," Conor answered.

"Who would have thought?" Conor felt himself pondering, after passion had taken its course, and the two of them lay in bed, bathed in the moonlight streaming through the open curtains.

"I didn't expect this," he said, turning to face Cheryl.

"It wasn't exactly at the top of my agenda either, but I can't say I'm sorry it happened," she admitted.

"What are we gonna tell Jessica?"

"I don't think Jessie needs to know everything that goes on in my life ... or yours,"

"I guess not."

"I know this was all unexpected, but I need to ask you something. A part of me can't help wondering whether all your houseguests get such special treatment?" she asked with a sly grin.

"I was gonna say unfortunately no, but I don't want to imply that this wasn't something special for me too. Because it was, or is."

With the clarity of a new day, next morning at breakfast, both Conor and Cheryl felt the need to discuss the events of the previous evening.

"I hope you don't think I slip into bed so easily with every person I meet," Cheryl said, warming her hands around her coffee mug.

"I didn't think that, and if you recall, there were two of us in that bed last night," Conor answered.

"I'm glad we both see it as something natural that just happened. At the same time though, I wonder if I've just made my life more complicated."

"How so?" Conor asked, gesturing as to whether she wanted more coffee.

"No thanks. I need to get going soon... I just meant in terms of what's going on at home."

"Maybe it's like you said, not everyone needs to know everything about all aspects of your life."

"Ha… That's for sure," Cheryl chuckled. "My friend doesn't even know I'm staying here. Jessie suggested and arranged it all… the sneaky devil. It just so happens that Barry is not one of Jessie's favourite people, so I'm sure she'll cover for me if he happens to ask. He's a bit of a control freak and likes to know where I'm going, where I've been and with whom etc."

"And you're okay with that?"

"It gets on my nerves sometimes," she admitted. "It doesn't help matters that we had a bit of a blow-up before I left. I'm not sure what I may be going back to."

"How long have you two been together?" Conor asked.

"We met about three years ago, but we've only been living together for the past year. That has been a challenge. It's let me see a side of him I'm not particularly fond of sometimes… Look, I'm sorry, but I really have to get going," she said, glancing at her watch. "We can talk more when I'm back tonight."

Several hours later, Conor had been absent-mindedly skimming the headlines in the newspaper when the phone rang.

"Conor?" the voice asked.

"Yes," he replied, not immediately recognizing the caller.

"It's Cheryl. I'm glad I caught you," she said, sounding rather flustered.

"What's up?"

"About an hour ago, while I was in a seminar at the conference, I got an urgent text message from my brother, asking me to call him. When I did, he told me that our Mom has taken a turn for the worse. She's been ill for some time, but this sounds serious, and he's asked me to fly home tonight. I called the airline right away and managed to book a flight out at 8:30 tonight. The conference should wrap early so I'll just have time to get back to your place, pack up and head straight to the airport. I'm really sorry about this. I was looking forward to spending more time with you."

"I'm sorry to hear about your Mom," he told her. "Look, I can drive you to the airport, so you won't be so rushed."

"Are you sure you don't mind? Thank you. That would be great. I'll call when I'm leaving the conference. Talk to you later."

Despite the distressing news, by the time Cheryl arrived home just before six, she appeared in control of her emotions.

"Fortunately, the people at the conference were very understanding so I managed to leave early," she explained, giving Conor a peck on the cheek. "I wish you and I had more time, but I need to be at the airport by 7:15 at the latest."

"We can easily make that," Conor assured her. "Why don't you go pack, and I'll pull the car out of the garage. Are you hungry at all? Do you want me to make you a sandwich or something?"

"I did have a small lunch, but I'm too hyper to eat anything right now. On second thought, maybe a sandwich would be good. With this late a flight I probably won't get dinner."

They were out of the house shortly after six-thirty, relieved to find traffic lighter than expected.

"I can't predict how things are going to go with my Mom, but I don't have to be back at work until Friday, so maybe I can stop here on the way back home," Cheryl suggested, as they were pulling into the airport parking garage. "Of course that's if you want me to come."

"For sure," he told her, removing her suitcase from the trunk. "When do you think you might come?"

"I can't say... Tuesday night, maybe Wednesday. It depends on what happens in Jamestown. Either way, I would have to fly home on Thursday at the latest... unless," she said, her voice trailing off as they waited for the elevator up to the ground floor.

"If you can, that would be great," Conor answered.

"I just made it," Cheryl said a few minutes later, waving her boarding card. "But they said I have to head for the boarding gate right away because I still need to go through security. I'd hoped we might have time for a drink, but it looks like our goodbye will have to be short and sweet," she said, opening her arms for a hug. "I'll call you from Jamestown tonight, once I know where things stand… if that's alright."

"I should be home. If not you can leave a message."

But she didn't call that evening, the next day or the next. In fact, Conor didn't hear a word until the middle of the following week, when Jessica rang.

"I heard about Cheryl's mom," she explained. "I managed to see her while she was here,"

"You mean she's not there anymore?" Conor asked.

"No, she left last Thursday."

"Oh…" Conor replied, trying not to sound surprised. "And how's her Mom?"

"She's okay. It turned out to be a bit of false alarm, which oddly enough seemed to piss Cheryl off. I don't know what that was all about. It couldn't have been the extra cost of flying home because she earns good money. At any rate, while she was here I tried pumping her on how things went with you, but she was pretty close- mouthed. All she basically said was 'it was okay.' Did something happen between you two?"

"What do you mean something?"

"I don't know. Like maybe you didn't get along. Cheryl can be pretty tempestuous at times."

"What did she say?" Conor asked.

"Oh, no you don't," Jessica said. "I want *you* to tell me how it went. I don't want you to tailor your tale of adventure to match hers."

Suspecting that Cheryl had not divulged details on what had taken place, Conor assumed Jessica was bluffing, hoping that Conor would accidentally spill whatever beans there were to spill.

"We got along fine. You were right. She is really nice," he proffered.

"That's it? She was nice? Did you guys do anything

together in the evening, like go out to eat, or whatever? Come on, Conor. Truth or consequences."

"You make it sound like it was a date. She was a houseguest. She was tired after a long day at the conference, so we just stayed here, had some wine and talked."

"What did you talk about?"

"A lot of things... About how you and I met for example. Stuff like that."

"Boring..." Jessica moaned into the phone. "I figured maybe you might have hit it off on another level. Didn't you find her attractive?"

"*She's fishing*," Conor thought, now certain that Cheryl had remained tight-lipped. "For sure, but as you know, she has a boyfriend. I don't think she was looking for any extracurricular activities, if that's what you're hinting at."

"Oh, brother. That jerk," Jessica growled. "I'm surprised she told you about Barry. Speaking of the devil, did you hear what happened when Cheryl got back to Victoria?"

"How would I hear anything about that?" Conor answered.

"Yeah, I guess not... Barry, the prince, was waiting at the airport with flowers and a limo. On the ride home he popped the question."

"Really?" Conor said.

"And the foolish girl accepted. I couldn't believe it when she told me."

"She called and told you that?"

"Actually I called her. It's funny you should ask. You'd think that someone who just got engaged would have been happy, but she sounded kind of subdued. Maybe she just curbed her enthusiasm because she knows I'm not Barry's biggest fan."

"So what did you say to her?"

"It took me awhile to say anything, which probably didn't go over too well. I ended up congratulating her. I mean she's a good friend. What else could I say?"

"Hmmph… I had the impression they hadn't been getting along," Conor said.

"Did she say that?" Jessica asked.

"She hinted at it. She didn't go into much detail."

"Ahhh… who knows with that girl. Cheryl can be all over the place. Anyways, I was a bit disappointed."

"About her getting engaged?"

"That too… but more-so about you and her. I confess, a part of me was trying to play match maker, and then look what happens. You each think the other is 'nice,' and she goes off and gets engaged to that jerk. Weren't there any sparks between you guys?"

"Jessica… what do you want me to say? Yeah, of course. In the span of a single evening we fell in love, set a wedding date, thought about buying a house, having kids etc.etc. Sorry to disappoint you. I enjoyed meeting her and found her pleasant company, despite the limited time we had together."

"Did you guys rehearse your answers? 'Pleasant company' is almost verbatim to what Cheryl told me. If I was the suspicious type I might think you guys were trying to hide something."

"Man oh man, Jessica… look, if you really wanna know. We started off just talking in the living room, enjoying a glass of wine. She complained about having a sore neck so I offered to give her a massage."

"A massage?" Jessica asked, her voice rising slightly.

"A neck massage, which led to her asking for a back massage. Suffice to say things got a little heated, and we ended up going upstairs for a night of passion. Satisfied?"

"There's no reason to be sarcastic, Conor. I was merely asking how it went. Cheryl would never sleep with someone so easily. She barely knows you. You're just trying to put me on."

"Goodnight Jessica."

*

One might be forgiven for thinking that five, at times, tormenting encounters in one year, would have been enough for anyone. But despite the theory of learning by doing, by the time 1979 drew to a close, Conor was no closer to comprehending the reasons for his cup having runneth over, nor was he any nearer to determining what it might take to establish a lasting relationship.

At that point, he had simply no way of knowing that within several years, he would meet someone who he would stay with for the next 40 years, adding credence to the old adage that, *'something worth waiting for, is exactly that'*.

✳

MOROCCAN MOMENTS

"Excuse me pal, but what the hell do you think you're doing?" Stefan shouted, as he grabbed the young boy's shoulder and pulled him away from his attempt to unfasten the safety pin meant to protect Carrie's knapsack from being plundered while still on her back.

"Pardon Monsieur," came the reply, accompanied by a look of feigned innocence as if he had done nothing more objectionable than accidentally nudge someone on a crowded bus. "Pardon," the boy repeated, as he slipped back into the shelter of his assembled allies. Stefan and Carrie had been encircled by the group of teenage boys within seconds of crossing the border. Given that several looked downright mean, Stefan's move to openly confront one of their brood may have not been the wisest of moves. Fortunately, because of the presence of other tourists, his action succeeded, discouraging not only the would-be thief but other members of the troupe from further harassment, allowing him and Carrie to make their way to the waiting bus.

"Why Morocco?" Stefan had asked Carrie several weeks earlier, as they sat on the balcony of their flat in central Berlin. "There's plenty of other places I haven't seen that are easier to reach. I mean we can't even drive there. What's wrong with aiming for southern Spain. Or Gibraltar?

"Gibraltar?" Carrie had answered scornfully. "Are you kidding? That place is one notch down from an amusement park."

"But I've heard it's like visiting a piece of Britain without the fog or the rain."

"That 'piece of Britain,' as you put it, is about as genuine as a three-pound note. Yeah, you see all these 'English pubs and shops when you're strolling down the main pedestrian street. They even have a 'Marks and Sparks' store," she railed. "But it all feels so fake. I've no idea why the Spanish are so keen to have it back. Besides… parts of the place are swarming with monkeys, not to mention their descendants."

"Their descendants?" Stefan asked.

"Tourists. They flock to the Rock, as the locals call it. I'm telling you, the whole place feels incredibly artificial."

"So you've been there before?"

"Once… and believe me, once is enough. To make matters worse, once you've escaped the tawdriness of the main shopping area, chances are you'll end up getting caught in a traffic jam. Spanish border police hold periodic strikes that cause lengthy delays. The time I was there, we were forced to sit in a hot car in this huge packed parking lot for almost six hours. Fun it was not. I suppose it's a way of protesting Britain's refusal to return the peninsula to Spanish rule. If it was meant to deter tourists from ever coming back, it was highly effective."

"Okay, then Morocco it is."

It took three full days to drive from Berlin to Algeciras, with the nights being spent ramped in the back of Carrie's Renault R 4, parked at an autobahn rest stop or deserted country road, where they were less likely to encounter nosey police, hungry coyotes or zealous serial killers.

Once in the confines of the southern Spanish port city, they were lucky enough to find a parking garage that wasn't going to charge more than the car was worth. The next phase of the planned ten day stay in Morocco started out easily enough by locating the ferry's ticket office. Considerably more difficult was trying to explain to an agent why they only wanted a one-way ticket to Ceuta, the Spanish governed enclave located on the north African coast..

"Why you no want return ticket?" he'd mumbled.

"We're going to Morocco."

"Why you no go Tangier?"

"We plan to do that on the way back," Stefan told him.

"Ceuta is Spain," the agent advised.

"I'm well aware of that," Stefan replied, turning to Carrie. "Why am I bothering to explain our itinerary to this guy?"

"I was wondering the same thing," she said. "Just give him the money and let's get out of here."

Tickets in hand, they were now facing a two hour wait until the next ferry was scheduled to depart. Once on board they quickly settled in on the upper deck lounge for what was expected to be a one-hour sea crossing.

"It says here," Carrie said, reading aloud from a guidebook she'd picked up at the ticket office while Stefan had been enduring the agent's inquiries. "Ceuta has been under the control of the Spanish since the 17th century, and even remained so after Morocco gained its independence from France in 1956."

"So how come the French didn't take over Ceuta as well?" Stefan wanted to know.

"According to this, France took over the Sultanate of Morocco in 1912 under the Treaty of Fez. For some reason Ceuta was left as a military post and a free port... Oh God," Carrie suddenly gasped.

"What?"

"I hope nobody asks me where I've been on holiday."

"What do you mean?"

"According to this book, Morocco is known by locals as al-Mamlakah al-Maghrribiyah. How the heck can you ever pronounce that?"

"All that just for Morocco?"

"It apparently means 'the Kingdom of the West."

"Does it say anything about the Berbers?" Stefan asked, glancing out at the calm waters of the Mediterranean.

"The Berbers?," Carrie said, flipping a page in the

guidebook.

"You mean the rug people?"

"The rug people?" Stefan repeated. "I'm not sure that's how they would like being referred to."

"I know who they are," Carrie answered, somewhat crossly. "What are you getting so uppity about? It's not as if I asked, 'are they the people who cut hair in Ireland?'"

"Fair enough."

"It says here they were one of the tribes that populated Morocco before it was even Morocco," Carrie continued reading aloud. "Listen to this. Not only was it once a Protectorate of France, over the centuries it was also colonized by the Roman, the Carthaginians, the Greeks and for a spell was independent under the Byzantines."

"What does it say about Ceuta?"

"Give me a minute," Carrie answered, as she flipped through several pages. "The city is separated from Morocco proper by a double ring of fences that completely surround its borders. Each fence is 20 feet high and meant to prevent the city from being overrun by African refugees."

Knowing they would be using public transport, the two travellers had packed light, limiting their luggage to two small knapsacks. Just how prescient that decision had been became apparent during the noticeably less strenuous jaunt from the port to the border crossing in the suffocating heat.

With passports and visas clutched in their hands, there was little trouble getting through the border control of both Spanish and Moroccan authorities. Once safely on Moroccan territory, they couldn't have gone more than a hundred yards, when they were accosted by a pack of young teenage boys, jabbering away in French and broken English, wanting to know if they needed a guide or wished to purchase what looked to be a packet of crumpled postcards.

"No thanks," Stefan told the one walking backwards in front of him. "Why would I need a guide? We're in the middle of nowhere."

"Where you go?" the boy wanted to know.

"We're on our way to Tetouan… if I'm pronouncing it right."

"Bus station, half kilometre."

"That's what I was told at the border, thank you."

"You need place to stay. I know very nice place. Cheap."

"We've got a guidebook, thanks. It lists hostels and pensions."

"No can trust guidebook," the boy said, just as Stefan glanced over to see another member of the pack attempting to undo the safety-pin holding the zippers closed on Carrie's backpack.

"Excuse me pal… etc., etc.

"Jesus… Off to a great start." Stefan said to Carrie, once the group had scampered off to hound other unsuspecting tourists. "That guy was trying to get into your backpack with you right there. I hope that's not a sign of what we can expect in the next ten days," he mused aloud, as they trudged along the ribbon of burning asphalt cutting through the barren landscape.

"I thought I felt something," Carrie admitted.

Once settled in on the rickety bus heading for Tetouan, some 40 kms. distant, Carrie wasted no time in scouring the guidebook for a place to stay. While she was busy perusing the various options, Stefan simply stared out at the passing scenery which seemed to consist of nothing more than sand, sand and more sand. Every so often however, the monotony was broken by a small village, its clay-walled buildings rendering it barely visible amidst the surrounding countryside.

Her diligence paid off as Carrie was able to find an inexpensive hostel a five-minute walk from the central bus station. Once checked in, they sought directions to the market and within 15 minutes were walking through narrow alleyways of the city's bazaar. Given that the market was relatively barren of other tourists, they quickly made prime targets for the desperate salesmen hawking everything from objects of copper and wood, to carpets, foodstuffs and barrels of brightly coloured spices, to name just a few. After being badgered by at least half a dozen men within the span of several minutes, they chose to accept an offer from one particularly persistent salesman.

"Please, you come my shop," he begged. "Not far."

Unsure whether the shop in question was just around the corner as he claimed, or at the end of a distant darkened alley, they followed reluctantly, increasingly concerned about ever finding their way out again than meeting some dire fate. As they continued to tramp along through a labyrinth of shops displaying various artefacts, they were about to call a halt to the expedition when suddenly their guide stopped and urged them to enter a shop. Waiting inside was yet another salesman who greeted the couple with a half bow before drawing aside a heavy curtain and ushering them into a room where every visible space on the walls and floor was covered by various sized carpets. Adding to the already exotic atmosphere, was a haunting form of Moroccan music, a mixture of an unidentifiable instrument and a Spanish flamenco-style guitar, emanating from a set of hidden speakers. Muted by the carpets, the music was the perfect accent to complete the dream-like atmosphere. Just then, an older man entered through a side curtain Dressed in a gandoura, a loose fitting, short-sleeve tunic that descended to his ankles, he quickly approached the pair with outstretched hands.

"Welcome…welcome, Madam and Monsieur," he said with a smile, that revealed several gold teeth. "Welcome to my shop. Please take seat," he added, gesturing towards a half dozen, cracked leather hassocks scattered around the room. "You like peppermint tea?"

Carrie and Stefan glanced at each other.

"Uhhh, I guess so," he answered.

Acting on a nod from the older man, one of the staff,

who'd been standing quietly off to one side, immediately withdrew two shot glasses from a nearby cupboard and placed them on a round brass tablet directly in front of the guests. He then withdrew a pouch from inside his garment and proceeded to fill both glasses with peppermint leaves. At this point another man came out from the back carrying a copper tea pot. With the expertise of an experienced server, he began pouring a steaming liquid, repeatedly raising and lowering the teapot above the tiny glasses without spilling a drop.

"Wow... that was quite the feat," Stefan whispered to Carrie as they jointly accepted the glasses and raised them to toast their host. "Any idea what we might be about to drink?"

"I hope it's peppermint tea," she answered. "At least it doesn't smell like anything bad."

"Yowza," Stefan wheezed, trying to hide his reaction after taking the first sip. "This stuff is sweet enough to dissolve all of my fillings, not to mention melting my crowns," he muttered through the clenched teeth of a smile.

"You like buy rug," the older man asked, gesturing to an ample stack piled on the floor. "Which one you like?" he added, gripping one corner of the top rug and flinging it back to expose the one underneath. "You like dark one, light one?" he wanted to know, as he repeated the flipping action several times.

"I'm sorry," Stefan said, setting his tea back down on the tablet. "I think there's been some sort of misunderstanding. When your colleague approached us in the market, we thought he was taking us to a souvenir store. We just arrived in Morocco today and plan to visit several more cities. It would be a little tough to jam a rug into my knapsack and even if I could, I wouldn't want to have to lug it around for ten days," he said with a grin.

"We can send to your home," the elderly gentleman suggested eagerly. "Not cost much."

"They look like nice rugs," Carrie told the man. "They really do. But I'm afraid neither one of us is really in the market for one."

"Oh, oh," Stefan whispered, having seen the abrupt change on the salesman's face upon hearing this news. "We're either destined for the white slave trade or as fodder for their farm animals."

Needless to say, it came as a relief when the aged host clasped his hands and said, "I understand sir. So sorry. I wish pleasant time in my country."

With business now concluded, no efforts were made to have them finish their tea, in itself a blessing. Instead, a round of rapid half bows were exchanged before the couple were accompanied back to the store entrance and left to their own devices to find their way back to the hostel.

The hours of daylight still remaining were spent roaming the streets, trying to get a feel for 'normal' life in Tetouan.

Early next morning, shivering from the remnants of the cool night air, the pair were back on the same streets, headed to the station to catch a train bound for Fez.

"It says here that Fez was founded in the 9th century," Carrie informed Stefan as they sat waiting in the station's second-class lounge. "At one time the city was considered to be the Mecca of the West and the spiritual and cultural capital of Morocco."

"Hmmm," Stefan replied, glancing up at the large clock on the wall which indicated the train was already ten minutes late. When they finally climbed aboard and made their way to their assigned compartment, they were pleased to discover they would have it to themselves for at least a portion of the journey. Once Tetouan had been left behind, Stefan's gaze was glued to the window, marvelling at the desert-like landscape with its mesmerizing shades of brown and yellow hues. Although the scenery appeared void of any signs of vegetation or civilization, the almost hypnotic terrain would occasionally give way to include low level mountains, and a series of distant wadis. From time to time a number of mini caravans were sighted, the three or four camels in the entourage accompanied by a heavily dressed owner walking alongside. All that was missing to complete the burgeoning 1001 Nights fantasy, was a Lawrence of Arabia figure galloping across the horizon, trailed by a lengthy column of dust.

After checking in at another cheap pension, the first stop on the agenda was the centuries old Medina, a sector of Fez that contained the local bazaar, or 'Souk' as it was known locally. Sauntering through its crowded narrow gangways, where locals far outnumbered tourists, the two of them felt as if they had somehow slipped back through the veil of time to a foregone era. With its shadowy nooks and crannies, periodically broken by beams of dust-filled sunlight streaming through the thatched roof covering the shops and alleys. the mystical aura was heightened by jangling oriental music, competing with the indecipherable shouts from booth owners doing their utmost to lure in passing customers. Aside from the sheer number of utterly fascinating visual and aural elements threatening to overwhelm their senses, Stefan and Carrie were confronted with odours stemming from the plumes of smoke rising up from various meats sizzling on grills. As they moved along the row of food kiosks, those scents were quickly replaced by that of assorted fresh fruits, vegetables and spices, the latter housed in large wooden barrels in front of stalls throughout the market. In yet another section, booths were filled with identical woven baskets, decorative blankets, articles of clothing and carved olive wood souvenirs, all waiting to be sold at prices well below those in Europe.

Amidst the shifting masses, most men were dressed in the Moroccan gandoura. Similar but not identical to the one seen in Tetouan, these traditional outfits hung like a cloak over its owner, many with an ornate gold pattern sewn into the chest area. These were usually topped by a round white skullcap (kufi). Women were primarily clad in black, body- length robes, highlighted with brightly coloured scarves. Some had chosen to wear the burka, the all-encompassing Muslim garment that covered the entire body from head to toe.

"Those must be terrible to wear in this heat," Carrie remarked, as they passed a group of women whose burkas left only a narrow cloth grating for them to see through. "But I suppose they're used to it," she added.

"I read in the guidebook that Morocco is pretty much a patriarchal society, so who knows how much choice they have in the matter," Stefan told her.

"When were you peeking in my guidebook?" Carrie wanted to know.

"Last night after you fell asleep."

With midday temperatures inching towards +30, and the strain of navigating through the crush of people taking its toll, their desire to further explore was being significantly dampened.

"Why don't we look for a less crowded place that can provide some fresh, if not cooler air," Stefan suggested.

"Fine with me," Carrie agreed. "As interesting as this bazaar is, I could use a break and maybe something to drink."

A short while later in a less traveled gangway, cold drinks in hand, they suddenly found themselves confronted by a scene that gave new meaning to the phrase "sweat shop". There along a row of stalls, boys not yet in their teens were crammed into a series of tiny, badly lit cubby holes, squatting over what appeared to be round brass plates. With a hammer in one hand and a small chisel in the other, each was busy stamping decorative symbols into the plate that would ultimately serve as a table atop foldable, wooden legs. All this activity was taking place in a loud, dusty and throat parching environment, hard to bear for even several minutes, let alone a whole day.

"I take it truancy is not a crime in Morocco," Carrie said, as they watched one boy for several minutes. "Why aren't any of these guys in school?"

"My guess is because school doesn't bring in money to help out the family," Stefan answered.

"It's so sad to see young kids stuck in such a dead-end, monotonous job," Carrie said. "It can't be good for their health either. The child labour laws here must be pretty slack, if they exist at all," she added. "Let's move on before I start crying or shouting."

Having born witness to most sectors of the Souk, they stopped at a small kiosk for lunch, munching on their first falafels, before eventually making their way to a part of the city recommended by a fellow tourist who'd been seated at the next table.

"It's really quite remarkable," he'd enthused. "You really should make the effort to take it in while you're here."

Following the directions he'd provided, they managed to locate the obscure entrance he'd warned about and climbed a set of narrow stairs to a flat rooftop that offered a bird's eye view of the city's renowned "paint pots."

"How come this wasn't in your precious guidebook?" Stefan prodded.

"I haven't got that far yet, I guess. Oh my God," Carrie groaned, as they edged toward the railing of the viewing platform "What is that awful smell?"

"It's gotta be coming from the dyes in those pots," Stefan told her, pointing to the twenty or more circular cement pots laid out as if pieces on a life-size Chinese Checkers board. "They look like giant, concrete ink wells," he added.

"They're breathing that stuff all day and nobody's even wearing a mask," Carrie commented. "How can they stand that?"

"Nobody looks much older than twenty. Maybe that explains it. The older workers have all gotten sick and left."

"I'm serious, Stefan. It must be horrible to work under such conditions."

"I wasn't joking," Stefan told her. "Maybe they do all get sick after awhile."

Despite the stench, they stayed long enough to watch young, bare-footed men, their pants rolled up to their thighs, stomping on raw leather hides immersed in pots filled to the brim with various brightly coloured liquids. Other hides had either been left to soak in adjacent pots or placed on racks to dry in the sun.

"The places around here all look like they're residential flats," Carrie pointed out. "How on earth do people put up with such a pervasive stink? We've only been here five minutes and I'm already having trouble breathing."

"If the smell isn't bad enough, think what the work must be doing to the skin on their legs," Stefan said.

"This may be a so-called highlight on a city tour, but sorry, I've seen enough," Carrie complained, as she urged Stefan to retreat to the stairway. "Remind me to never buy a coloured leather jacket," she said, as they returned to street level. "Who needs a canary yellow leather jacket anyway?"

Following a visit to the royal palace with its lengthy reflecting pool and elegant fountains that could rival the Taj Mahal, the rest of the afternoon was spent traipsing through the quaint narrow alleyways of the Medina, fending off a seemingly endless phalanx of yearning salesmen.

"Have you noticed that nearly all the people who've been trying to sell us things, both here and at the Souk, are men?" Stefan asked when they had stopped for a drink at an outdoor cafe.

"Now that you mention it.," Carrie answered, glancing at the passing crowd. "But it fits. Women probably aren't allowed to take up such positions."

"You could be right," Stefan answered, taking a sip of his cold cola. "Hey, I don't know about you, but with all this walking, I'm starting to feel kind of whacked."

"It's probably the fumes from that paint place," Carrie replied.

"That didn't help. I wouldn't mind grabbing an early dinner somewhere and heading back to the pension. We've got a long train ride ahead of us tomorrow."

Opting for a restaurant a mere stone's throw from their pension, the two of them enjoyed a traditional Moroccan dinner, declining repeated offers of peppermint tea from their waiter.

"You seem to have made quite the impression," Stefan said, as the dishes were being cleared.

"What are you talking about?" Carrie asked, gently tapping her mouth with a napkin.

"Every guy in the place hasn't taken his eyes off you. since the moment we walked in."

"You're crazy," she said. "Really?"

"I'm serious… No, don't look," he told her, as Carrie was about to survey the room herself. "It's not the first time I've noticed it. When we were at the Souk, there was a point where I was walking a few steps behind you. I could see how heads were turning, fingers pointing, whispers being shared… it was as if you were some sort of celebrity."

"I honestly hadn't noticed."

"You were probably too busy fending off sales guys, but yeah, you've been a magnet since we crossed the border at Ceuta. I picked up on it in Tetouan too, but here the gawking has been more blatant. I suspect it's the blond hair and blue eyes," Stefan continued. "Not to mention your other noticeable attributes," he added with a smile.

After refusing the complimentary dessert on the grounds that they wanted to wake up with teeth, the two of them departed under the continuing gaze of other patrons, both male and female. Back at the pension just after nine, they fell into bed exhausted, asleep within minutes.

"Excuse me… do you speak English?" Stefan asked the clerk behind the thick, glass window, when his turn finally came. "Can you tell me the difference between second and third class?" he continued, without waiting for an answer to his first question.

"Third class cheaper," came the sullen reply.

"I assumed that," Stefan said. "I'd like to know what the difference is we'd be paying for."

"Why don't we just take the third class tickets, Stefan," Carrie demanded impatiently, glancing at the long line of early travellers behind them. "It can't be that intolerable, can it? As long as it doesn't smell of dye."

"I guess it's what you'd call more 'local colour'," Stefan cracked a half hour later, as they made their way down the narrow aisle of the creaking carriage that was filled with both two and four legged passengers.

"I kind of like it," Carrie confessed, squeezing herself on to a wooden bench in an already crowded compartment. "If this is good enough for the locals, it's good enough for me," she added, nodding hello to fellow passengers, none of whom appeared to be tourists. "Look at it as an adventure," she scolded Stefan, who had occupied the last remaining seat across from her, his knapsack cradled on his lap.

"I hope it's an adventure that doesn't include being pecked by a chicken or shat on by a goat," he replied, making sure his feet were clear of any curious animals, as the train lurched into motion.

"Do you have the feeling we're being stared at? Or at least you are," Stefan asked. "Especially the old guy by the window, the one with the turban."

"What about him? Carrie asked.

"He's gonna end up with a stiff neck from trying to steal so many glances at you. Maybe you should think about dyeing your hair while we're here, so you don't stand out so much. I can recommend a place where you could probably get it done cheap," Stefan joked, as the man's gaze shifted accusingly to him.

"Not funny, Stefan. I can still smell that place. It's in my pores. And by the way... how do you know this 'old guy' doesn't speak English. Don't be so insulting."

"I'm not being insulting. I'm just pointing out that you are the centre of attention…again.”

"So what if I am? It's not hurting anybody. I don't see any other tourists so naturally we're something unique. I'm sure these other people must be wondering, 'are they poor, cheap or just crazy?'"

"Shouldn't we be humming Marrakesh Express right about now?" Stefan asked, six hours later, as the the train was entering the outskirts of the place made even more famous by the 60's song. With the train having slowed to almost a crawl, the first thing to catch their attention were the numerous minarets and tiled archways serving as entrances to the old part of the city. As had been the case at the Ceuta border crossing, within seconds of leaving the bustling train station, they were surrounded by a gaggle of wanna be guides, each professing the wish to 'practice their English'."

"Sorry," Stefan told a teenager who had more or less elbowed out his competitors. "We don't really need a guide at the moment."

"I know a cheap hotel, sir."

"Thanks, but we already have a place in mind," Stefan explained, turning to Carrie. "This guy doesn't sound like he needs to practice his English any time soon. "

Increasingly frustrated by the young man's persistence, despite repeated attempts to dissuade him as they walked along the street, Stefan finally stopped to settle the matter. "I don't know what it will take to convince you that we are simply not interested in engaging your services. We just want to be left alone."

"But sir…"

"No, hold on. I don't seem to getting through to you"

"Stefan," Carrie said warily, sensing trouble brewing.

"It's not your English that needs practice, it's your manners. Be so kind as to stop harassing us."

With that he and Carrie walked off, leaving the would be guide to search for other prey.

"That wasn't exactly the auspicious welcome I was hoping

for," Carrie said. "You were kind of hard on him, don't you think?"

"Did you want him hanging around for the whole day?" Stefan grumbled. "He just wouldn't take no for an answer."

"I don't know about you," Carrie said, in a tone somewhere between exhaustion and boredom, as she looked out over the city's infamous central bazaar, from the outdoor cafe they had come to after checking in. "We just got here, and I already find this place incredibly hectic. It seems a lot more touristy than Fez. Maybe it's too soon to judge but I liked it a lot better there."

"It is a bit much," Stefan agreed, nodding to the waiter as he set down a bottle of cola with Arabic script. "But maybe it was the long train trip. And things didn't exactly get off to a great start, being molested by that guy at the train station. But we haven't really given the place a chance yet. Hopefully there are interesting things to see and do away from this circus," he added, pointing to the relentless activity in the square.

Hoping to learn whether Stefan's speculation was justified, Carrie pulled the guidebook out of her daypack.

"Did you know that Morocco was inhabited by hominids over 400,000 years ago?" she asked him.

"No, but I'll call the newspapers," Stefan answered. "What are hominids?"

"We are," Carrie explained. "At least we're part of a group that includes orangutans, gorillas, and chimpanzees."

"Who was around back then to note that we 'hominids' were here?"

"It doesn't say," Carrie said. "It only says that the first recorded history began with the Phoenicians between 8 or 9 BC."

"Weren't the Phoenicians the guys who invented the blinds?" Stefan said with a straight face.

"Funny boy," Carrie said. "As I was saying... The Berbers... there's your Berbers again... were apparently here, at least on the coast. In 40 AD the Romans annexed the whole area before being sacked by the Vandals in the 5th century."

"I'm not sure I need to know all this."

"Wait there's more."

"You don't say."

"The 6th century saw the beginning of the Byzantine Empire. The Muslims showed up in the 8th and Morocco itself was established at the beginning of the 9th. That was under the Idrisid dynasty and a certain King Baga. After the Napoleonic Wars, North Africa became increasingly ungovernable by the Ottoman Empire seated in what is now Istanbul."

"I thought you wanted to find out more about Marrakesh," Stefan said, visibly agitated. "I should have turned *you* loose on that guy at the station. You would have scared him off with your tsunami of information. Are we done?"

"Just a little more," she whined playfully. "Morocco then became the resort of pirates under local chieftains," she added, before turning to another section of the book. "Interesting."

"What?"

"What they say about Marrakesh. Besides this market, it lists a number of things to see, like the Bahia Palace, the Majorelle Gardens, a mosque built 500 years ago, and a couple of museums. But the majority of places it recommends are outside the city."

"Such as?"

"Camel rides in the desert, day trips to remote villages in the Atlas mountains and stuff like that."

"That's something I wouldn't mind doing... hiking into the mountains. But we probably don't have enough time to organize that, so why don't we check out some of the things *in* the city?"

"I would like to... but not today," Carrie said in mild protest. "I feel beat. While we've been sitting here, it struck me that we've been on the go non-stop since leaving Berlin. I think it's all catching up with me. I know our room is kind of..."

"Dank and depressing," Stefan cut in.

"My thoughts exactly, but I wouldn't mind going back there for a little rest."

"Fine by me," Stefan assured her. "Might do us both some good."

But what was intended to be a 'little rest,' ended up lasting until darkness had descended on the city.

"We must have needed that," Carrie called out from the bathroom, as she splashed cold water on her face, rejecting the option of drying off with a grungy looking towel. "I feel a lot better, but I'm starving. Why don't we head back in the direction of the central square and have a good dinner somewhere."

It was while on a search for a decent looking restaurant, through streets as busy as they'd been hours earlier, they happened to pass by a bar with an enormous picture window. Directly behind the window, facing out towards the street, a roomful of men sat transfixed, staring up at a television mounted above the window.

"Hey, get a load of these guys," Stefan said, stopping to look. "Man, why didn't I bring my camera. This would have made an incredible photo," he mused.

"What are they watching?" Carrie asked, threading her arm in Stefan's as the two of them stood there.

"I suspect it's a soccer game. But look at them, All fifty or sixty of them are looking in exactly the same direction. They're either anticipating the next goal or the second coming."

"Muslims don't believe in Jesus, do they?"

"Who said anything about Jesus? I almost feel like running back for my camera, but by the time I got back it would likely be too late."

"Probably just as well," Carrie told him. "Isn't it Muslims that believe having their photo taken robs them of a piece of their soul?"

"I thought that was North American Indians," Stefan replied. "But you may be right. I remember taking a photo on a public street in England one time, and this Arab guy came running up to me demanding that I delete the photo because I had taken it without his permission."

"So what happened?"

"I don't remember. I think I just ignored him and walked off. It was a public street so what the heck. Anyway, forget the camera. The image of these guys is already burned into my brain forever."

"Do you have the feeling this place is much less nerve-wracking than it was this afternoon?" Stefan said as they walked through the central market. "Even the vendors seem less aggressive. Or maybe they're just burned out and wanna go home. Should we take a look around before dinner?"

"I'm awfully hungry, Stefan," Carrie complained. "Can't we come back tomorrow?"

"We can, but I think it's probably more relaxed at night. Hey… look over there," Stefan urged. "Even the snake charmers seem to be in a better mood," he added, pointing to several reptiles that were being coaxed out of the wicker baskets by tunes played on a small gourd.

"What is that thing?" Stefan wanted to know, pointing to the instrument that had a hole at one end and two pipes attached at the other,

"I think it's called a pungi," Carrie told him. "I saw a picture of one in the guidebook."

"Am I imagining it or is that guy playing Stairway to Heaven on that thing?" Stefan asked, as they stopped to watch one snake wiggling up out of its nest.

"I'm sure," Carrie answered. "I think you've been out in the sun too long," she added, taking his arm and dragging him away. "I'm curious how they can train a snake to do that, although I must say that snake looked suspiciously rubbery to me."

"Can't you just see the headlines," Stefan asked. "Tourist

uncovers fake snake scandal.”

"Well, it did," Carrie argued, as they continued their search on streets running off the square. When they did finally agree on an establishment, dinner ended up taking much longer than expected. In a sour mood when they hit the street, because the meal, when it did arrive, had not been worth the wait, they returned to the bazaar, traipsing around for a good hour. Not in the least bit tired after their afternoon nap, it was close to midnight when the pair straggled back to the pension. Shortly after taking to bed, a couple in the next room started up, shrieking in an indecipherable language. Rooted in either anger or ecstasy, their confab lasted well past 3:00 a.m.

Although they didn't need to be back in Berlin for another week, early next morning, Stefan and Carrie decided to blow off visiting Casablanca to head directly for the port of Tangiers, a city that conjured up images of sinister, trench-coated characters lurking in dark alleyways, waiting to kidnap unsuspecting tourists to use as hostages in exchange for captured foreign spies.

"Tangiers was founded as a Phoenician colony somewhere around the 10th century," Carrie recited as the train started its five-and-a-half-hour journey north to where the Mediterranean and the Atlantic merged at the Straits of Gibralter.

"Hey, Carrie," Stefan half moaned. "Don't get me wrong. Your interest in learning about the places we've been visiting is admirable, and I like history as much as you, but there's a limit. Go ahead and read if you want, but please don't overload me with anymore facts and figures about Romans, Spaniards etc."

"Okay. I'll zip to the present instead" she told him. "Or at least the near present... like 1923, when Tangiers became an international zone managed by colonial powers and a destination for diplomats, businessmen, writers, spies and bohemians."

"Hey... that's more like it. Spies and bohemians," Stefan echoed. "Dens of iniquity, with the chance of being turned into incurable opium addicts."

"You've been watching too many movies, lad," Carrie said, ignoring Stefan's flight of fantasy. "The city's dubious status came to an end with Moroccan independence, between 1956 and 1960."

"So what you're saying is the place is a few decades past its prime. What does it say there is to see and do now, remembering that we only have a day, two tops?"

"The Medina," Carrie answered, flipping to a new page.

"Been there.. done that," Stefan retorted. "Hard to beat the one in Fez."

"It apparently has beaches worth visiting and something called the Casbah Museum."

"Make a note of that one," Stefan suggested. "Something called the Casbah has got to be interesting."

"Perdicaris Park, Cap Spartel, and ..."

"Hey, like I said, we only have one day," Stefan repeated, which Carrie took as a sign to stop the lecture and let him gaze out the window in silence.

But as can happen with the best laid plans, shortly after the train rolled to a stop at Tangiers central station, they emerged out into a torrential downpour.

"Now what?" Carrie asked, as they huddled beneath the awning of a nearby cafe.

"Hey, I don't want to be a spoilsport," Stefan began. "But this doesn't look like it's going to let up anytime soon. I looked on my phone and the forecast is more of the same for the next couple of days. Seeing we haven't booked a room yet, why don't we see if we hop a ferry back to Algeciras for this evening? Truth be told, I'm beginning to feel a little Medina-ed out."

"I'm glad *you* said that. I was thinking it was just me," Carrie admitted. "If the rain stops we can just wander around for a few hours. If it doesn't, maybe there's a museum worth visiting. Either way we can try and catch a ferry later this evening. I remember passing a tourist agency in the main hall of the station. So first the ferry tickets and then lunch."

"The buildings all look the same as do the people," Stefan said, as they toured the old town, the rain having let up during lunch. "Just like all those other places we've been."

"It's still the same country in case you hadn't noticed," Carrie ribbed him.

"But this place really does give off mysterious vibes, don't you think?" he asked.

"Vibes?" Carrie echoed. "What is this 1968?"

"You know what I mean. You expect Orson Welles to waddle by in a wrinkled, white suit and Panama hat, a fat stogie stuffed in his mouth."

"Back to the movies are we?" Carrie said. "How about if Bogart slinks past with a sneer and a cigarette dangling from the corner of *his* mouth," she countered.

"Sorry, but that was Casablanca," Stefan corrected.

"Okay, Mr. Know it all... maybe Bogart was here on a secret mission."

Following a late afternoon jaunt through Perdicaris Park, the two wearied travellers hopped a bus to the port, where after collecting their boarding cards, they made their way to the crowded foot passenger lounge.

"This is probably going to seem a little odd, seeing we've been together for almost two years," Carrie said. "I should already know the answer."

"Answer to what?" Stefan asked.

"If this was your first time in Africa," she said, glancing at the ships on the other side of the lounge windows.

"First time in West Africa," Stefan told her. "I was in Egypt for a few days in 1981. It's very different from what we've seen here."

"In what way?" Carrie asked.

"Well for one thing, there's less people here. If you thought Marrakesh was hectic, Cairo would blow you away.

Even back then the place was insanely overcrowded."

"Were you just in Cairo or did you get to see some of rural Egypt?"

"Except for the Nile delta, I'm not really sure there is such thing as 'rural' Egypt. If there is I didn't see much of it. The only time I saw any vegetation or farmland was from the bus between the Suez Canal and Cairo. Everything else was pretty much desert. But I did manage to see the pyramids in Giza."

"Excuse me, sir."

His conversation interrupted, Stefan turned to see a man in his mid-thirties standing in front of him, flanked by two larger specimens. All three men were dressed in Western style clothing.

"Excuse me, sir," the man repeated. "You are taking ferry?"

"Yeah." Stefan answered.

"I am an officer with customs control," he said, briefly flashing an identification card written in Arabic. "May I please see your passports?"

"Why that?" Stefan wanted to know.

"No worries, sir, it is routine. I must check if all is in order," the man informed him.

Reluctantly, Stefan dug his passport out of his knapsack as Carrie did the same. Once they were handed over, the self-designated leader quickly flipped through each of them, while his two colleagues stood there looking menacing, arms folded across their chests like bouncers at a disco.

"I'm sorry, sir. I must check something in my office. You stay here, yes?" he asked, holding the two passports in the air.

Feeling a sense of foreboding, Stefan glanced at Carrie who looked equally ill at ease.

"Uhh... to be honest, I'm not terribly keen on relinquishing our passports to a virtual stranger," Stefan said. "Our ferry leaves in less than half an hour. How long is this going to take?"

"Ten minutes, sir, no worries," the man answered, already

moving away, followed by his two lackeys.

"I don't know about this," Stefan said to Carrie, after the men had disappeared into the crowded terminal. "Did you get a close look at their ID's?"

"No better than you," Carrie answered. "Besides I can't read Arabic either. For all I know they could have been showing us their fishing licences."

"The question is what are we going to do if they're not back in time? We still have to go through security and they won't let us board without passports."

"It's too late now," Carrie moaned. "I don't know what they would have done if we'd refused to hand them over. We should have asked to have a closer look at their ID's. Why were there three of them? Let's just hope they're on the up and up."

For the next fifteen minutes, Stefan's eyes alternated between the ticking clock above the check-in counter, and the section of the hall the "officials" had vanished into. With only ten minutes left before boarding would be completed, Stefan was on the verge of approaching a uniformed guard to complain when the three men reappeared. Looking somewhat disgruntled, the leader simply handed back the two passports without a word.

"You know what I think?" Stefan said, once he and Carrie had cleared security and were waiting to board the ferry. "I think those guys were trying to earn a little 'Baksheesh.' They figured if they stalled long enough, we'd panic and come looking for them, willing to fork out some sum to get our passports back."

"Who knows. I'm just glad we got them back in time. It would have been a terrible way to end the trip."

A short while later, standing on the rear deck as Africa receded into the churning wake, Stefan asked. "So now that it's all behind us, what was the highlight?"

"Hard decision," Carrie mused. "There were so many. That boy trying to break into my knapsack, the tooth dissolving tea in Tetouan, the stinking paint pots, the nervy kid at the Marrakesh train station and those three clowns just now…"

"Seriously," Stefan said.

"Without a doubt the Souk in Fez," Carrie replied. "That's a place I won't forget anytime soon. But then, that goes for the whole country."

Shaking off a shiver from the brisk breeze that arose as the ferry arced northeast towards Europe, Stefan gestured at the upper deck lounge door. "And the low point?" he asked, holding it open for Carrie.

"Leaving," she answered.

✻

LUNACY AT THE LÜNERSEE

For those of you who've never been exposed to it before, let me tell you, the world of treasure hunters can be a peculiar and often pathological place, saturated with swindlers, fraudsters, rogues, charlatans, con artists, and confidence men. Someone who once occupied a stellar position within that murky constellation was R.G. Thomason, or Roger as he preferred to be called by both friends and enemies.

The first time Roger and I crossed paths was in the spring of 2004. Somehow he'd managed to get hold of my name and number from a mutual acquaintance. After introducing himself as the President of Seek & Find, an 'exploration company,' he claimed to have founded, he got straight to the point, enthusiastically dispensing details of a project he had in the works, finishing up with the news that he was seeking someone to fill the double role of key researcher and cameraman. Despite the shady reputation conjured up at the mere mention of 'treasure hunter,' I expressed an interest, readily agreeing to a subsequent face to face meeting, albeit via Skype. The grainy image on the screen came as a bit of a shock, with my first thought being, *'he certainly doesn't look the part'*. Having pictured someone in a sharkskin suit with slicked back hair, I was surprised to see the figure of a grey haired, barrel-chested, grandfather. Already in his 80's by that time, Roger simply came across as the last person you would think capable of lying through his teeth, an obvious advantage in his line of work. As I would soon come to learn, hornswoggling had been his way of life for a long time. Having learned at an early age of P.T. Barnum's famous adage, 'there is one born every minute,' Roger had spent years developing methods of how to convince people he was doing them a favour by allowing them to participate in what he promised would be a "once in a lifetime expedition." I key element of this flawless strategy, which was basically deception groomed to perfection, was to plant just enough seeds of truth to make his grandiose schemes appear feasible if not altogether plausible.

Eager to lure me on board, Roger had boasted at length about his prodigious track record, rattling off an astonishing number of investors who'd been willing to fund his fantasies in hopes of basking in the anticipated glory. Potential investors however, had not been the only targets vulnerable to his web of intrigue. His uncanny ability to cajole had been used to equal success to feed the voracious appetite of ambitious production firms looking for a worldwide scoop. Roger's presentations may not have always been airtight, but they were certainly impressive. In addition to receiving a detailed researched report revealing names, places and dates, prospective clients would be dazzled with polished videos of the team in action, working with what he claimed was state of the art equipment that included metal detectors and ground-penetrating radar that could locate objects buried up to three metres.

Once financial backing had been lined up, if not yet secured, Roger's sights were then set on local hotel and restaurant owners near the site of the planned expedition. Visions of multiple and swift benefits, stemming from what Roger claimed would be the publicity and tourism resulting from any discovery, were dangled before the proprietors. In exchange for this presumed windfall, owners were expected to provide free accommodation and meals for Roger and his team during the span of the expedition.

Looking back, I would like to think that had I been aware of these tactics when I first accepted the position, I would have turned and walked away. Then again, who could resist a yarn about the legend of a buried Nazi treasure, spun by a raconteur as persuasive as Roger? But to be perfectly honest, it wasn't entirely a case of not having known what I was getting myself into. I had previously undertaken other research projects, and knew that I would not only be facing the daunting task of long drives to distant archives, but also the long-winded speeches of archivists who had nothing better to do than recite a list of do's and don'ts while in their sacred halls.

Once having orally agreed to accept the job, I was sent an array of documents outlining what it was that had initially garnered Roger's attention. The legend he'd focused on that year, had revolved around the Nazi concentration camp at Dachau, one of the Nazis' numerous gates to Hell. The first of its kind, the Dachau KZ had been established in 1933, its sole purpose to incarcerate opponents of the Nazi regime. That lengthy list had included Jews, homosexuals, criminals, people perceived as work-shy, and anyone else the Nazis wished to neutralize. Those unfortunate enough to have passed through its gate had anything of value immediately confiscated. While articles belonging to non-Jews were routinely registered and kept in the 'Effects Storage Area', ostensibly to be returned upon the prisoner's release, possessions belonging to Jewish prisoners fell under the direct jurisdiction of the SS, and remained unregistered on the understanding that their owners were not ever likely to be freed. Given the sheer number of prisoners detained from Dachau's inception to its liberation in 1945, it's not difficult to imagine the enormous amount of wealth that was accumulated. This garnered treasure had not only consisted of cash, jewelery and other personal items of value, but also the gold teeth extracted from prisoners upon their death. Although most of this illicitly obtained booty had been sent in some form to the Reichsbank in Berlin, research suggested that SS personnel at Dachau had also helped themselves to portions of it. As I discovered in my research, details of what allegedly became of the hoarded trove began to leak out in the months directly after the end of the war. The prime source of this information had been an Austrian physician by the name of Wilhelm Gross. Gross had apparently been treating imprisoned Nazi war criminals at the time, one of whom had been an SS officer stationed at Dachau. Facing an uncertain future, this SS officer chose to reveal the story of a treasure buried somewhere in the mountains of Austria. Whether Gross had believed the story or not, he chose to keep it to himself until 1952, at which time he shared it with a U.S. Army intelligence officer by the name of Dr. Edward Greger. No credible evidence could be found as to why Gross had selected Greger, stationed in Austria at the time, to be the recipient of the burgeoning legend. According to Gross, in the weeks before the German surrender in May 1945, the Commandant of the Dachau concentration camp had ordered that the stored 'treasure' be removed, ostensibly to prevent it from falling into the hands of the approaching Allies. He and three SS colleagues had loaded the plundered wealth, collectively valued at several million dollars, into four large, metal boxes usually used for storing ammunition. Gross told Greger that the condemned man he'd treated right after the war, had claimed to have been one of the four SS officers. Under cover of darkness, the boxes had then been put on trucks and smuggled out of the camp. Once out of the camp the group had headed south, travelling either early in the morning or late in the evening to avoid possible patrols, friendly or otherwise. Using only back roads, they'd made their way into Austria via the Arlberg Pass before heading up the Brandnertal to where the road ended. It had apparently taken the men several days to reach this point.

According to the legend's chronology, doubts had been raised as to whether four men could have lugged such heavy boxes up a treacherous mountain trail to the Lünersee, a pristine Alpine lake not far from the Swiss border. Having conducted his own research, Greger countered such arguments, saying there was evidence that the four had abandoned their trucks at the base of the trail and used two mules taken from the local village, presumably Brand, to transport the boxes up to the lake. Given that the Allied armies had yet to reach the isolated region, the four Nazis concluded that the Lünersee would be a safe location to bury their loot and proceeded to do so along the lake's rocky shoreline. Their plan was to then escape across the Swiss border, returning to retrieve the hidden treasure at some future point when they deemed it safe to do so. But given that there was no honour among the thieves, let alone trust, the men reportedly drew a crude map indicating the exact location of the buried treasure, splitting it into four pieces with each culprit receiving his share, thereby theoretically limiting the chances that anyone could return and abscond with the ill-gotten gains on his own.

But according to Gross's informant, only three of the four thieves actually headed into Switzerland. The fourth had returned to Germany, hiding out with his family, before eventually being captured, tried and sentenced to death for his crimes. It was while awaiting execution and undergoing medical treatment from Gross that this fourth man had allegedly decided to reveal his secret.

Further research indicated that Edward Greger had believed Gross' tale and had agreed to help him search for the treasure. But before an expedition could be fully organized, Gross mysteriously disappeared. For reasons unknown, Greger chose not to act on his own, a decision that would prove costly, for four years later, in the summer of 1956, construction began on a hydroelectric dam at the Lünersee. Upon its completion in 1958, the subsequent increase in the lake's water level, meant that anything that might have been buried along or near its shoreline was now under seventy-five feet of water. Without the means to resolve this new development, Greger's interest in the legendary Nazi treasure remained dormant for many additional years. That changed in the summer of 1990, when a severe drought in the region forced officials to authorize the release of water from the dammed lake, temporarily returning it to its original depth.

Parallel to that event, clues as to the identity of Gross' original secret informant emerged from research being carried out by a US federal employee named Robert W. Kesting. Amidst the documents Kesting discovered while investigating a 1946 war crimes trial involving Dachau, was an interrogation statement made by a man named Josef Jarolin. A professional soldier, Jarolin had joined the SS in 1935, serving first at the Sachsenhausen concentration camp, before being transferred to Dachau in 1938. Similar to Gross's mysterious informant, Jarolin had later been captured, tried, convicted, and executed for the atrocities he'd committed at the Dachau sub-camp at Allbach. According to his interrogation statement, Jarolin had claimed that the Dachau Commandant had conspired to smuggle a treasure out of the Dachau camp, and that he, Jarolin, had witnessed trucks loaded with valuables leaving the camp. Prompted by this 'new' information, which more or less supported the story delivered by the still missing Gross, Edward Greger now decided to travel to the Lünersee. Using coordinates based on the crude instructions that had been supplied by Gross, Greger and an associate claimed to have pinpointed the treasure's exact location. But in spite of a thorough and exhaustive search with metal detectors, the pair were unable to find any sign of it. The question raised by their failure was not so much whether the treasure existed, but rather whether someone had beaten them to it before the dam was built.

Confusing as it all was, this extensive research was passed on to Roger, who in turn, promised to compensate me as soon as financial backing for the expedition had been secured. Armed with the new research material, Roger now approached potential investors with the added claim of having tracked down the descendants of two of the four SS men and had seen two portions of the legendary map. Remarkably, at no time did investors see fit to ask Roger to produce evidence to back up this audacious claim, content, it seems, to simply accept his assertion that this 'exclusive knowledge', had been used to determine the precise location of the buried treasure.

Although a formal contract had yet to be signed, Roger was confident he would receive the necessary funding to undertake an expedition. Hoping to use the granting of official permission as an incentive to close the deal with investors, he wrote to Austrian authorities, seeking authorization to search the area around the Lünersee. In his attempt to gain those rights, he alluded that financial backing had already been confirmed, informing officials that such an expedition would bring world-wide attention to the area, and inevitably help increase the local economy through an increase in tourism. In his response to Roger's request, the State representative reminded him that should permission be given, Austrian law dictated that 50 percent of any discovery would belong to the explorer, and 50 percent to the owner of the property, that being the state. The official went on to suggest that should any treasure be found, as the President of Seek and Find, he should consider donating a portion of it to a charity fund for Holocaust victims.

As the months dragged on without an answer from Austrian authorities, Roger took it upon himself to present them with additional 'facts', hoping that it would not only speed up the glacial pace of bureaucratic decision making, but also serve to calm wavering investors. Based on additional research I had conducted in the interim, Roger revealed that the Commandant involved in the theft at Dachau, had been SS Col. Eduard Weiter. According to Roger, Weiter and several SS officers had left Dachau camp on April 26th, 1945 with a contingent of prisoners; *an excellent way,* Roger had emphasized, of camouflaging the transportation of stolen goods. He then went on to identify Weiter's accomplices as SS Lt. Colonel Wilhelm Ruppert, and Capt. Michael Redwitz, both of whom he claimed, had had exclusive access to the storage areas at Dachau where the confiscated valuables had been stored. The fourth man, Roger declared had been Josef

Jarolin. The implication was that these were the men responsible for absconding with the treasure. Roger then went on to point out that even though Redwitz, Ruppert and Jarolin were tried, convicted and executed in 1946. that did not eliminate them as the perpetrators. Col. Weiter's alleged complicity, was reduced but not ruled out by his suicide on May 6th, 1945. All four men, Roger insisted, had had the time, motive and opportunity to carry out the theft before meeting their respective fates.

In his application to Austrian officials, Roger had estimated the initial phase of the expedition would take seven days. If something were to be detected, an additional 3-4 weeks would be needed for excavation. He also informed them that because the four men were believed to have buried their loot by hand, no heavy machinery would be needed to extract it, thereby eliminating any risk to the environment. In conclusion, he gave them his assurance that should the treasure be found, it would be removed, photographed, inventoried, and distributed in accordance with Austrian law; all under the supervision of the proper authorities.

Roger's concerted efforts paid off and by the end of the month, official permission had been granted. Events moved rapidly after that and within weeks various contracts were signed. Two members of the production company Roger had convinced to come on board, flew into Munich a week later and made their way to a hotel in the village of Brand. Meanwhile, Roger, Terry, his vice-president and senior technician, and Jenny, a secretary who'd been coaxed into coming with no salary, but a free trip to Europe, arrived a day later, holing up in private quarters down the road. For reasons that were never explained, arrangements were made for myself and Adam, the sound operator, to stay in the same hotel as the two producers, Darren and Sharon. On the night of our arrival, the four of us sat down for dinner to get acquainted.

"So what's your take on Mr. Thomason," Sharon had

asked shortly after we'd ordered.

"In what sense?" I replied.

"Is he legit? Do you think there really is a treasure?" she asked.

"A little late to be asking that question don't you think," Darren inserted. "Besides, he's working for Roger. What's he supposed to say?"

"I really don't know," I admitted. "The research produced a huge amount of contradictions, but I suppose it's not impossible they did make off with the valuables. Whether they buried it at the Lünersee and whether we can find it... that's something else entirely."

"Before signing the deal with Roger, we did a little investigating of our own," Darren confessed. "He's undertaken quite a few expeditions in his career, but strangely enough we couldn't find anything that looked like it had ended with a major discovery."

"I wouldn't know about that," I told Darren. "I was hired to do research... which I did... as well as be the cameraman. If you don't mind me asking, why did you get involved if he has no record of successes?"

"Now that's a question I wouldn't mind hearing the answer to as well," Sharon piped up, looking directly at Darren.

"There's always a risk factor with these things," he declared. "I know there's no guarantee we'll find anything, but if we do, it will be a world exclusive. We had some heated discussions back at head office in the States about whether we should take this on, but ultimately we decided to go for it. If it turns out to be a dud, we'll just write it off."

The first day of the shoot got off to a late start due to a malfunction with the cable car. Once the logistical task of transferring equipment and crew up to the lake had been completed, the team made use of the remaining hours to scout locations in a jeep supplied by the Austrian authorities.

As we all soon saw, the Lünersee is a breathtakingly beautiful body of greenish-blue water surrounded by an imposing ring of high, snow-capped peaks. It is a fairly small lake, measuring only one and a half kilometres long and 750 metres wide. Thanks to a gravel service road that circles the lake, it didn't take long to explore the shoreline and pinpoint the various landmarks that Roger claimed fit to the map he'd purportedly seen.

On the morning of the second day, once on site, a tense argument broke out between Roger and Terry, as to which location was the best to begin exploring. Terry reluctantly acceded to Roger's decision, only to have trouble getting the metal detector to deliver a signal. Ah yes, Terry... a rather gangly, painfully shy individual who often found it difficult to summon up the self-confidence to look you in the eye as you spoke to him. If anyone could be described as a metal detector nerd, it was Terry. But whatever level of technical knowledge he possessed in order to operate the sophisticated equipment, it failed to be enough that morning.

"It's a new system," Terry struggled to explain to a skeptical Darren, after almost twenty minutes of inactivity. "I haven't really had the chance to get to know it fully yet."

"Was there some reason you didn't take the time to familiarize yourself with it before coming to Austria?" Darren wanted to know.

"I'm sure it's just a minor adjustment," Roger told the producer. "It's possible the mountains are affecting the signal," he bluffed.

But it wasn't just a minor adjustment that was needed, and after a full hour of fiddling with dials and cables, Terry remained baffled. In a desperate attempt to determine the problem, he got on the phone to the manufacturer, whose head office happened to be in Istanbul, Turkey. If the surrounding mountains hadn't been disrupting the functioning of the detector as Roger implied, they certainly were playing havoc with Terry's cell phone reception. So there was poor old Terry, stranded on a rocky outcrop near the shoreline, yelling into his cell phone, trying to explain the situation to a technician who only spoke limited English. Having tired of the unfolding spectacle, and perhaps suffering from the higher altitude, Roger had in the meantime laid down on a grassy knoll, his half-open shirt making him look for all the world like a beached whale that had washed up on the Lünersee's shore.

"I think I saw this movie," Darren grumbled, as Terry continued to spout unintelligible words into the phone. "The Marx brothers starred in it."

Realizing there was little to do beyond waiting and hoping, Darren and Sharon decided to go for a stroll around the lake, assuming that by the time they returned, Terry would be hard at work. But by the time they got back just after one, Terry was still fiddling with the non-functioning detector. A dejected Darren declared the day a washout, suggesting that he, Sharon and Herr Schmidt, the Austrian official chaperoning us, return to the hotel in Brand. Given that it was Roger who had hired us, Adam and I felt it prudent to stay put, a wise decision as it turned out, as two hours later Terry finally got the detector to work, and we were actually able to capture some footage of him in action.

"Who are those guys with Herr Schmidt?" Darren asked the next morning, as he joined us in the hotel breakfast room.

"After you left yesterday, Terry managed to get the detector working and he marked out three potential sites," I explained. "Roger called Herr Schmidt right away, and I presume he arranged to bring in these three to help dig. Things may be looking up."

"Well, let's hope today is more productive than yesterday," Sharon added.

Within the hour, the party, which now totalled eleven, had made their way back up to the lake, and were circled around the first site Terry had designated.

"According to my readings, there is a large metal object approximately one to two metres down within this perimeter," Terry said, pointing to the red string he'd stretched out the previous afternoon to form a two meter by two metre square on the side of a hill.

"If you don't mind me asking," Darren began. "How did you come to conclude that this is where we should be digging?"

"We calculated co-ordinates using the two sections of the map I saw," Roger cut in. "From there we were able to reduce the number of possible locations."

Responding to a brief nod from Herr Schmidt, the three men shed their uniform jackets, retrieved what looked to be brand new shovels from the jeep and began digging in the hard ground.

"That's enough," Darren told me, after I'd shot ten minutes of them in action. "This isn't a story about Austrian shovelling techniques," he kidded. "Although if we don't end up finding anything, we may have to pad that aspect a bit. In the meantime, I'd give it a rest."

Approximately three hours later, the diggers had managed to open up a square hole almost a meter deep. At this point, Terry called a halt to the excavating and climbed into the pit with the detector.

"I don't have a signal anymore," he said, an announcement that quickly dampened the moods of both Darren and Sharon, not to mention the three diggers.

"So what do you suggest we do now?" Darren asked, directing the question to Roger.

"I'd say we give Terry a few more minutes.," Roger answered.

"Sometimes, magnetic waves can affect the accuracy of the readings," he lied. "There probably a lot of iron in these mountains. That could be throwing the readings off."

"So like what?" Sharon whispered to Darren, once Roger had walked over to give Terry some new instructions. "Roger didn't know there would be mountains in the Austrian Alps? I'm tempted to say the only magnetic waves around here are coming from a few 'loose screws'… but I'm not quite there yet."

Still unable to detect a signal after a further fifteen minutes, Terry sheepishly admitted that perhaps his calculations had been slightly off. Moving to a spot several metres closer to the shoreline, he declared that this is where the team should now dig. The news did not sit well with anyone, least of all the three men expected fulfil the task. But dig they did and several hours later, a second hole approximately the same size as the first, had been created. Repeating his performance in the new pit. Terry proudly told the group that this time he had a signal, albeit 'a weak one'.

"I think we should continue to dig," he advised.

Half an hour later, one of the shovels struck something metallic, sending what sounded like a gunshot, echoing across the lake. Various members of the group, who had been passing the time in various spots near the hole, quickly crowded around its periphery.

"Success beckons," Roger crowed somewhat prematurely, as the other two diggers stopped to watch their colleague scrape away the last bits of dirt and pull out a rusted, piece of metal.

"Is that what I think it is?" Darren gasped in disbelief, taking the object in his hand. "It looks like a bloody tin of luncheon meat. for Christ's sake," he said.

"That's exactly what it is," Herr Schmidt confirmed, accepting the tin from Darren, while casting accusatory glances at Terry and Roger. "I doubt they had luncheon meat back in the Nazi era," he added mockingly, after reading the faint label. "More than likely it was left here by one of the workers when they built the dam."

"Unbelievable," Darren groaned. "A full day of digging and all we have to show for it is a discarded can of luncheon meat. Great… just great," he fumed.

Insisting they not waste any more time and energy digging at any other sites, without reasonable assurance it would be more successful, Darren suggested that he and Sharon return to the hotel to re-evaluate the state of affairs, a decision greatly welcomed by the team of diggers.

"I'm sorry chief," Terry said lamely, once the others had driven off in the jeep. "The thing was giving off strong signals. I thought it might have been a chest."

Not about to castigate his vice-president in the presence of a cameraman and sound operator, Roger simply told him, "False calculations can happen, Terry. We all know that. But I think we need to review our information and make sure your measurements for the third site are accurate. I know you don't have x-ray vision, but if we're going to ask them to dig again, we have to be as sure as we can."

"But chief... "

"Terry," Roger said more firmly, cutting him off in mid-sentence. "We're here to find the treasure and we're going to find it. There's bound to be some false starts. The producers have to accept that."

That evening, after dinner at the hotel, conversation briefly turned to the day's disappointing results.

"God almighty," Darren began, hoisting his second mug of beer. "How did we let ourselves be talked into financing part of this fiasco?" he asked Sharon, who knew her partner was not looking for a response. "Look," he added, directing his comments to me. "I'm not looking to blame anyone. I can only blame myself. I know you haven't worked with Roger before, but did you run a background check on him before you accepted the job? I mean really... Seek and Find? Talk about false advertising."

"I did look at their web site," I told him. "But you know how distorted those things can be. I found it interesting that he had been on so many expeditions, but it came as news to me when you said you hadn't found any record of major discoveries."

"Darren, you said yourself there would be a risk," Sharon interrupted. "We've still got a few more days to come up with something. Maybe we'll have more luck tomorrow."

"I'm not sure what you're basing that on," Darren answered.

"Of course, what good is an empty can of luncheon meat without a rusted fork and knife?" he added, taking a hearty slug of his beer.

"But there's no point in belabouring this tonight. I've got to send an update to the boys back home, so why don't you all have another drink on me, and we'll see you in the morning," he added, getting up from the table. "So good night, gents... Sharon."

"Is his head on the line if all this goes south?" I asked, after Sharon had made no motion to follow him.

"Not really," she answered. "Darren is a co-owner of the company. His partners may not be pleased if we don't come up with anything, but they know the risks. Maybe this is none of my business, but do you have any idea who some of the investors are? We paid Roger a fee for the rights to document the expedition, but he was pretty closed-mouthed about who he got the main funding from. All he would say is that the investors wanted to remain silent partners. Maybe because they want to avoid being publicly humiliated," she added with a smile.

"Sorry, but I'm not privy to such information. Roger's secretary, Jenny... she hinted something about a rich dentist in Texas, but she didn't get specific, and I didn't feel it my place to ask."

"I understand," Sharon said. "We should have done more research on our own. Let's just cross our fingers for tomorrow."

With memories of the previous day's 'findings' still fresh in everybody's mind, communication between the various parties, which again included Herr Schmidt and his team, remained sparse on the ride up to the lake.

"They're leaden," Darren said to no one in particular, after Terry's calculations and subsequent hours of digging at the third site had produced nothing more than a four-foot long, piece of cable. "That's why they're called pipe dreams," he continued. "And right about now, I'd say ours are headed for the bottom of the lake to join the missing treasure. If there even is one... What can I say? We've spent thousands for a discarded tin of luncheon meat and a piece of cable. That's it... we're done. We're going home."

"But we've planned for three more days," Roger protested.

"You have to have patience in this line of work."

"Patience for what? Sorry Rodge, old buddy, but we can't afford to waste any more time and money. We don't need a full set of rusted cutlery. After yesterday's fiasco, I suspected this might happen, so this morning I had a little chat with the hotel manager. He was very understanding and said there would be no problem with us cancelling our remaining days. It's too late to drive back to Munich today, so we'll be outta here first thing tomorrow morning. I suggest you and your team also quit while you're behind."

With visions of an award-winning documentary now jettisoned, Darren and Sharon gathered up their belongings and clambered aboard the jeep, joined by Herr Schmidt and his team.

"Good luck boys," Darren called out as the jeep pulled away. "You won't be hearing from us."

With no producers left to tell us what they did and didn't want, and no desire to watch Terry fumble any further with his gear, Adam and I said our goodbyes, choosing to walk to the cable car station rather than wait for the return of the jeep.

Months later, back in the States, Roger continued to renege on his promise to pay for the research, despite my repeated requests. Fortunately, much like the arrangements that had been made for our accommodations, before the shoot began, the production company had insisted that Adam and I be paid directly by them. That codicil turned out to be a silver lining and helped to soften the blow of the other tardy payments.

A year or so later, by which time memories of the swindle at the Lünersee had become considerably less vexing, I happened to be scrolling the Internet when I stumbled across a web site that showed that Seek & Find were now involved in the hunt for a pirate's lost treasure somewhere in southern Louisiana. "*So,*" I thought to myself, "*The old goat managed to convince one more set of gullible investors into funding yet another pie in the sky expedition eh.*"

If it hadn't been apparent at the Lünersee, it was now abundantly clear that as far as Roger was concerned, success was simply something secondary.

❃

A CUBAN CHRONICLE

"You have *got* to be kidding!" Lars moaned, his shoulders drooping at the sight of a half-dozen long lines of passengers waiting to pass through passport control. "There's at least ten entry stalls here. Why are only half of them open? Have they been taking lessons from the Post Office?"

"Complaining isn't gonna make things move any faster, Lars," his partner, Sara told him, as they assessed the situation. "From what I've heard, they don't take complaints lightly in Communist countries. So unless you want to spend part of our vacation, not to mention an extended one, in the clink, I suggest you belt up and get in line."

"Should we at least stand in different lines in case one is faster?" Lars asked.

"What's the point of that? You can't change if one of us gets to the desk first, unless you want to incur the wrath of the hundred others behind us."

"So in other words we can look forward to standing for at least an hour in a hall that reeks like a locker room on a rainy day," Lars grunted, before taking his place behind a woman with a bouffant hairstyle, making a mental wager he would beat the Bermuda- shorted man in the adjacent line, to the glassed-in cubicle housing the passport officer.

"I thought Americans weren't allowed to come to Cuba," Lars whispered over his shoulder, as the line inched forward. "I know Cuba's been cut off from the rest of the world for ages but what's with this woman's hairstyle? Did we somehow land in 1965?"

"Shhh, behave yourself," Sara admonished. "Just because you're wired from the flight is no reason to be obnoxious."

"Who needs a reason?" Lars answered. "But really... Don't

you think she looks like LadyBird Johnson?"

"Excuse me," the brunt of Lars' mocking said as she turned to face him, "Did I just hear you mention Ladybird Johnson?"

"Uhhh… Yeah," Lars answered, feeling his face redden. "My girlfriend and I were debating which President had invoked the embargo on Cuba and is ultimately responsible for this line-up."

"It's terrible, isn't it?" the woman said. "I don't understand why the people who run this place don't do something about it. It's the same thing every time I come. But what can you do?... By the way, it wasn't Johnson who instigated the embargo. It was actually Eisenhower. Kennedy, Johnson and all the others just followed suit and kept it in place."

"Am I right in thinking you're not American?" Lars asked, momentarily distracted by a flickering neon light directly overhead.

"Canadian," the woman told him. "Americans are still not officially allowed to come here, although I understand there are many loopholes. Is this your first time in Cuba?"

"Yes it is," Sara said, joining the conversation.

"On vacation?"

"Not really," Lars said. "We don't want to stay in one place. We want to travel the entire country and see as much of it as we can."

"Is that not a vacation?" the woman asked.

"To me a travel vacation is an oxymoron. Sort of like progressive conservative or quality sleaze," Lars said.

"Lars," Sara cut in. "I'm sure this woman is not interested in quibbling over semantics. It makes you sound like such a snob."

"On the contrary," the woman replied, taking time to move a foot or two ahead as the line shifted. "I agree with your partner. Travel should inspire and be an education'. That's especially true here in Cuba. It's fascinating to see how residents have been deprived of so many things, yet they've adapted and survived."

"I take it this is not your first time here," Lars said.

"Oh God no," she said with a laugh. "I've lost count of how many times I've been here. My husband and I had been coming here since the late 80's. He died two years ago and this is my second time back since he's been gone. But there's still so much to see and experience, even after all this time."

"Wow... since the late 80's," Lars said. It must have been really different back then."

"Things have changed a lot, but I must say I don't consider these all-inclusive resorts an improvement. We never stayed in hotels. It's much more interesting to stay with the locals where you get to see how Cubans live... or at least some Cubans."

"So if you've been here so many times, you must know quite a bit about Cuban history," Lars said, noting that their line had inched ahead of the man in Bermuda shorts. " I mean back before Castro."

"Yes, but unfortunately for many people, Cuban history goes back no further than 1959, when Castro overthrew the corrupt Battista regime. Back then the place was crawling with the Mafia."

"So much of Cuban history is distorted," Lars said. "I can remember being taught that Christopher Columbus 'discovered' America. First of all, how can you 'discover' a place that was already inhabited? And secondly, Columbus didn't even land on mainland America. He waded ashore in Cuba."

"That's right," the woman answered, shoving her suitcase forward with a nudge of her foot. "It appears we're going to be each other's captive audience for awhile... my name's Dorothy," she added, extending a hand.

"Lars Kierey."

"Sara Fennell."

"Do you hear that?" Lars suddenly asked.

"Hear what?" Dorothy replied.

"The song on that guy's ear phones… The one who's just in front of you. It's loud enough to make out what it is."

"I wasn't really listening," she said.

"It's *I'm Still Standing*. How fitting is that!"

"If you're interested," Dorothy broke in. "While we're waiting I could tell you a bit about the place. I like to think of myself as a bit of an amateur historian when it comes to Cuba."

"That'd be great," Lars told her, glancing at Sara.

"Sure, I'd like to learn more about it as well," Sara said.

"As you mentioned, when Columbus arrived in 1492, Cuba was already home to three indigenous peoples: the Taínos, the Ciboneys, and the Guanajatabeyes. At the time the population was thought to have been between fifty and three hundred thousand.

"So many?" Sara asked.

"So they say. The Guanajatabeyes were the first to inhabit the island. Then the Ciboneys, who were thought to have come from South America. And finally the Taínos, who ultimately became the largest indigenous group. They reportedly arrived from the West Indies in the 1400s. They might have remained the largest group if the Spanish conquistadors hadn't managed to decimate their numbers within 70 years."

"I've read that the US ruled the roost at some point as well," Lars said.

"That came much later," Dorothy continued. "Cuba was Spain's main colony in the Caribbean for four centuries and America was the primary market for products like sugar, tobacco, rice and coffee. But the Americans had long coveted the island a mere 90 miles from its coast, so in 1898, they assisted Cuba in achieving its independence from Spain. Over the following decades the Americans proceeded to intervene militarily on behalf of American businesses, which had invested heavily in the country. Then in the first half of the

20th century, U.S. mobsters showed up and used the island as a money-laundering playground. That all changed in 1959 with Castro."

"Man, that woman can talk," Lars said, after both he and Sara had finally cleared passport control and found themselves in the bustling arrival hall. "I bet she could have gone on for another hour."

"Probably," Sara agreed, as she struggled to avoid the constant flow of other patrons. "But a lot what she had to say was really interesting. She was virtually a walking encyclopaedia."

"Now that we know everything there is to know about Cuba, we can turn around and go home again."

"In an hour or two we'll probably have forgotten half of what she told us. How old do you think she was?" Sara asked.

"Judging by the hairstyle and the Doris Day ensemble…"

"Don't be mean," Sara snapped.

"I'm not being mean," Lars protested. "She really looked like she just walked out of the 50's. I'd say she's probably pushing 70. Did you see where she went? She was just ahead of me but it took that zombie of an immigration officer so long to take my photo and stamp my passport… I don't see her anywhere in this throng," Lars said, as they continued to weave their way towards the main exit.

"I didn't see her. Maybe she was meeting someone. I guess she wasn't that interested in extending our history lesson. I'm still not sure she didn't hear your crack about the Ladybird comparison."

"It's too bad she's disappeared. I'm sure she could have given us a few tips about places that are off the beaten track."

"I guess we'll just have to explore for ourselves," Sara said, as the two of them walked out the exit doors into stultifying heat.

At first count, there had to be well over fifty vintage cars in the airport parking lot, each more spectacular than the next. Too wearied by the experience at passport control to peruse them all, Lars quickly selected a red and white 1956 Chevy convertible in pristine condition to transport them to their lodgings.

"How much to Vedado?" he asked a young man dressed in white slacks and a University of Colorado T-shirt, who was casually leaning against his pride and joy. The man, who was trying his darnedest to impersonate a snarly Latin version of James Dean, albeit with slicked back, Elvis styled hair and a self-rolled cigarette dangling precariously out of the side of his mouth, told him, "Ten dollars."

"Fine," Lars replied, looking for the latch to release the trunk.

"No, no," the young man said. "It is broken. Your luggage must go in the back seat."

"That appears to be the only thing wrong with this car." Lars noted out loud, as he climbed into the front seat, relegating Sara to the rear. "How have you managed to keep it is such great shape what with the embargo and all?" he asked, as the engine roared to life and the young man eased past his randomly parked competitors.

"Cubans are masters of makeshift," the young man answered.

"It seems your car isn't the only thing in good condition," Sara said, while trying to keep her hair from fluttering in the wind as they left the airport grounds and on to a four-lane highway. "Where did you learn your English?"

"Everyone takes English in school," he explained. "Plus I have learned much from tourists. As you know we are only 90 miles from the home of the brave," he added with a sarcastic grin.

Their first glimpse of the effects of a decades long embargo was visible on the drive to Vedado. The roads were virtually inundated with vintage cars, many not nearly in as good shape as the taxi they were in, but with no hindrances such as traffic lights or stop signs anywhere to be seen, they made good time, rolling past buildings with crumbling facades, fronted by unkempt lawns and overgrown foliage.

"I guess we can save on buying a map," Lars said to Sara, as the taxi pulled off a main thoroughfare onto a heavily treed street.

"Why is that?" she answered, still struggling to keep her hair from lashing across her face.

"I haven't seen any street signs to let you know where you are. Just some stone tablets at street level that are impossible to read from a moving vehicle. How do people unfamiliar with the city, get to where they want to?"

That was obviously not a problem for the young driver, as he cruised past large houses that suggested the area had once been an affluent neighbourhood. After being dropped off in front of a five-storey apartment house, they were buzzed through a locked gate into a courtyard, before ascending to the 4th floor in a rickety elevator that groaned and screeched the entire way. It was an elderly, grey-haired gentleman in a white shirt that was waiting for them as the doors squeaked open.

"Bienvenidos to Havana," the man said, extending his hand, first to Sara and then to Lars. "And welcome to my home," he added, gesturing for them to enter through the open door directly across from the elevator.

"Man, can you believe how big this place is?" Lars whispered to Sara, after the man had guided them into the living room and excused himself to inform his wife of their arrival. "I bet there must be half a dozen rooms. I wonder if they're all as stuffed as this one. I've never seen so much kitsch in one place. It's amazing. I thought there was an embargo."

"Lars, behave yourself." Sara scolded. "This man is our landlord for a few days, so don't start off by insulting his taste in decor."

"Hmmm," Lars murmured disapprovingly just as the man returned with a woman in a blouse and ankle length skirt, her neck and hands loaded with significant amounts of jewelry.

"Welcome to our home," the sixty something year old said. "It's nice to meet you. Would you care for something to drink?"

"Water would be nice," Sara answered, as Lars nodded in agreement.

For the next fifteen minutes the foursome engaged in small talk, during which Lars and Sara learned the elderly couple were retired Professors.

"What did you teach?" Lars asked, directing the question to both of them.

"I taught History and French, and my wife taught Philosophy," the man explained.

"So you would be a good person to talk to about the history of Cuba's relations with its neighbour to the north," Lars said.

"I'm afraid that would take a long time to discuss fully," the man told him. "Perhaps while you are here, we can find the time for such a discussion. But for now I'm sure you both must be exhausted from the trip. Why don't I show you to your apartment so you can get some rest. It's just down the corridor from us."

"Sara, come in here," Lars called out, while his partner was in the bedroom unpacking. "You gotta see this."

"Oh my God," Sara gasped as she entered the living room. "What were they thinking?" she asked. "The walls, the rug, the lampshade... even that small television is pink. I can tell you one room I won't be spending much time in, thank you very much. It gives me a headache just looking at it," she added, quickly returning to the bedroom.

"I don't know about you, but after being cooped up in the plane for so long and then the wait at passport control, I feel half brain dead," Lars complained, as he watched Sara methodically arrange her cosmetics on the bathroom shelf. "What say we go for a walk in the neighbourhood once you're done. I need to move a bit. Maybe we can grab dinner somewhere and get back before jet lag really kicks in."

With Sara in full agreement, the two of them set off for a stroll through Vedado, often walking on heaved sidewalks thrust upwards by the roots of large trees.

"Judging by the size of some of these houses," Lars noted, "even if they've seen better days," he added above the rumble of vehicles as they neared a major road, "people around here must have had money at one time. I wonder if most are single-family dwellings or if they've been split up into smaller units."

"Go knock and ask," Sara quipped, as they passed a house where the sound of a blaring television was escaping through an open window.

"Yeah, in my perfect non-existent Spanish. That could prove interesting."

Next Day…

"I didn't realize this was part of the deal," Sara remarked next morning, as she and Lars sat on the terrace, enjoying breakfast served by a maid employed by the owners of the flat. "Thank you," Sara added, nodding her appreciation as the woman set down a bowl of fresh fruit and coffee in front of them.

"I forgot to mention it," Lars said, taking a sip of his steaming coffee, while surveying the distant skyline of downtown Havana, highlighted by the distinctive dome of the Capitol. "Something else… this morning when I got up, I happened to look out the kitchen window, where you can see the sea. I was just thinking about the fact that we are here in Havana, when every once in awhile I would see these bursts of white, cloud-like plumes arching up along the horizon. I couldn't figure out what the heck they were for the longest time and then suddenly it dawned on me," Lars added boisterously. "You know what they were?"

"No," Sara answered, looking at him over the rim of her mug.

"I could see laundry fluttering on the line on the rooftop directly below us so I figured it must be incredibly windy out.

We don't notice it here because we're on the lee side."

"The what side?"

"The lee side. The terrace is out of the wind."

"So tell me already," Sara said. "What was it?"

"Waves… huge waves crashing against the breakwater along the Malecon," Lars explained.

"The Male… what?"

"The Malecon. It's the oceanside drive. After we're done with breakfast we can walk down and take a closer look."

Twenty minutes later, Lars and Sara were on the Malecon, staring at the enormous waves shooting twenty to thirty feet up in the air after hitting the cement wall of the breakwater.

"Wow… the power behind those waves must be incredible," Lars marvelled, as a group of kids in their early teens appeared out of nowhere, and started racing back and forth to the breakwater trying to see if they could touch the wall and run back before the next wave rolled in and drenches them, not to mention possibly knock them flat on their backs. Despite being at least fifty feet from this action, it wasn't long before glasses, hair and clothing were caked with a coating of sea salt carried by the strong gusts of wind.

"I dare you," Lars said, tilting his head at the kids.

"Oh I'm sure," Sara answered. "It's always been my dream to be squashed like a bug by a killer wave and then get washed out to sea. Saves a bundle on funeral expenses."

"Okay… if you'd rather not."

Later that morning, after a much-needed shower and change of clothes, they decided to head into 'old Havana'. It was only a short walk to a major artery, where Lars quickly flagged down a taxi that had no sign indicating it was operating as such.

"How did you know this was a taxi," Sara asked, as the two of them squeezed in the back seat of a 1952 Plymouth, already occupied by three other passengers.

"I'll bet there's not one taxi in Havana that actually has a taxi sign on the roof. I read somewhere that literally every car in Havana is a potential taxi. If you spot a car with a number of people inside it's more than likely a group taxi. The more passengers, the cheaper the fare. When I spotted this one, I figured it had to be a taxi."

"My hero," Sara said, as she scrunched up her shoulders in a vain attempt to get comfy. "But what happens if people have different destinations?" she asked.

"I guess we're gonna find out."

Fortunately, they weren't the only ones wishing to be dropped off at the Capitol building, a structure reportedly built from the design of its counterpart in Washington. Almost immediately Lars' attention fell to a block-long row of vintage cars parked out front and he insisted on walkig over for a closer inspection. With all the makings of a car museum or fairground exhibition of old timers, what was different about this display was that the owners were eagerly competing for customers to take a tour of the city.

"How much?" Lars asked a dark-skinned man in a Panama hat, standing beside a bright red, 1958 Oldsmobile convertible.

"One hour $20.00," the man answered.

"Sorry," Lars replied. "That's a bit too expensive according to our guidebook."

"How much you pay?" the man asked.

"I figured $10 would be fair."

"I take $15."

"Done deal," Lars responded, his hand already on the passenger door handle.

Although cruising through the Havana in an open convertible on a warm, sunny day was an exhilarating experience, it came with a catalogue of noise. From start to finish they were bombarded by the sounds of bleating horns, squealing tires, hissing brakes, roaring motorcycles, and the rumble of constant construction, not to mention roaming packs of howling dogs. But despite the at times irritating aural accompaniment, both Lars and Sara had been enjoying the drive immensely until suddenly, a loud bang jarred them back to the here and now.

"I think we just got a flat tire," Lars said, noting that the rear of the car was now tilting sharply to the left.

"If it's just a flat," Sara quipped wryly. "Whose wheel is that bouncing wildly down the Malecon in front of us?" she asked, as the Olds screeched to an unceremonious stop.

"Good point," Lars replied, as he caught sight of the errant wheel. "Fortunate that there's no oncoming traffic so it's not going to end up in somebody's windshield."

Acting as if it was a regular occurrence, which it may well have been, the driver slowly got out to inspect the damage, taking a cursory look at his rapidly shrinking wheel before calmly dialling a number on his cell phone. Within minutes a replacement was pulling up behind the crippled Olds, and '*what a replacement*', Lars thought, as he laid eyes on a 1942 blood red, Chevy coupe.

"Can you believe this," Lars gushed, as he walked around the car, admiring its features. "What a beautiful car."

"It's nice, but it's not worth fawning over," Sara told him.

"Are you kidding? Do you have any idea what this car would be worth back home? A fortune... that's if you could even find one."

"Steady lad. You look like you're about to drool. It's just a car."

"Just a car?" Lars mocked.

"Hopefully one where the wheels are on tighter," Sara added.

Once underway again, Lars was eager to ask the new driver how he'd managed to maintain such a priceless vehicle. That plan was quickly thwarted however, with the discovery that the total extent of the new driver's English was, "nice car, no Señor?"

Returned to the spot where the tour had begun, Lars was in the process of offering the new driver a tip, when he was interrupted by a tap on his shoulder.

"You like tour?" a man, who looked to be in his mid-thirties asked.

"Yeah, it was great," Lars replied, as Sara was rearranging her wind-blown hair, in the reflection of '58 Buick's side mirror.

"You like I show you sites of Havana?"

"We just saw a whole load of them thanks," Lars told him.

"I can show many more. Not cost much," the man insisted.

"Thanks but no thanks," Lars repeated. "We just want to find a quiet place and maybe have a drink," he added, as he and Sara started to cross the street.

"I know perfect place for drink," the man told them, walking alongside. "It Hemingway's old hang-out. Not far from here."

"No offence, but we'd just as soon scout out a place on our own. Maybe some other time."

"You like cigars?" the man persisted.

"I don't smoke and neither does she."

"That okay. You buy good Cuban cigar as gift. Factory right behind Capitol. I show you. You pay cheap if I take you."

"Sounds like the deal of the century, but like I said, neither of us smoke and I wouldn't give any as gifts. So if you don't mind, we'd just like to be left alone."

Fortunately, this last plea got through and the man turned on his heel and walked away.

"You know at some point I wouldn't mind seeing a cigar factory," Sara admitted once their assailant was out of sight.

"Me too, but I didn't want that guy pestering us the whole time. Maybe we can check it out after we grab a drink," he said, spotting a large sign indicating that 'Hemingway's Haunt' was indeed just a block away.

"I wonder if this place was as boring and crowded in Ernie's heyday," Lars asked, raising his voice to overcome the din of noisy patrons, as the two of them sat observing people line up to take selfies with a seemingly unflattering portrait of Hemingway propped up at one end of the bar.

"Wanna bet half the people in here have never read a word of Hemingway," Lars grumbled.

"Have you?".

"I tried one of his books a few years ago but didn't like his style."

"So there you go… Come on then. There must be a quieter place to have a drink," Sara said, prompting a quick exit. With no other decent watering hole in the vicinity, they ended up buying soft drinks from a vendor and retreating to a nearby park from where, as it turned out, it was a short distance to the aforementioned cigar factory. After dispensing with a somewhat exorbitant entrance fee, which Lars couldn't help grumbling about, he and Sara were directed to join a line of visitors entering a roped-off area that overlooked the factory floor. From there they had a bird's eye view of a large room where 40 to 50 women sat at desks rolling dried tobacco leaves into various versions of the famous Cuban cigars.

"Phooey… It doesn't smell too great in here," Sara remarked as they watched one woman complete her task with the finesse and speed of experience. "I wonder how they get rid of the smell when they go home every night."

"Probably by just smoking one of them, thar ceegars," Lars joked.

After purchasing an exemplar from the sales shop to see what all the fuss was about, they returned to the nearby park and asked a passerby for a light. Taking a deep puff, Lars immediately coughed out the inhaled smoke, desperately gasping for air.

"That good eh?" Sara kidded.

"Whoa… that heap strong," he said, handing Sara the stogie.

"No thanks," she told him. "I'll just watch. It doesn't smell that bad. How does it taste?"

"Like dried donkey dung."

"I take it you're speaking from experience."

Choosing to walk the several kilometres back to the flat rather than take a taxi, they stopped at a roadside kiosk to purchase a clump of what Lars quickly coined "Baby bananas."

"These things are miniature. Half the size of the ones back home," he said, handing the seller a fistful of pesos he'd obtained earlier in the old city.

"Ugghh," Sara said, spitting out the chunk she had bitten off. "They may look cute, but they taste horrible. It's a really bitter taste."

"No pleasing you eh?... First the cigar and now the bananas," Lars taunted, tossing his own portion in a nearby bin.

Back at the apartment block, they were just getting out of the elevator when the Professor emerged from his own door. Lars used the opportunity to ask whether he could recommend a good restaurant in the area.

"El viejo Gringo," the Professor answered without hesitation. "It is the best in the neighbourhood and very reasonably priced. It is not far from here."

Although it was not quite seven p.m. it was already dark by the time the couple left for The Old Gringo.

"How exactly are we gonna find this place with no street signs?" Sara asked, as they walked along a busy street.

"And not exactly an overabundance of streetlights either," Lars pointed out. "According to the Professor it's three blocks up, turn right and halfway down the street."

Lars's optimism however, turned out to be premature. Having retraced their steps several times over the span of an hour, they finally spotted a small sign in the yard of a house on a residential street.

"This must be the place," Lars said, holding open the door and following Sara down a set of stairs into a dimly lit basement.

"Buenos Noches Señora … Señor," a woman in her 40's greeted, before showing them to the last empty table. Despite the small space, only large enough to accommodate six tables, the ambience was relaxed, with a interesting assortment of art objects and captivating photos adorning the walls. Once having ordered, they passed the time recalling some of the day's events.

"That's it, I'm hooked," Lars declared, after his first sip of a mojito. "This tastes incredible. You should have ordered one."

"I'm sticking with wine, thank you," Sara told him, raising her glass. "The menu said it's from Chile, and it's also very good."

Following what both felt had been a sumptuous meal, they departed, promising the proprietor they would definitely return.

"I never really thought about it till now," Lars said, as they strolled arm in arm along a now eerily, empty street, enjoying the warm night breeze and clear, starlit sky. "But we never asked the Professor whether this was a safe area to walk in at night."

"I'm sure he would have said something if he thought it dangerous," Sara replied. "I wonder where everybody is. It's not even ten o'clock."

Next day...

With the memory of the previous evening's walk still fresh, they decided to return to the old city on foot. They were just passing the historic National Hotel, famed for its association with organized crime and glitzy Hollywood stars of the 40's and 50's, when they were joined by a well dressed individual.

"Looks like we have company," Sara whispered to Lars before the man spoke.

"Señor, Señorita... Buenos Dias.... welcome to my country," the man said. "A country that I love so deeply, I have devoted my life to spreading knowledge of it to visiting tourists," he continued without a let up. "Everything you would like to know about my wonderful Cuba, I can provide," he boasted, as they walked along the Malecon.

"That could take awhile," Lars goaded him. "I'm not sure we'll be here that long."

"You make joke sir, but I tell the truth. I know so much about my country."

"Hey, I believe you," Lars said, interrupting the man's 'Spiel'.

"But we're not here for a history lesson. We came to explore the country on our own terms."

"I understand sir," the man replied. "Then I wish you the best of times in my land." And with that the salesman turned and walked back in the direction of the National Hotel.

"Well that was a pleasant surprise compared to that guy yesterday," Lars commented. "I understand people are just trying to make a living, but it was starting to seem like every time we turned a corner someone was trying to sell us something or be our guide. It was starting to get on my nerves."

"Well you saw how this man reacted when you remained polite and said no thanks. Just keep doing that," Sara advised.

Entering the old city from its western border, they soon found themselves in narrow streets pulsating with life. Residents of all ages were out in full force, patiently sharing space with the numerous tourists, many of whom were day-trippers in from the all-inclusive resorts of Varadero. Navigating their way past push carts full of fresh fruits, vegetables and even unrefrigerated meat, as well as makeshift garages where young men had set their antiquated cars up on cylinder blocks in the middle of the street in order to repair them, the pair eventually made it to the central square, where overhearing a departing guide addressing his group, they learned that buildings in the square had been recently renovated.

"Do you really think this was what Cuba looked like

decades ago?" Lars growled, as they surveyed a plaza framed by buildings painted in an assortment of gaudy colours. "If it was, I'm glad we're visiting before the entire city looks like this. It's about as authentic as something straight out of Disneyland."

Abandoning the square, they returned to more untouched sections of the city, occasionally running into clusters of red and white uniformed school children obediently marching along behind their teacher.

The remainder of the day was spent exploring the old city's cluttered neighbourhoods, peering into darkened entranceways and courtyards, absorbing all the idiosyncrasies of a city where life had been bent but not broken. At one point, yearning for a snack, they ventured into a small grocery store to purchase some sandwiches. It was while they were standing in line at the check-out, that a tall, thin man directly behind Sara, started up a conversation.

"Excuse me, You are tourists, yes?" the man asked.

"Yes," Lars answered, thinking the question pretty superfluous.

"Where do you come from?" he wanted to know, setting his basket of groceries on the counter as he spoke.

"Canada," Sara told him.

"Ah yes, I know it. Toronto Maple Leafs...Montreal Canadians."

"That's us," Sara said, trying to be polite as the line slowly moved towards the cashier.

"Yes. Canada is a rich land. Not like here."

"Oh, oh..." Lars whispered to Sara.

"Here we are not so rich," the man continued. "Here it is hard for someone like me, someone with four young children," he added, pausing to let that image sink in. "Perhaps you could help me."

"How so?" Lars asked, sensing he was being set up, but willing to play along for now.

"I need milk powder to help feed my children, but it is very expensive. Perhaps you could help me out. I would be very grateful."

"*If this is a scam, it's a pretty original one,*" Lars thought, as he glanced to Sara to see how she was reacting to the overture.

"How much is milk powder?" Lars asked.

"It is $5.00," the man answered, holding up a package from his basket.

"Five dollars? That seems like a lot for a bag of milk powder," Lars stated.

"That is for four bags sir."

Now fully aware he was being had, Lars nonetheless offered to pay for two bags, an offer to which the man immediately agreed. Once out on the street, Lars remarked about the recent transaction.

"Did you notice the guy only took two bags and gave the other two back to the cashier?"

"I didn't," Sara said, gently pulling Lars out of the way of an oncoming car in the narrow street.

"In other words he never intended to buy four," Lars said. "I also saw that she only rang up a dollar something for the two he kept, so where did the $5.00 come from? But I have to give it to him. The guy was a smooth operator. I mean, who's gonna call his bluff and refuse to help starving kids?"

"I'm a bit surprised you didn't balk but just see it as your good deed for the day," Sara told him. "I've no doubt we're going to run into more of his kind while we're here. When that happens, do what you did with that guy near the National Hotel... just smile and say no thanks. Having said that... as much as like old Havana, I could use a break from all the noise and hectic pace. I'm up for calling it a day. If we choose to walk, we could still make it home before dark."

Next day...

Early next morning, Lars was woken by the sounds of a barking dog, coming from an adjacent rooftop.

"It'll stop sooner or later," Sara assured him "Besides, it's almost eight o'clock. Didn't we tell the professors wife we'd take breakfast at eight thirty? That's just enough time to shower and get dressed."

Right after breakfast, first item on the agenda was to confirm their reservation for a rental car, scheduled to be picked up the following day. After completing the formalities at a small rental office on the grounds of the National Hotel, Lars suggested that they hop a bus to Cristóbal Colón Cemetery.

"You want to go to a cemetery?" Sara asked, slightly aghast.

"I forgot to mention it to you. This morning when you were in the shower, the Professor knocked on our door and gave me this brochure," Lars explained, pulling the booklet from his camera bag. "Amongst other things, he strongly recommended going to see this cemetery, but to do so before it gets too hot. He even told me which bus we need to take. From what I've read, it looks pretty impressive."

Still unsure about whether she truly wanted to visit the cemetery, once aboard the proper bus, Sara began reading the brochure.

"Have you read all this?" she asked, several pages in.

"I actually only glanced at it."

"It sounds incredible. Listen to this. *'The cemetery was named after Christopher Columbus and is considered to be one of the most important and largest in all of Latin America. It's rectangular shape measures 800 metres by 620 metres.'*"

"That's huge," Lars said. "That's almost a kilometre."

"There's more," Sara told him. "*It houses more than 800,000 graves with one million interments and more than 500 mausoleums. It's especially known for its elaborate statues most of which are made from marble'*... and here's something rather strange. It suggests 'Patrons should *not plan for a lengthy stay'*."

"Does that mean us?"

"No... It's referring to the dearly departed," Sara said with a smile.

"Explain."

"It says that *because space is at a premium, the remains of the deceased are removed after three years and stored in a separate facility.* That's pretty weird, don't you think? Where do people go to pay their respects after three years?"

"No idea," Lars answered. "I don't imagine one can be buried here for free, so I wonder how people are compensated for what ultimately is an empty grave?" Lars mused aloud. "I'm glad the Professor told me about it. It sounds like quite the place. By the way," he added, putting the brochure back in his knapsack. "I think the next stop is ours."

And impressive it was, capturing the pair's interest for well over three hours, as they wandered its numerous pathways and examined its impressive monuments. Back on the bus, headed downtown, Lars informed Sara that he was also interested in visiting the Museum of the Revolution. The Professor mentioned it as well and he certainly was dead on with the cemetery... pun intended."

"I'm not sure I'm keen on something like that," Sara told him.

"Do you know where this museum is?"

"I think we actually passed by it on the way to the central square. It's apparently housed in the old Presidential Palace, which seems pretty fitting given that Batista was still quartered there when Castro came to town."

"Where have I heard that name before?" Sara asked. "Hey, look at that building over there," she added abruptly.

"Where?"

"That one on the far side of that plaza. It looks like an outline of the face of Che Guevara... over on that wall."

"It looks like it's made out of some sort of metal tubing," Lars commented, just as the bus turned up a side street and Che disappeared behind a clump of trees.

"Anyways," Sara said, turning back to face Lars. "Who was this Batista guy again?"

"Dorothy mentioned him... during our history lesson at the airport," Lars reminded her. "He was the last President of Cuba. Word is that he was basically in the pocket of organized crime and led an incredibly corrupt regime. When he fled into exile in January 1959, he apparently helped himself to over $40 million as spending money. He later moved from the Dominican Republic to Spain where he died in 1973."

"When did you become so well informed?" Sara asked. "I guess we really didn't need that guy who claimed he knew everything there was to know about Cuba, did we?"

"You're not the only one who's been reading up on Cuba's history. I did some snooping after we decided we were going to come here."

'*Overkill*' was the description Lars placed on the revered museum after having only been there for half an hour. "I know this place is meant to show and honour various phases of the 'struggle'," he told Sara, who had changed her mind to join him at the last minute. "But from the glut of photos on these walls, I get the feeling someone recorded everything and anything to do with it. And I mean everything. This is way, way too much to take in," he said as they ascended the stairs to the next floor.

In addition to the surplus of photos, the three floors housed countless artefacts, displaying virtually every object that had ever been touched by prominent participants.

"It's all a bit much," Lars said, after they had cut short what could already be considered a whirlwind tour. "Most Cubans probably appreciate Castro having gotten rid of that Batista creep, but who's interested in seeing a towel Fidel may have used while still in the mountains?"

"I didn't see that," Sara told him.

"I could go back and take a photo of it if you like," Lars kidded. "You could show the neighbours and something to tell the grandchildren someday. But seriously, enough sight-seeing of the Revolution. Seeing as we're leaving tomorrow, I'd rather head back to the Capitol for another long look at the cars."

"But we'll be coming back here before we head home," Sara said.

"I know, but it's a sunny day. Who knows what it might be like in a couple of weeks. Let's take advantage of the good weather."

On the way back to the Capitol, they couldn't help noticing the number of residents out on their balconies, seemingly content to be doing nothing else but leaning on the ornate iron railings, observing the world beneath them passing by.

"Would you mind if we stopped and picked up some Aspirin?"

Sara asked, as they noticed a long line of people waiting to get into a pharmacy. "I don't know if it was the wind from our tour the other day, but I feel I'm fighting off the beginnings of a cold."

Knowing the cars could wait, they took their place in line behind a distinguished looking man clad in a rather tattered suit jacket. Upon seeing his fellow customers, it wasn't long before the man started up a conversation.

"I'm afraid you may be in for quite a wait," he announced in perfect, accent free English.

"That's okay," Lars told him. "We're not really in any rush."

"That's fortunate because here in Cuba there's no such thing as being in a rush... at least successfully," he explained. "Everything takes longer."

"Is that mainly because of the culture? That people are just more laid back? Or can you blame it on the embargo?"

"It probably has more to do with the fact that wages are so meagre. Few people see the need to provide quick and efficient service."

"Do you think it would be different if the embargo wasn't in place?" Lars asked, pleased to have met someone who wasn't trying to sell him something.

"The embargo has certainly affected people's lives. If it was lifted the economy would undoubtedly improve. But the government also bears some responsibility for the terrible shape of the economy. It often serves their purpose to blame everything on the embargo."

"Do you mind me asking what you do for a living?" Lars asked cautiously.

"I used to be an assistant professor at the University, but I was dismissed because I refused to tow the Party line in my classes."

"But how do you support yourself?"

"I receive a small pension and make ends meet by doing odd jobs, such as giving private English lessons."

"This probably sounds like a dumb question but is there no chance for you to emigrate?"

"I have applied numerous times, but each time they refuse. They claim my work as a Professor gave me access to sensitive information. That's an exaggeration of course. It's more a case of their being afraid I would discredit the government somehow if I was allowed to move to a country like the US."

"So you are more or less a captive in your own country," Lars said.

"That's a pretty accurate assessment," the man said with a degree of resignation. "I'm sorry, but it's my turn at the counter. It's been nice chatting with you. I hope you enjoy the rest of your stay."

"I feel sorry for that guy," Lars said to Sara, as they watched the man approach the counter. "When an articulate, intelligent guy like that is not allowed to teach and is forced to eke out a living, it makes me wonder what our Professors might have agreed to, to afford the lifestyle they have. Too bad we couldn't introduce him to someone like Dorothy. I think they would have hit it off and it might have been a ticket out of here for him... Say, is it just me or do the staff behind the counter look as if they're acting in slow motion? I think we can forget about the cars today. At this rate we'll be lucky to be out of here by sundown."

But they did manage to acquire the desired Asprin and made it home before darkness descended. Following another delicious meal at the Old Gringo later that evening, they returned to the flat early enough to say goodbye to the Professors, pack up, and be in bed by ten.

Next Day...

With knapsacks loaded and secure, and the flat keys left on the kitchen table as requested, the two made their way to the National Hotel on foot, arriving just as the car rental office opened.

"What kind of car am I going to get today?" Lars asked the man behind the counter, as he handed over his driver's license for inspection. "I reserved a compact but I don't see any in the lot."

"We give you a Gee sir."

"A G? What's a G? You sound like a cheerleader?"

"Lars," Sara said in a firm tone. "The man's just doing his hob."

"I just want to know what kind of car we're getting," he replied.

"Gee is Chinese car, sir," the man explained, as he pecked at his keyboard with two fingers. "It is good car," he assured Lars.

"I'm not fluent in Mandarin," Lars said, when he first laid eyes on the designated vehicle. "But my guess is that Gee is Chinese for piece of junk. This thing looks so flimsy I could almost pick it up."

"As long as it gets us where we want to go," Sara sighed.

"That in itself is debatable," Lars replied. "If we get into an accident, we'll be toast," he added as he pried open the door and was met with a blanket of stale air.

"What is with this car?" Lars fumed. "We've been admiring these vintage cars, most of them over 50 years old, and here is this relatively new one, that smells like someone died in it 50 years ago. They're probably still in the trunk."

Despite his dissatisfaction, Lars knew there was little alternative but to take the G and drive. Armed with a map he'd picked up at a bookstore the day before, they were soon cruising west on a four-lane highway, past what they initially believed were the outskirts of Havana. But no sooner had they settled in for what they hoped would be a relaxing drive to Viñales, the highway suddenly morphed into a two-lane road, leaving them to navigate through an exclusive neighbourhood, bristling with fancy villas sequestered behind high brick walls.

"If I didn't know better, this area could easily be mistaken for a section of Beverly Hills or Belair," Lars snarled, as they passed one dwelling with a uniformed guard outside its gate. "I was going to say I wonder who lives here... but in all likelihood it's high-ranking government officials. Quite the contrast from old Havana."

"I'm curious how they rationalize such a blatant display of wealth to the comrades lower in the pecking order?" Sara said,, taken aback by the sheer affluence of the dwellings. "Revolution, what revolution?"

Once the suburbs and satellite cities of Havana had receded, Sara adjusted her seat back for the three hour drive and admitted she wanted to take a little nap.

"But you'll miss all the stunning scenery," Lars warned.

"I can see it on the way back," she answered. "We do have to come back the same way don't we?"

"As far as can tell there's just the one main road... so nap away."

Although he hadn't been aware of at the time, before leaving for Cuba, Lars had unknowingly fallen victim to what could be called a booking scam. Thinking it prudent to reserve a 'Casa' ahead of time, he had forked out $25 to a local agency, for each of the three reservations he'd requested. The city of

Viñales represented the first of the three reservations, and upon arriving at the designated house, he was not pleased to learn that the room had already been rented out to someone else.

"I'm sorry," he said, his teeth clenched as he spoke to the middle-aged proprietor who had answered the door. "But what's the sense of paying to reserve a room only to find out it's gone? Didn't you get any notice from the agency that I had reserved a room?"

"Not sure, Señor. My daughter deal with agent."

"Do you at least have another room?" he asked the woman.

"Sorry we full, but we have neighbour who also rent room, Very nice, Same price."

"And where is this neighbour?" Lars wanted to know. "Can we at least take a look at the room before deciding?"

"No problem, Señor," she assured him.

"Well that was certainly $25 well spent," Lars grumbled, when he returned to the car. "And you want to hear something else? The rental cost of the room is the same price as the reservation fee. Somebody is asking a killing. But the woman said there's another room just across the street so let's go check it out."

After a quick tour of the facilities, Lars agreed to accept the alternative lodging, somewhat mollified when told they could still have their home-cooked meals at the original Casa.

"I think I'm going to have a word or two with that agency when we're back home. That's the last bloody time I pay for a reservation," Lars said, as they unpacked in their gloomy, windowless room. "Did you count how many people asked us if we needed a room? Every time we stopped at an intersection, someone was at the door of the car. We didn't need a reservation at all."

"Who was to know?" Sara said, hoping to avoid an argument.

"We have a room now and we'll know better next time."

"Look," Lars said, glancing at his watch. "It's only one o'clock … We didn't come all this way to sit in our room, especially this dreary one. Why don't we take off and see some of the countryside."

"But we just spent three hours in the car," Sara complained. "I wouldn't mind resting for awhile."

"You can rest on the beach," Lars told her.

"Beach? What beach?"

"When the woman at the other Casa was checking to see if this room was available, I was scanning a rack of brochures. I noticed one that said something about an 'exclusive, remote beach' a few miles west of Viñales. Anything's more inviting than this room."

Armed with directions from the owner of the new Casa, they had only been a few miles west of Viñales when Lars spotted two young women hitch-hiking.

"Hey why don't we give those two a lift. If they're locals, maybe they know where this beach is," Lars said, pulling over to the side of the road.

"Since when do you speak Spanish, Señor?" Sara asked.

"Maybe they speak English," he replied, watching the two young women in the rear view mirror as they ran up to the car. "If not we'll figure something out. What's beach in Spanish… Playa? And what's remote?"

"Your sense of judgement," Sara quipped.

"Gracias, Señor," said the one with her hair pulled back into a pony tail, who appeared to be the older of the two. The greeting was quickly followed by something neither Lars nor Sara could understand, as the two tossed in their luggage and scrambled into the back seat.

"Sorry, but we don't speak Spanish," Lars explained.

"Where you go?" the woman asked, as she leaned forward.

"There's supposedly a remote beach west of Pino del Rio. Do you know it?" Lars asked.

"We go Pino del Rio," the woman answered with a big smile.

"That works out well, but it's the beach we're looking for. It's somewhere…"

"I don't think you're getting your point across, Señor," Sara interrupted.

"Uhhh. Playa… something," Lars said, glancing up at the woman in the mirror as he pulled back on to the road.

"Playa Bailén?" the other woman suddenly said.

"Yeah… Si," Lars answered. "That's the one. Do you know how to get there?"

"We go Pina del Rio," the first one repeated.

"I got that part," Lars told them. "It's Playa Bailén, we're looking for. It's not shown on the so-called map in our guidebook."

Over the remaining distance to Pino del Rio, conversation had been sparse. Upon entering the town, the woman who had initially done all the talking suddenly asked if they could be dropped off at a pharmacy.

"We here to visit our abuela," she told them.

"Abuela?" Sara repeated.

"Uhhh," the woman answered, looking to her companion.

"I think is grandmother," the second one announced.

"Si, grandmother," the first woman echoed, seemingly proud of her pronunciation. "Grandmother needs medicine."

"No problem," Lars answered. "Just tell me where."

But when the drop off point was reached, it was only the younger woman who got out."

"Isn't this where you wanted to get off?" Sara asked the other woman.

"No… I come with you. I show you Playa Bailén."

"I don't think that's necessary," Lars said. "According to this map, there appears to only be one road west from here. The road to the beach must run off of it somewhere and there's bound to be a sign. I think we can find it on our own."

"Is no problem, Señor," she insisted, leaning back to show she had no intention of leaving.

"But when we get to this beach, assuming we can find it…

we may want to stay for awhile. How are you going to get back to Pina del Rio?" Lars asked.

"No problem, Señor," the woman repeated.

"Now what, Señor?" Sara said, scrunching up her forehead.

"Whether we want one or not, it seems we now have a guide," said in a lower voice. "But for the record, she's volunteering her services right? I'm not gonna let her charge us."

"We'll see," Sara replied.

Approximately fifteen minutes later, still on the same road west out of Pina del Rio, they'd been the only vehicle visible for several miles.

"Are you sure this is the right way?" he asked.

"You turn here," the woman suddenly shouted, pulling herself forward on the back of Lars' seat.

"Here?" Lars repeated, automatically slowing down. "But there's no sign. Are you sure this is the road?"

"This road to Playa Bailén. I know. You must turn."

"Okay... I guess I don't have much choice," Lars said, leaving the paved highway for a dusty, rutted road. "Man," Lars muttered, after they had ventured several miles down the road. "When they said 'remote' they really meant 'remote'," he said quickly rolling up the window to keep out the dust. "I mean talk about desolate. There's no signs of civilization anywhere. All we need now is for the Gee to break down."

"Banish the thought, Señor," Sara advised him. "Sorry, but are you sure this is the right road?" she added, turning to the woman.

"Si, si... right road." the woman answered.

"What do you think we should do?" Sara asked Lars in a quieter tone. "Who knows where she's leading us."

"Well unless she has a gun in her purse, I don't think we have too much to worry about."

"But we're miles from anywhere. She could be ..."

"She's been with us the whole time since we picked her

up, and she hasn't used her phone, so it's unlikely she's arranged an ambush or anything. We've come this far, let's give it another few minutes. If there's still no sign of the beach, we'll just tell her we've changed our minds and head back to Viñales."

As fate would have it, it was just as Lars was determined to use the next opportunity to turn around when the whitecaps of the not-so-distant sea came into view.

"Well what do you know," he said, as they pulled to a stop next to a concrete building at a parking lot void of any cars.

"Is this really it?" Lars asked, as turned off the engine.

"Si ... Playa Bailén. Beach other side of trees."

"Well this certainly was worth all the effort," Sara moaned. "Now what?"

"Well we've seen the remote parking lot... I guess we should take a look at this remote beach" Lars suggested, as all three passengers climbed out of the car.

"If we're gonna stay here for awhile, what are we going to do with our friend?" Sara asked, when the woman was a few feet ahead.

"She told us it was not a problem if we stay, so I'll just thank her and say goodbye. It looks like there might actually be somebody in that building over there so maybe she can arrange to get a ride back. Why don't you and our trusted guide wait here. I'll be right back."

The building turned out to be a restaurant, with bare concrete walls and a floor to match, upon which were a number of empty plastic tables and chairs that gave the place the ambience of a deserted bunker. The lone figure slouching behind the counter when Lars walked in, suddenly jerked to attention as if Lars was the first customer he'd seen in weeks, which all things considered, could very well have been true.

"Buenos Dias," Lars said. "Do you speak English?"

"A leetle, Señor."

"Great, maybe you can tell me, if there's a bus that goes back to Pina del Rio from here?"

"Bus… no, Señor. No bus."

"Okay … yeah, well… how come that doesn't surprise me," Lars mumbled to himself. "In the meantime, can I get a couple of cokes from you?"

Returning to the car, Lars was surprised to see Sara standing there alone.

"So where did she go?" he asked, handing Sara a drink.

"I may have pissed her off," Sara admitted. "I had the feeling she was hinting for some sort of compensation for her troubles and when I tried to explain that we were grateful and case closed, she walked off in a huff."

"Walked off where? You can see for miles around here. Where did she go?"

"The last I saw of her, she was headed towards that small shack," Sara said, pointing to a tumble-down hut not far from the restaurant.

"Okay… so if that problem is solved, why don't we grab the blanket from the trunk and head down to the beach?"

"Do you think it's safe to leave the car here like this?"

"It should be unless there's a gang of international car thieves hiding behind the sage brush over there. Besides, they'd have to be pretty friggin' desperate to want to steal this thing."

"I don't know," Sara shuddered. "This place kind of gives me the creeps," she said, as they passed through a thicket of trees out on to a seemingly endless beach. "I've never seen a beach so empty. It must go on for miles and there's not a soul in sight. I'm not sure I wanna stay here."

"It is kind of spooky," Lars agreed, flipping the blanket into the air and straightening it out once it had settled on the sand. "Can you at least see the car from here?" he asked. "Ever since you said you thought you pissed our guide off, I've had this vision of her wanting to seek some sort of revenge."

"I can't see it. I think you'll have to walk back to the edge of the trees."

"Okay… Just for my own peace of mind, I'm gonna take a

quick look to make sure she or nobody else is hanging around the car."

"Anybody else? Where are they going to come from?. Drop from the sky?" Sara kidded.

Ignoring the jibe, Lars started off towards the trees. Having left his shoes and socks by the blanket, he was enjoying the feel of the warm sand on his feet when all of a sudden he felt stabbing pains on the soles of his feet. Looking down he saw that the source was dozens of barbed thorns half buried in the sand. Only halfway through this tortuous field at this point, he was temporarily frozen to the spot, trying to decide whether it best to back track or push through to the trees. In the end he chose the latter, yelping and cringing with each further step until reaching safer ground. Dropping down on a clear patch of sand, he began extracting the tiny spikes protruding from his flesh. Once the stinging nettles had been removed, he hobbled far enough to make sure the car was still where he'd left it.

"Well that was certainly a joyful trip," he groaned, plopping back down onto the blanket and examining his aching feet. "At least they're not bleeding."

"What happened?" Sara wanted to know.

"I accidentally stumbled into a field of … I don't know what they were… but boy did they hurt. I was going to go for a swim but there's no way I'm going to expose my wounds to salt water. I know you're not terribly impressed with this place so let's get out of here."

"Not a minute too soon as far as I'm concerned," Sara answered, quickly getting to her feet. "We would have been better off staying in Viñales."

"Look, why don't you take the blanket back to the car. Here's the keys."

"What are you going to do?"

"Well for one thing I'm going to put my shoes back on… ever so carefully," he told her. "And so should you. Then I'm going to hobble over to that shack to see what became of our guide. As much of a pain as she is, we can't just leave her here."

"Says who?" Sara replied, as she gathered up her belongings.

But there was no sign of the missing navigator at the locked shack. Limping back to the car, Lars was glad to see all four wheels still in place. Confident they could find their way back to Viñales without the benefit of a guide, they bid farewell to the remote beach, with Lars unable to refrain from yelling, 'Come on, Silver, Come on, Scout' out the open window, as they drove off in a cloud of dust.

Next Day...

Still smarting from their unpleasant encounter with the remote beach, at breakfast the next morning, the pair decided this day would be spent closer to home. Acting on a tip from fellow tourists staying in the Casa, they placed a call and booked a riding tour into the nearby mountains, only a short drive from the Casa. Just as they were walking into the courtyard where the horses were stabled, a young man in his early twenties emerged from a nearby barn to greet them.

"Not too sure about this," Lars mumbled, after the man, who had introduced himself as Raphael, accepted their payment and gone off to collect the saddles. "Did you catch a glimpse of those horses in the corral?" he asked Sara. "They all looked a trifle malnourished and a little worse for wear. I mean their backs were sagging so much, they almost looked like two men in a horse costume."

While waiting for Raphael to return, the two of them walked over to the fence for a closer look. Just at that moment, one of the animals swung its head around towards them with an expression that seemed to say, 'whatever you do, please don't sit on me.'

"Are these the horses we're going to take?" Lars asked Raphael when he came out of the barn with the first saddle.

"Yes sir," he answered, tossing the saddle on the top rung of the fence.

"Uhhh... They don't look too healthy. Are you sure they're up to it? Especially in this heat?" Lars asked.

"They are fine sir. They are used to ride," he assured.

As it turned out, the horses were fitter than they looked. Fitter in fact than their riders.

"Did you know the tour was going to be five hours?" Sara asked Lars, as she struggled to walk to the car after the tour had ended.

"I'm going to be bow-legged for a week, and my butt is so sore it must have blisters."

"It did go longer than I expected," Lars agreed. but it was worth it, don't you think? I've never seen mountains like that before. Sort of like those in Vietnam's Hai Phong Bay but without the water. I found them fascinating."

"They were unique, but I found the stopover at the tobacco drying house equally fascinating, though I could have done without that 'Coco loco' drink the farmer offered me."

"What was in it?"

"Didn't you see him chop open the fresh coconut? He did it so quickly I'm surprised he still had all his fingers."

"No. I was wandering through the racks of drying tobacco leaves."

"He emptied the contents into a glass and added what he claimed was 100-proof rum. I could hardly get it down. I'm lucky I didn't go blind."

"I thought you just said you liked the stopover."

"I did. It was interesting to see how the tobacco is harvested and dried. Plus I was just glad to get off the horse for awhile."

"Did you try any of the cigars?"

"You know I don't smoke, and I certainly wasn't about to try a honey, pineapple or grapefruit flavoured one."

"Did you try to get your nag to gallop out on the trail,?" Lars asked, as he watched Raphael remove the saddle from his trusty steed.

"Are you kidding?" Sara answered. "Did you?"

"I tried kicking my heels in her ribs a couple of times, but each time Caramelle, who should have been called Molasses, would just turn her head and snicker. at me. I'm convinced her genes somehow got mixed up with those of a turtle. Only once did she come close to acceding to my wishes, delivering a gallop that only lasted for about four seconds. I could have easily gotten off and jogged alongside."

"I suspect my muscles are going to ache tomorrow," Sara confessed, as she waddled back to the car. "But all the same, I'm glad we did it. To top it off, I think I got a bit of a sunburn."

That evening, at dinner in the Casa they had originally booked, they were served a chicken/pork concoction with a mix of cooked vegetables.

"You like?" the house owner asked, eager to deliver a second helping from a steaming pot.

"Not for me, thanks," Lars said, holding up both hands. "I'm stuffed, but it was really good."

While awaiting dessert, Lars fell into conversation with a couple seated at the next table. Unbeknownst to him the Swedish pair happened to be the ones who had unknowingly usurped their reservation.

"Do you dance Salsa?" the attractive, blonde-haired woman asked.

"Not if I can help it," Lars answered with a grin.

Unsure how to respond, the woman paused for a moment before Sara came to her rescue.

"Ignore him and maybe he'll go away," she joked.

Having been relieved, the woman went on to describe a club not far from the Casa, where she claimed visitors could enjoy watching what was billed as 'Salsa night.'

"I don't think I could dance if my life depended on it," Sara told her. "We were riding for five hours today and I'm sore all over."

"Oh, you must not dance," the woman's partner said in a

serious tone. "It is fun just to watch. Some people are very good. You should come."

Once desserts were finished, the foursome made their way to the club, chatting as strangers do, along the way. But no sooner had the group entered the courtyard, the Swedish pair wished them 'a pleasant evening' and moved off to sit with people they already knew. Alone at a table bordering the dance floor, Lars and Sara were enjoying the first round of mojitos, when a music man on a makeshift stage, suddenly started up, prompting a half dozen dancers into action.

"Some of these people must be professional dancers," Lars said, halfway through the third song, which to his ear was barely distinguishable from the first two. "That couple over there, the woman in the white dress and the guy with the scarf knotted around his neck. They dance as if they're made of rubber. They must have been practicing for years."

Two strong mojitos later, Lars's admiration for the dancers' antics had shifted considerably.

"The more I watch them, the more I figure it can't be that hard," he said, his words slightly slurred.

"So like what, you're suddenly a Salsa expert?" Sara asked playfully. "If you're so talented, let's see you get up there and show them how it's really done."

"If I hadn't been on that donkey of a horse all day, I would," Lars muttered in response.

"That's a convenient cop out. You just don't want to make a fool of yourself in front of all these good dancers."

"It's not that," Lars protested. "As far as I can tell all you need to Salsa is to act as if you're dancing on hot coals in bare feet."

"I think there's a little more to it than that, Señor. No more mojitos for this muchacho, ladies and gentlemen."

Next Day...

Although the problem had been noticeable on the drive to the remote beach, Lars had initially brushed off the irksome bucking, assuming it was simply 'par for the course' for such a poorly built car. But next morning, on the way back towards Havana, the Gee not only started bucking more frequently, but also seemed to peak out at a top speed 100 kmph, not a bad thing given the condition of the roads. Increasingly frustrated by the car's performance and not eager to be stuck with such a lemon for the remainder of the trip, he made the spontaneous decision to pay a return visit to the rental office.

"Who knows what else can go wrong with this heap?" he told Sara. "We're planning on heading for Cienfuegos anyways, so it's not really out of the way to go back to Havana."

"Holy shit," Lars cried out, as they were pulling into the bay of the National Hotel later that morning.

"What now?" Sara shouted back, having been aroused from a half sleep. "What's the matter?"

"You know what that is?" Lars said.

"What what is?" Sara asked, somewhat irked.

"Over there by the main entrance," Lars said, as he squeezed into an empty slot just outside the rental office. "It's a 1959 Thunderbird convertible that looks like it just came right out of the showroom. Why couldn't we rent a car like that? That was my dream car for years when I was a kid," he raved.

"Go see if the keys are in it," Sara joked. "I'll create a slight distraction and meet you on the Malecon."

"Don't tempt me, lady. If we weren't on an island, I'd seriously consider it. In the meantime, let's get rid of this hunk of junk."

Following some last-minute coaching from Sara, Lars entered the rental office, intending to politely request a replacement auto. He was only able to get as far as uttering, 'the car I rented a couple of days ago,' before the man at the desk immediately cut him off.

"No problem, sir. We give you brand new car," he assured Lars.

"I obviously wasn't the first customer to complain about the Gee," Lars muttered, as he and Sara sought the licence number of the car they'd been assigned.

"Shit," Lars said suddenly.

"Now what?"

"The T-Bird is gone."

"And?"

"I wanted to check out the interior and maybe even see who it belonged to."

"Probably some retired Mafia boss," Sara mocked. "Look, here's our car," she added, pointing to a shiny blue Gee, still covered in tiny droplets of water from having recently been washed. "I hope this one at least works."

"It means a hundred fires," Sara read aloud from the guidebook as they headed southeast out of Havana on a multi-lane highway.

"What does?" Lars asked, swerving to miss yet a pothole, one in a series of random, significantly sized craters.

"Cienfuegos," she told him.

"What do they need so many lanes for?" Lars complained, changing lanes to get out from behind a smoke-belching truck. "There's barely enough traffic to fill two. They could have settled for fewer lanes, and used the extra money to fill in some of these potholes. How can people drive here at night? Hitting one of these pits would wreck even a good car. God knows what they would do to a Gee."

"Then how about slowing down a bit, Mr. Speed Demon... it's not as if we're in a hurry. Cienfuegos is only a three-hour drive. I'd like us to get there in one piece."

Despite his tendency to drive beyond the speed limit, Lars was forced to slow their pace when the four-lane highway suddenly ended and they were thrust on to a two-lane road.

"We could easily be in Manitoba," Lars commented, suddenly paying more attention to the countryside. "If it wasn't for the fields of sugar cane."

"And the palm trees," Sara added.

"And the people waiting for a bus that might or might not come," Lars said, pointing to yet another group congregated under a bridge, sheltering from the heat. Others more skeptical about the reliability of public transport, could be seen huddled in the back of a dump truck or squeezed into the one of the few private jalopies capable of lengthy drives. On the rare occasion a bus was actually spotted, it was packed to the hilt, belching out billowing clouds of thick, bluish smoke as if fogging for mosquitos.

"Getting from point A to B in this country appears to be a challenge," Sara said, as another dump truck offering standing room only, rattled past in the opposite direction.

"That's one of the reasons I like picking up hitchhikers," Lars told her. "Makes life a little easier for them and hopefully a little more interesting for us."

"Yeah, I can remember just how interesting," Sara snorted, recalling the remote beach saga.

With no hitchhikers or other diversions to delay them, other than a number of vultures perched precariously near the road's edge, waiting for an accident to happen, they arrived in Cienfuegos shortly after two.

"Tell me this isn't happening," Lars said angrily to no one in particular, when informed by the proprietor of the Casa, that the room they'd reserved had been allocated to another guest.

"I send you to other Casa. Is also nice place," the woman quickly added.

"Sorry, but something must have gotten lost in the translation," Lars told her, making no attempt to disguise his sarcasm. "Why bother accepting reservations only to ignore them?"

"Many people no show," the woman answered. "We take customers first serve."

"I think she means first come, first serve," Sara inserted, taking hold on Lars' elbow. "Cool down, Lars. The woman said she could recommend another place."

"What is it with you and harmony?" Lars asked bitterly, when the woman had gone off to find the address of the alternative accommodation.

"What do you mean?" Sara asked.

"You never get angry… No wait, I take that back. I've seen you get angry with me plenty of times. But don't you ever get upset with strangers because something in their behaviour was objectionable?"

"Sometimes," Sara replied, miffed by the generalization.

"This woman for example," Lars continued. "She's responsible for having given away our reservation. Doesn't that bother you?"

"I'm disappointed, but I get the feeling that's what they all do. I'm sure the other place will be fine."

"But this one's right on the water, that's why I booked it in the first place. Did you get a look at the patio? It juts out into the bay with an incredibly view of the harbour."

With few other options available, and tempers simmering, they drove to the new Casa in silence, only to discover the 'nice place' was in the middle a gravel parking lot in what looked to be the industrial section of the city.

"We're not staying here for weeks," Sara told him, as they collected their luggage and rang the bell. "With no other houses nearby, at least it will be quiet."

Not wishing to let the unexpected switch in Casas spoil his mood more than it already had, Lars suggested going for a walk to clear his head.

"I think that's an excellent idea," Sara told him, aware that her own frame of mind was threatening to tip. "I could use a little R & R to absorb some of the adventures we've already had. I can only take in so much before it all starts to become a blur. I can use the time to look in the guidebook and to see what there is to see in Cienfuegos. I might as well do the same with Trinidad, seeing as that will be our next port of call."

Relying on his good sense of direction, Lars wandered off

towards the harbour, taking note of buildings and landmarks along the way to assure he could find his way back. Several blocks from the new abode, he happened past an overgrown field of tall grass and weeds, that on second look revealed itself to be an abandoned amusement park, complete with rusting ferris wheel, broken merry-go-round and paint-chipped booths that had once offered fair goers the chance to win prizes.

"So this is what the world might look like after a nuclear war," he thought to himself, regretting that he had left his camera at the flat.

As he was approaching the harbour, Lars couldn't help noticing that the tide was out, exposing a dense thicket of mangrove trees that stretched along the coastline. Eager to have a closer look, he started across a broad, wet plain. Although the ground underfoot had initially been hard, compacted sand, it wasn't long before it began to turn to a mucky gumbo, each step becoming more and more arduous. Without warning, the gumbo abruptly gave way to a gooey slime in which he found himself sinking up to his ankles.

"Shit…If I get stuck here and the tide comes in, they'll never find me," he thought. Deciding that a closer inspection of the mangrove tress was not worth such a fate, he struggled to extract his mud coated shoes and headed back to safer ground.

"What the heck happened to you?" Sara asked, when she caught a glimpse of him in the doorway with muddied shoes and splattered pants.

"I was brutally attacked by a clump of mangrove trees," he told her. "Although they should really be called 'mangled' trees."

"What on earth are you talking about?" she said, setting the guidebook aside.

"You wouldn't believe how gnarled the roots of those things are. They make an almost impenetrable barrier. I made the mistake of trying to get a closer at them look without realizing how soft the ground was. I was lucky to get out of there."

"Well at least your little misadventure seems to have taken your mind off the cancelled reservation."

Only able to have a bland tasting dinner in the centre of town that evening, they returned to the Casa just after ten, unaware that the tranquility they had so enjoyed that afternoon would prove to be fleeting. In bed by 11:00, both had trouble getting to sleep thanks to a myriad of nocturnal sounds.

"I can deal with the crickets and the occasional barking dog," Lars said, feeling wide awake. "I can even handle the odd car racing past. But who the hell rides a horse through the city at midnight?" he added.

"The start of a cattle drive?" Sara joked, giving him a playful poke in the ribs. "Or maybe a one-man posse out to steal the wheels off our Gee?"

"Serves him right if it is," Lars replied, rolling over on his side. Fortunately for all concerned, shortly after the loud clopping hooves had faded, all other irritating sounds ceased as well.

Next Day...

By next morning, the tension of the previous day had been forgotten. Right after breakfast, which had included an unidentifiable and unpleasant tasting fruit served by the Casa owner, Lars and Sara returned to the centre of Cienfuegos for a little sight-seeing.

"I know you may find this hard to believe," Lars remarked as they walked along a busy street. "But Cienfeugos has a feature that outdoes Havana."

"Granted we haven't that much of the city yet, but I find that hard to believe," Sara replied.

"The vintage cars."

"I might have known... you and your cars," Sara echoed.

"No really... For someone like me, who's old enough to remember them in their prime, being able to see them up close without people pestering you to take a tour is a big plus."

Equally impressive were the old buildings bordering a park in the central square. Amongst the most august was the city hall. With twin turrets and an ornate, white-stuccoed facade, it stood as a prime example of the Spanish culture that had once dominated the area.

"This building has obviously been renovated," Lars said admiringly. "But unlike its counterparts in Havana's central square, it's managed to keep its authentic, old world charm and doesn't resemble a gaudy fun house at a county fair."

"I didn't realize Cienfuegos is not really on the coast," Sara commented, reading from the guidebook while stopped at a sidewalk cafe just off the square.

"According to this map, it sits on the edge of a large bay. The actual sea looks to be a few kilometres away. Lars, look at this," she added. "There's a place called Playa Rancho Luna that looks like it's right on the coast. Maybe we can go for a swim or snorkel ... or just chill in the shade with a good mojito."

Although relatively easy to find, Playa Rancho Luna did not quite live up to their expectations.

"I think we can forget about snorkelling," Sara said, standing at the shoreline, the warm, murky water lapping at her feet. "Where is the brilliant turquoise sea that was in the glossy brochures?"

"I'm not sure Cienfuegos is going to make my list of places to return to," Lars remarked, as they retreated to the shade of a palm tree to relax.

"It's strange how easily your mood can shift," Sara said, gazing out at the sea. "I really liked Havana and Viñales, if you exclude that 'remote' beach fiasco. But I'm finding it a chore to enjoy Cienfuegos. I hope Trinidad is more interesting. From what I've read, just outside the town there's an all-exclusive resort that looks to have a decent beach."

"In the guidebook," Lars pointed out. "Who knows what it looks like in real life."

"Well, let's at least keep it in mind," she said. "It's called Playa la Boca."

"Then I vote for leaving this one-horse town tomorrow and taking our chances in Trinidad. To help celebrate, why don't we splurge on a good meal in the town square. Maybe our landlord can recommend a place that's better than where we were last night."

"La Verja," the elderly man who had greeted them upon their arrival, told them later that afternoon. "It is best restaurant in Cienfuegos."

"I was tempted to tell him, 'that ain't saying much,'" Lars told Sara, when they were back in their room.

"I'm glad you restrained yourself. Hopefully he's right and there will be something worth remembering about Cienfuegos."

Later that evening, immediately upon entering La Verja, they were approached by a white-jacketed waiter.

"Buenas tardes. Bienvenidos a la Verja," he said, before guiding them to a table.

"If La Verja is truly Cienfuego's best restaurant, it doesn't seem to rank as one of the most popular," Lars remarked, once the waiter had left them alone with their menus. "We're the only customers. Do you think we're just too early?"

"I know southern people tend to eat later, but they have to cater to tourists as well" Sara said, while perusing her options. "All I know is that I'm hungry."

While in the midst of considering what to order, a man in a light-coloured suit appeared and seated himself at a piano not far from their table. Without any introduction, he broke into a low-key version of a song Lars couldn't quite place. Several bars in, the pianist was joined by two women in floor length gowns. Standing behind their respective microphones, they began singing what Lars finally recognized as 'The Girl from Ipanema.'

"Must be kind of depressing playing to an empty house," Lars said, nodding his gratitude as the waiter set down two mojitos. "And the last time I looked Ipanema was in Argentina."

"Don't be so petty, Lars," Sara growled. "*They* look like they're enjoying themselves even if you're not."

"They're paid to act jolly. Who wants to come and listen to a dejected…"

"I can think of worse ways to earn a living," Sara interrupted. "At least they don't have to work outside in the stifling heat. By the way, did you notice that La Verja means The Fence? It's written on the back of the menu."

"Don't look now, but our private concert is about to be gate-crashed," Lars told her. "Another couple just walked in."

Despite the surplus of empty tables, the waiter seated the new arrivals directly adjacent to Lars and Sara. Perhaps because of their limited audience, the trio decided to take a break after only four songs. With music no longer a distraction, the neighbouring diners soon fell into conversation.

"First time in Cienfuegos?" the grey-haired gentleman in a suit and tie asked in a thick English accent.

"First and probably last I'm afraid," Lars answered.

"That's rather disheartening to hear," the man replied. "I take it you haven't been overly awed by the place."

"One could say that."

"I'm afraid I can't confirm or refute your opinion as we just got here this afternoon. Name's Eric by the way… and this is my wife, Angela."

Clearly not as interested as her husband in chatting, Angela simply nodded before returning her gaze to her menu. "We're from England," Eric announced. "Central England… Small town near Nottingham. You've probably never heard of. And you two?"

"Canada," Sara answered, glancing at the still silent Angela.

"I'm Sara and this is Lars. Don't pay him much mind. He's always critical of something. Cienfuegos may not be Paris, but it's not that bad."

"It's too bad we're leaving tomorrow," Lars inserted." We could have taken you around to see all the things not worth seeing."

"Where are you off to?" Eric asked, directing his query to Sara.

"Trinidad... the city... not the country," she told him.

"That's where we've just come from... the city not the country," Eric explained.

"You didn't happen to stay at the all-exclusive resort did you?" Lars asked. "What was the name of that place Sara?"

"Playa la Boca."

"Playa la Boca," Lars repeated.

"Not familiar with the place," Eric said. "We prefer to stay in private homes. Nicer way to get to know the real Cuba, if you know what I mean."

"So you didn't see the beaches there at all?"

"No, 'fraid not. We English are not beach people, especially those of us from the north. What is worth seeing in Trinidad is the old town with its churches and barrios. We quite liked it, didn't we, Angela?"

"Hmmm," his wife murmured.

"Well that's good to know," Sara said.

As the exchange between the threesome continued, Angela being content to remain within the pages of her menu, several more patrons arrived. With the trio of musicians returning to the stage, further conversation was brought to an end.

"Well I wish you a more pleasant stay in Cienfuegos than we've had," Lars told Eric, just as the waiter arrived with their meals.

Next Day...

"Does it say anything in your guidebook about Cuba being known for meteorites?" Lars asked, when they were underway the next morning.

"Meteorites?" Sara parroted. "Not that I know of. Why do you ask?"

"What else can be causing these huge potholes? I thought the highway near Havana was bad. There's so many of them here, I haven't risked going more than 70 in case I have to swerve around them and there's oncoming traffic."

"I don't see slowing down as a major problem. We're not in any hurry. Besides, the guidebook says it's only 83 kilometres to Trinidad."

Shortly after passing a sign indicating there was less than 20 kms. until Trinidad, Lars happened to spot two young women hitch-hiking.

"What are you doing?" Sara asked, as he slowed and eased the Gee off on to the shoulder.

"I thought I'd give those two women a lift," he told her.

"Have you forgotten what happened the last time you decided to pick up a couple of hitchhikers? Besides, did you see how much stuff they have? We don't exactly have a lot of room."

"We can make it work," he assured her. "Maybe one or both speak English and can give us some tips about Trinidad."

"Muchos gracias Señor," the taller of the two said as they reached the car.

"Da nada," Lars answered, using up almost half of his Spanish. "Hang on a moment," he added as the woman started to load their belongings into the back seat. "Let me put some of your luggage in the trunk so you'll have more room."

Once the trunk had been rearranged to accommodate the new baggage, Lars was about to climb back in the car when he noticed that the left rear tire was flat.

"Shit. How did that happen?" he fumed." I didn't notice anything while we were driving. How could it go flat so quickly?"

"Better still, where are we gonna get it fixed on a Sunday?" Sara asked, having gotten out to inspect the damage. "We do have a spare don't we?"

To no one's surprise, least of all Lars, rather than coming equipped with a full size spare, the Gee only a mini-sized tire to offer, along with the advisory to have it replaced as soon as possible and not drive faster than 50 in the interim. To add to the current problem, getting at the 'spare', meant removing everything Lars had just finished putting in.

"¿Habla español, señor?" the taller woman asked once they were roadworthy again.

"No sorry," Lars answered. "Do you speak English?"

"Un poco," she answered, before breaking into a flurry of Spanish with her partner that at times sounded more like an argument than a discussion.

"I know place that fix tire," she told Lars, once that discussion has ended.

"Really? That would be open today?" Sara asked.

"Si. A friend of mine work every day. I take you there."

Hobbling into Trinidad in the disabled Gee, Lars followed the woman's instructions through the crowded streets, eventually pulling into a courtyard that looked more like an auto graveyard than a repair shop. At the sight of their car, two men who had working on a vehicle up on blocks, stopped what they were doing and walked over. One of them greeted the taller woman with a hug, which was then followed by a brief explanation in Spanish.

"Si, si," Lars heard the man say, when the woman pointed to the tire. "Ees no problem. We fix for you, sir."

Less than an hour later, with the tire now fixed and the mini-spare back where it belonged, both Lars and Sara thanked the men and women for their assistance and set off to find the last of the trio of Casas he'd reserved in Canada.

"No way," Lars muttered aloud as they arrived on a busy, two-lane street bearing the name they had been looking for. "These houses are virtually right on the road. There's no front yard at all. And look at all this traffic. Where is somebody supposed to park? There's no way we're stayin' here."

"You can't not show up. We've got a reservation," Sara

said.

"Watch me. We've already been tossed from two previous reservations… it's time to reverse the action. We gotta be able to find a better place than this," he said, as they drove past the designated house number.

"Well I for one am not in the mood for Casa hunting in this heat," Sara complained. "Why don't we just look for a hotel for tonight and conduct a search tomorrow?"

With Lars in full agreement, it wasn't long before they were strolling into the lobby of a 4-star hotel in the centre of town. As an added bonus, a short discussion with a sympathetic receptionist resulted in a reduced rate for the one night.

"Because today is Sunday, I can give you a better price," she told them. "But I can only offer you one night. Tomorrow we are fully booked," she explained.

"One night is fine," Lars said, as he signed the register and handed over his passport. "I'm sure we can find something else tomorrow. Say… can you tell me how far we are from the sea and where the nicest beaches are?" he asked, as he accepted the key to their room.

"Si, Señor," the young woman answered. "Playa Ancon is a very nice beach."

"How far is it?"

"It is not so far. About fifteen minutes by car."

"What about Playa la Boca?" Sara asked, as she opened to shuttered door to their balcony to look down at a courtyard of tropical splendour.

"I'd rather go for the one the receptionist recommended," Lars answered. She's probably more reliable than the guidebook."

With the clock having just inched past three, they wasted no time unpacking, made the short drive to Playa Ancon and hit the beach running. Needless to say it was a relief to discover that everything that had been missing at Baailén and

Rancho Luna, was there in excess at Playa Ancon, with pure white sand, crystal clear, blue waters and a long strip of palm trees to relax under. Far from being overcrowded, it had just enough patrons to make for a comfortable mix, with a different language being spoken every few metres.

"This is a part of Cuba I came to see and experience," Lars raved after the two emerged from a half hour of snorkelling.

"It is beautiful," Sara agreed. "It's like swimming in a bath tub. And the view underwater is amazing. Why don't we see if we can stay at the hotel down the beach? I could take lounging for a day or two."

"Why don't you chill out here and I'll walk down so see if they have anything available and how much it would cost," Lars suggested, tossing his mask and snorkel on the towel. "And maybe I can grab us something to eat at one of the kiosks."

"Sounds perfect," Sara cooed, as she stretched out on her towel, half in the sun and half in the shade.

Walking along the hardened, wet sand at the water's edge, the closer Lars got to the multi-storey hotel, the more crowded the beach started to become. Just before turning up towards the hotel's beachfront entrance, the sound of joyful shrieks caused him to glance out into the water. There, approximately fifteen metres away, two men, clearly in their 60's, were cavorting with two considerably younger women. Slowing his pace, Lars watched as the friskiness switched to what could only be called public necking, the two men kissing and caressing their young companions, unconcerned with any onlookers.

"Pretty obvious what that's all about," Lars thought as he kept walking. *"The old farts could be a little more subtle. At least they're not wearing baseball caps with the maple leaf."*

Although the hotel turned out to be fully booked for the next week, Lars' jaunt had not been in vain. Thanks to a friendly clerk, he'd left with the address of a private Casa a mere kilometre up the coast.

"The guy highly recommended it," Lars told Sara upon his return. "He said it has four apartments and is right on the sea."

He also said it's not expensive. It's on the road back to our hotel so we can easily stop by and see if they have a room free."

As luck would have it, the Casa did have something available, and they were able to book a room for the following two nights before returning to the hotel. A day that had seen its fair share of challenges, was brought to a close with a delicious seafood platter at the hotel outdoor restaurant Sara had seen from the balcony.

Next Day...

After having taken full advantage of the extensive buffet on the hotel's terrace, right after breakfast they tossed their belongings in the car, left it parked in the hotel lot, and started off towards the town square.

"Is it my imagination or do some of the locals waving to us, have a look of resignation?" Lars asked, as they made their way along a narrow cobblestone street, lined on both sides with a row of brightly painted houses, on the front steps of which some dwellers sat perched.

"I hadn't really noticed," Sara answered. "But it doesn't look like a very affluent part of town, so maybe it's not your imagination."

Following a visit to a memorial park bordered on three sides by three different churches, and full of statues honouring long-gone heroes, they left to wander through some of the neighbouring streets.

"Aye yai yai," Lars muttered, as they rounded a corner to see a weary-looking donkey coming up the street, pulling a wagon loaded with sugar cane stalks stacked to an improbable height. "If the driver hits the wrong cobblestone, that load lis going to tumble into the street," he said.

Further along on the same street, they halted briefly to watch a group of youngsters, many yet to enter their teens, engaged in a game of soccer on the barrio's harsh pavement, using overturned pails as goal posts.

"A future Messi in the midst?" Sara asked as they walked on, trying not to disrupt a game that had way too many players.

"Never know," Lars answered. "But I read somewhere that Cuba is better known for its baseball players and boxers."

Over a late lunch back at the hotel restaurant, they discussed possible ways to spend the afternoon, knowing they wouldn't be able to check into their new Casa much before six.

"So much of what we've seen since Havana has been flat," Sara said. "I wouldn't mind driving up into the mountains north of the city. Maybe we'd get a sense of where Castro and his comrades were holed up before the march on Havana."

"Sounds fine to me," Lars told her. " I could do with a change of scenery."

Not long after, a whining Gee was chugging its way up a steep and winding road surprisingly free of potholes.

"I don't know how anyone could live around here," Sara commented, as they continued to climb. "This forest is so thick, if there had been any rebels around, the army must have had fun trying to track them down."

"I don't want to disappoint you but, Castro's headquarters were further east," Lars said. " Somewhere around the city of Santiago which is quite aways from here."

"Well, even if it's not exactly breath-taking, with just trees, trees, and more trees," Sara exclaimed. "At least you got your change of scenery."

"Let's give it another few kilometres," Lars suggested. " If nothing grabs our interest we can head for the Casa and maybe go for a walk on the beach."

With the exception of stopping for a cold drink at an isolated bar literally in the middle of nowhere, and that had hopefully seen better days, they were soon retracing their tracks towards Trinidad. In the interim however, dark rain clouds had moved in, making the prospect of a walk along the beach, a less than thrilling option.

Fortunately, their room was ready sooner than expected so they were able to check in early. Given that the threatening rain had not appeared, rather than returning to the city for dinner, they accepted the owner's offer to dine on the rooftop patio overlooking the sea. Later that evening, they quickly learned that their fellow diners seated at the next table were fellow Canadians.

"What part?" Lars asked, now relaxed and in a good mood.

"Oh, it's small town in Saskatchewan. You wouldn't know it," a man in his mid forties told him."

"Try me," Lars urged.

"Turtleford."

"Northwest of North Battleford?"

"That's right… don't tell me you've heard of it."

"Not only heard of it, I've actually been there, or at least through it."

"Get out," the man said, looking briefly at his wife, unsure if he was being led on. "You're probably the first person I've ever met, outside of locals, who's heard of it, let alone been there. Explain."

"An old girlfriend's grandfather had a farm a few miles north of there," Lars began. "She and I went up there to visit… that was years ago. It wasn't my favourite place in the world, but that might have had something to do with the fact her relatives expected me to help clean out the barn while we were there. Not my idea of fun by a long shot."

"That's funny, but not surprising," the man chuckled. "Running a farm is no cake walk, so you take help where you can get it. Even if it needs a little persuasion. What was their last name? Farmers have to come into Turtleford for supplies from time to time so people get to know people."

"Harrison," Lars told the man. "I don't recall his first name. He had two sons who also worked the farm. One of them might have been named Andrew."

"Nope. The name doesn't ring a bell," the man confessed. "You ever heard of them Jane?" he asked his partner, who merely shook her head and resumed jotting her thoughts on a post card. "Is this your first time in Cuba?" the man continued, still not feeling a need to introduce himself.

"It is. We've been here for … what's it been Sara, eight days?"

"I've lost count as well."

"How long are you planning to stay in this area?"

"Not sure. Probably only one more day. We still want to take in Santa Clara and we've heard the beaches on the northern coast are nicer than the south, so we may want to check that out as well."

"That's true… I think they are nicer up there. If you can, you should try and make it to Cayo Santa Maria. It is very exclusive."

"As in all-exclusive, you mean?" Sara asked.

"There are four or five big resorts up there and others are being built. But they are not terribly expensive."

"We don't know what 'not terribly expensive' means because up to now we've been staying in Casas," Lars told him.

"I doubt you'll find any private Casas up there. Cayo Santa Maria is on the end of a peninsula. To get to it you have to travel across a lengthy causeway. I didn't see any private homes there."

"Something to keep in mind," Lars said.

"You know if you're going to be here for a day or two more, you should book a day trip on a catamaran. There's one tour out to an uninhabited island where you can swim or snorkel. They even toss in lunch as well. We did it last year… It's a full day adventure. Can you remember what it cost us, Jane?"

Jane's answer was a mere shake of the head.

"Another thing to keep in mind," Lars added.

Seeing the owner approaching with their meals, the man

wished them a "Bon appetite,"before turning to examine his own menu. Having overheard the tail end of the conversation regarding the boat tour, the Casa owner explained that she happened to know the tour operator and would gladly call to see if tickets could be reserved for the next day.

"Do you know how much it is?" he asked.

"I believe it is $45.00 per person," she answered.

"That sounds pretty reasonable if it's a whole day. What do you think Sara?"

"Why not," she answered, nodding her appreciation for the woman's offer.

Just as the were finishing dessert, the Casa owner returned to confirm that she'd been able to book two places for the next day's tour, scheduled to leave port at 9:00 a.m.

"I will give you directions and arrange for an early breakfast," she promised. Ordering two mojitos to polish off their meal, they excused themselves from Jane and her nameless husband and retreated to a corner of the patio to relax and enjoy their drinks.

"Lady Jane wasn't particularly talkative tonight eh?" Lars remarked quietly . "Must be related to Angela," he added, as the two of them watched the fiery, red ball descend into the watery horizon.

Next day ...

It was just after 8:00 the next morning, when Lars and Sara found themselves walking up the gangway of a large catamaran docked in a harbour south of Trinidad.

"Yow... this thing is a lot bigger than I expected," Lars said, as they made their way to the stern where they could sit under a canopy to protect themselves from the blinding sun and gathering heat- "I bet this thing could hold 50 people with no problem."

"Oh God, I certainly hope not," Sara said, as she leaned down to tuck her day pack under her seat." I'm looking forward to a nice, quiet sail, so I'm glad there's no where near that number today."

As the clock ticked down towards their scheduled departure time, it looked as though Sara was likely to get her wish. But with less than five minutes to go, Lars happened to glance over to an adjacent jetty where a group of boisterous tourists was disembarking from a bus.

"Oh man, am I glad they're not coming on this boat" Lars muttered. " They look like a pretty rowdy crew."

"Don't worry," Sara said. They wouldn't all fit on this boat anyway. There must be another catamaran somewhere."

But there wasn't, and it was only when the bus driver realized he had mistakenly pulled onto the wrong jetty, that the loud group were re-directed and subsequently stormed aboard their catamaran.

"So much for my peaceful, leisurely journey, " Sara overheard the woman adjacent her moan. "How can people drink beer so early in the morning? And from the looks of it, some of them have been at it for while."

With seats in the stern of the boat already filled, the latecomers were forced to occupy spaces in the bow, leaving them prone to the prospects of a merciless sun for the next hour or more. Due to either the early start, or the after effects of a previous night's partying, once the boat had cleared the harbour, the group quieted down and remained so until the speck of an island became visible in the distance. It was at that point the captain of the catamaran announced that guests who wished to go snorkelling should remain onboard once the boat docked. After other guests had gone ashore, which included most of the party animals, the boat backed out under motor and moved to the far end of the island where it laid anchor.

"For the next forty-five minutes, guests will have the opportunity to snorkel and swim in some of Cuba's finest waters," the captain advised over the intercom. "We only ask that you do not stray too far from the boat as the waves on this end of the island are fairly high today and the currents notoriously strong."

The captain was correct. Snorkelling while bobbing in swells up to 3 feet was more work than fun. While Sara preferred to float on the surface, gazing down through the clear waters to the bottom some fifty feet below, Lars made several attempts to reach it. Each time however, his own buoyancy and limited breath forced him back to the surface. Although the captain had promised participants forty-five minutes, the dozen or so swimmers hadn't been in the water for more than twenty when an alarm bell caught everyone's attention.

"Please return to the boat, immediately;" the captain ordered. "The waves are becoming larger and the current stronger. I'm afraid it is too dangerous to stay here."

Within minutes of going ashore at the dock, Lars and Sara took to the water again, this time snorkelling in calmer, shallower waters just off shore. Some distance away from Sara, Lars had been gliding over a large bed of kelp when he decided to take a break on a small, open patch of sand. Unbeknownst to him however, another swimmer had already laid claim to that location. It was just as Lars tried to touch bottom with his extended toe, that a sand-coloured sting ray buried in the sand, shot out from beneath his foot, sending up a plume of disturbed sand, and scaring the living daylights out of him.

"Shit, I just stepped on a sting ray," Lars shouted to Sara, some twenty yards away. Sticking his masked head back under again, he caught sight of the startled sting ray as it turned back to face him.

"Oh oh, I think it's a good idea to get out of the water," Lars told her.." That thing didn't like me intruding on its territory, let alone stepping on its head."

Not wishing to test how perturbed the tiny ray may have been, Lars and Sara quickly scrambled on shore, just in time to join the other day trippers for the buffet lunch being served on the dock.

"This hamburger tastes like," Lars began, scrunching up

his face to show his displeasure. "Actually I don't know what it tastes like, but it sure isn't a hamburger."

"I'm not a big fan of this fish either," Sara admitted. "But I guess one can't expect gourmet food on an uninhabited island. We should have thought ahead and brought something with us."

"The safest thing to do is just have a coke. Coke kills anything."

By late afternoon, a good percentage of the party animals were either still in the process of remaining bombed or bemoaning severe sunburns. One might have been forgiven for thinking the return trip would thus be a peaceful journey, and it may have very well been, had it not been for the captain's sudden decision to morph into Disco Bob less than ten minutes after clearing the dock. Any hopes of relaxing on the now calm sea, were quashed when guests were treated to a barrage of heavy metal music. Having never been much of a fan of AC/DC, Motley Crue and others of their ilk, many guests, Lars and Sara included, were understandably even less so by the time the boat arrived back in port.

Selecting to go for a final meal in the town centre before returning to the Casa, afterwards the tired, and somewhat sunburnt couple took a last stroll through Trinidad's streets, where in the dwindling light, many residents were out on their porches, enjoying the cooler evening air and listening to music wafting out from open windows.

"At least it isn't heavy metal," Lars said with a smile, as they walked along arm in arm. Back at the Casa just after nine, the end of the day was marked by a return to a rugged, rock-strewn section of the beach, hours too late to witness yet another spectacular sunset.

Next Day…

"So run this by me one more time. Just who was it that recommended we come to Remedios?" Lars wanted to know, as they pulled along curbside, next to a heavily treed park in the middle of the town. They had made good time travelling the 152 km. from Trinidad, passing through the provincial towns of Sancti Spiritus and Placetos, neither of which had been enough of a draw to divert them.

"I can't remember," Sara answered. "Wasn't it that woman we picked up outside of Trinidad? The one who helped us get the tire fixed. God that already feels like it was weeks ago."

"I think you're right. I vaguely recall her having said something about a cousin owning a Casa. This is the address she gave us, he said, glancing at a piece of paper and then at the house they were now parked in front of. "But this place looks more than just a little run down. It doesn't even look like anyone's living there. I'm not exactly up for staying here, but the drive was pretty strenuous, so I'm not keen on trying to make it Santa Clara today either. Why don't we just search for another Casa that looks a little more inviting?"

Leaving the car, they scouted the periphery of the park, eventually spotting a sign attached to the ornate facade of a colonial-styled house.

"This one looks pretty decent," Lars said. "Why don't we see if they have a room, and how much it costs?"

"I second that idea, but if you don't mind I'll just sit in the park for a bit. I could do with some more fresh air after being cooped up in that car all morning."

A few minutes later, Lars returned to the park to find Sara dozing on a bench. Perched at one end, provocatively eyeing Sara's day pack, was a large black raven.

"You have a neighbour," Lars told Sara, jarring her out of her snooze, as the bird flapped away. "Or had one...Do you have food in there?" he asked, pointing to the pack.

"Just some peanuts, but they're in a tin. So what did you find out?"

"It's probably the nicest place we've stayed in so far, except of course that pink palace in Havana I was particularly fond of," he said, joining her on the bench. "Anyway, they have one room left and it's only $25.00. But there's a catch."

"Isn't there always? Wait don't tell me... You reserved it but chances are it will have been given away before we get back,"Sara said only half jokingly.

"No. I told the woman we would take it and left a deposit. But we'll have to pay an extra $3.00 to park in a locked garage two blocks away."

"Obviously, she didn't see what we came in," Sara replied. "Who would steal that?"

"I told her the same thing but she said that without a doubt it, or parts of it, would be stolen if we left it on the street. It's only $3.00. Wait till you see the bedroom. It has an antique brass bed, with a nice firm mattress. We'll have to share the bathroom but it's been modernized and even has a bath that you can soak in it tonight. They also serve dinner on a patio that makes you feel like you're in the middle of a Spanish hacienda. There may not be a lot to see or do in Remedios, but we can at least enjoy the pleasant surroundings."

"So we've lucked in," Sara said, getting up off the bench. "After you then, Señor. "

Knowing they had no further need of the car, Lars got directions from the Casa owner and saw to it that the Gee was locked up in a garage within a gate controlled courtyard three blocs away.

"I don't care what it costs. I'm going to spoil myself and have whatever looks most appealing on the menu," Sara declared, after both of them had showered and rested up. "And let's really splurge and have wine as well. We deserve it."

One filling meal, and a full bottle of Chilean red wine later, the pair tumbled into bed around ten, falling asleep within minutes. Just after 1:00 a.m. however, they were awakened by the sounds of a couple having a ferocious argument in the next room.

"What's all that about? Lars groaned when the squabble

showed no signs of abating. "Why doesn't the owner tell them to pipe down? If that keeps up, I'm going to go say something."

"Unless you're going to take a crash course in Spanish, I'm not sure how much good that will do," Sara advised. "You have no idea who these people are and what they're arguing about. And no, before you accuse me, I'm not trying to be harmonious. You don't want to get mixed up in a domestic dispute and have them both turn on you."

"I'm too lazy to get up and trundle over there anyways. If we spoke Spanish, we'd at least know what they're fighting about."

As quickly as it had begun, the dispute suddenly ended. But before Lars and Sara could fall asleep again, the silence was replaced by the sound of bedsprings squeaking at regular intervals.

"I don't believe it," Lars said, rolling over to face Sara. "This place is turning into a menagerie. First they fight like cats and dogs and now they're humping like rabbits."

"True..." Sara said. "But whatever it was they were wrangling about, I'm glad to hear he's now teaching her a lesson."

Next Day...

Unlike several previous days, on this morning Lars and Sara granted themselves the luxury of sleeping in. Right after a late breakfast they sauntered across the street to investigate a small market that had been set up in the park. In each of the dozen or so wooden booths, men were attempting to sell goods they claimed to be genuine, local souvenirs. Business was far from booming, and as Lars and Sara made their way through the market separately, both were seen as prey by the zealous vendors.

"So what did you end up with?" he asked her when they met up at the opposite end of the market from which they'd started.

"I had to control myself," Sara admitted. "There was some nice jewellery that interested me, but I held off because I couldn't figure out where I would actually wear it. And you?"

"No idea why, but I bought two hollowed out coconut shells that have eery-looking faces painted on them."

"They sound horrible. Show me."

Removing the masks from a bag, Lars held them up one by one for inspection.

"Jesus Lars…" Sara gasped. "They really are horrible looking. And what are those sayings written beneath each face?"

"I have no idea."

"I hope you're not planning on hanging those hideous things somewhere at home. And who knows what those sayings translate as. Probably some evil curse."

"I'm sure I can find some use for them. The old guy selling them was so friendly, I felt I should support him. Didn't you see him? The one with the Yankees baseball cap, and a huge Cuban stogie."

"You sentimental old fool," Sara jibed. "He saw you coming."

A short while later, having retrieved the car from its secure location, Lars was loading their luggage into the trunk when his attention was nabbed by a group of young school children clad in matching red and white uniforms. Shouting and carousing as they made their way through the park, their antics prompted him to grab his camera from the back seat. Hoping to get a candid shot, once in the park he planted himself beside a large tree and waited. Despite his precaution however, no sooner had he done so, one of the children spotted him,. Within seconds the entire group had swerved towards him, smiling, waving and clowning for the camera. Although the shot still made for a unique and lasting memory of Remedios, it was only later when viewing the result that he noticed the angry face of a teacher in the background, obviously less than pleased by his action.

Just before noon, they departed Remedios, heading further north, covering the 70 kms, in just over an hour, which included crossing over the causeway which for awhile was flanked on both sides by water as far as one could see.

"Seeing as our buddy from Saskatchewan didn't recommend any specific hotel, why don't we just try the first one we see to find out how much this little adventure may cost us."

"Sounds as good a plan as any," Sara replied.

Lured in by a sign that indicated , Villa Las Brujas was a few kilometres hence, not long after they turned off on what appeared to be a newly paved road.

"Do you know what that means?" Sara asked, the guidebook in her lap as they continued on through a forest. "Villa of the Witches;" she told him without waiting for an answer.

"Sounds promising," Lars said, just as the forest opened up to reveal a large parking lot.

"Judging from the looks of these cars, this place must be very exclusive, not to mention expensive. There's even a couple of Mercedes here."

"We've come this far, we might as well check it out," Sara said, as she got out of the car. "That is if we can find the place."

Built into the tropical landscape to the point where you almost couldn't see it, Lars and Sara were forced up several false garden paths before finally locating a wooden building encircled by palm trees and shoots of bamboo.

"Buenos Dias," Lars said to the smartly dressed receptionist from behind a long marble counter in the plush elegant lobby.

"Buenos Dias, Señor," the woman answered in a monotone of superficial friendliness..

"We're looking for a room for a few nights," Lars explained."Do you have one free, and if so what it would cost?"

"Do you have a reservation?" she asked in accent free English, a look of mild disdain on her face.

"No," Lars admitted

"If you have no reservation I'm afraid I can't help you," she said. "We are fully booked for the next two months."

"Two months?" Lars said in disbelief. "Really… wow… but can you tell me how much a room would be if one were available?"

Acting as if Lars had assigned her an enormous task, the woman let out a deep sigh, reached for a glossy brochure from a nearby rack, and laid it down on the counter in front of him.

"You can find all the information you seek in here," she informed him. "But as I say we *are* fully booked."

"Yes, I understood that," Lars answered. "Is there another hotel on the island that you could recommend?"

"We are not in the habit of recommending other hotels, sir," she said, her smile tightening into a smirk.

"Excuse me, but were you sick that day?" Lars asked, as he picked up the brochure.

"I'm sorry?" the woman answered.

"I asked if you were sick that day," Lars repeated.

"Laaarrrsss," Sara warned, grasping his elbow.

"I'm not sure what you are referring to sir," the woman said.

"Lars," Sara repeated. " Let it go. She said there are no rooms available. "

"The day in Grade three when they taught the rest of us the benefits of having manners."

Despite her apparent command of English, it took a moment before the receptionist realized the inference of Lars' comment.

"I'm afraid I will have to ask you to leave, sir," she said with a scowl. "There are other clients I must attend to."

"Did you really have to do that?" Sara asked, when they were back in the parking lot.

"That woman was so uppity, she deserved to be put in her place," Lars answered, glaring at Sara across the roof, as he inserted the key in the door. "You can't tell me you didn't notice how snotty she was. All we were doing was asking about a room."

"If you react like that with every receptionist... good luck getting a room," Sara snarled, as she fastened her seat belt.

"If every receptionist is a high-nosed at that woman, I don't want to stay at any hotel here," Lars shot back. "But look... rather than fight about it, let's just try another hotel."

Although the receptionist at the next establishment further down the highway, was much more friendly, she was also the bearer of equally frustrating tifings, ultimately passing them over to the assistant manager.

"Sorry, but I'm a bit confused," Lars said, as he and Sara sat in her office. "The receptionist told us you have rooms free but can't offer one to us directly. That we would have to go to another hotel to book a room here. Is that right?"

"That's correct sir," the woman replied, resting her folded hands on the top of her desk.

"But that makes no sense whatsoever," Lars said calmly.

"I'm afraid those are the rules sir. I didn't make them. As far as I know they are set by the government."

"The government," Lars repeated. "But why would they do something like that?"

"I do not know, sir. All I can tell you is that if you would like a room here, you will have to reserve it at another hotel."

"Does that work in reverse?" Lars asked.

"I'm sorry;" the woman said with a puzzled look.

"Can I book a room at another hotel through you?"

"Yes sir, that is possible."

"But wouldn't your hotel rather have us stay here?" Lars asked, aware that he was provoking her.

"Of course," she said calmly. "But you have to reserve from a neighbouring hotel."

"Okay look," Lars said, leaning forward with one elbow on

the woman' desk. "Why don't we do it like this. My girlfriend will stay here while I go to the next hotel… assuming it's not fifty kms. from here… and see about reserving a room here. Would that work?"

"As you wish sir, but I am too busy to have your girlfriend sit in my office. She is welcome to wait in our lounge."

"You gotta deal," Lars said, extending his hand, which the woman reluctantly accepted.

"What a convoluted way of doing business," Lars grumbled once they were in the lobby.

"I agree, but at least we're getting somewhere," Sara replied.

"I don't want to witness what other hoops you may have to jump through at this other hotel… not to mention your possible reaction, so I'll gladly wait here until you're back."

It took the good part of an hour until Lars returned, declining to discuss details other than to confirm he'd obtained the prized certificate.

"Let's just say it was a high wire act without a net, but we have it now, so that's all that matters."

"Thank you, sir," Sara said, wrapping her arm around his waist as they walked to the reception desk with the document. "You know as much as I've liked staying at the Casas, it will be nice to visit the 21st. century, if only for a couple of days," Sara said, once the recptionist had processed their reservation and they were walking down a long carpeted hallway to their room.

"I don't know what's on your agenda, Mr. Kierey," Sara said, tossing her knapsack on the double bed and moving to inspect the bathroom facilities of a room that could have been anywhere in the world. "But the first thing I'm gonna do is stand under a hot shower for an hour."

"Fine with me," he told her, punching off the television whose screen welcomed them by name. "It'll be another couple of hours until the buffet opens, so I think I'm going to go for a swim. I don't know if you saw it while you were waiting, but the pool is actually a series of pools connected by a number of channels. It looks like you can literally swim from one end of the resort to the other. If you feel like it you can meet me there once you're out of the shower."

Despite the fact the resort had well over 300 rooms, Lars found himself sharing the pool with only one other guest. After breast-stroking past the middle aged woman several times, initially acknowledging her presence with a simple nod, Lars ultimately decided to break the silence.

"First time in Cuba?" he asked, while she was still several yards away.

"Oh heavens no," she answered, altering her course to swim closer. "We've been here many times."

"Is that a Canadian accent I'm hearing?" Lars asked, choosing to stand, but crouching so the water was still up to his neck.

"It is indeed," the woman told him. "Alberta to be more precise. And yourself?"

"First time," Lars admitted. "Also from Canada... Ontario to be more precise."

"And how long are you here for?" she wanted to know.

"We just got here this morning, but we've been in Cuba since the 12th. We're only staying here for a couple of nights and then plan to drive to Santa Clara before returning to Havana."

"I've been here a week already, and have yet to make it to the beach," the woman told him, in what almost sounded like a boast. "I'm content just to float around in the pool."

"Really?" Lars said, culling the surface of the water with his hands as he spoke. "I don't mean to be impertinent but couldn't you do that in a pool in Alberta?"

"It's too cold in Alberta right now. I have all I need right here. I'm basically here to do nothing," she explained.

At a loss as to how to respond, Lars simply wished her a pleasant stay, telling her he wanted to explore the other pools and swam off towards one of the channels.

"Can you believe someone would come all the way to Cuba and not bother to go to the beach?" Lars said, as he and Sara continued to load up their plates at the crowded buffet that evening.

"I mean it's right over the bloody embankment."

"Maybe she doesn't like the salt water," Sara suggested, signalling to one of the uniformed chefs that she would like a slab of roast beef. It took awhile to find an empty table but once they had, Sara was eager to tell Lars about a discovery she'd made in their room.

"The hot water cut out after two minutes?" Lars joked.

"No," she said dismissively.

"Bed bugs?"

"Lars, be serious," she urged. "Did you know you can go scuba diving here?"

"Really?"

"There was a booklet about it in the room. They provide lessons in the pool if you've never done it before," she explained.

"And you don't need a diving certificate?"

"Apparently not," she said. "I would be interested in giving it a try. Why don't we ask at reception after dinner."

Luck was with them, and within minutes of inquiring, they were registered for a beginner's lessons set for the next morning.

"I can see how for some people this 'exclusivity' isn't hard to take, even if the mojitos at dinner were watered down to the point of recognition," Lars said, as they strolled through the grounds that evening, enjoying the warm night air. Stopping at one of the numerous outdoor bars dotting the landscape, they treated themselves to several rounds of the free drinks.

"This place does have its benefits," Sara reflected, as she looked around at other guests. "But you sure don't get the sense you're in Cuba."

"I guess that's why they call them 'tourist ghettos'," Lars

said. "I suspect a lot of the people who come here, like that woman in the pool I told you about, are satisfied with chilling and maybe taking a day trip into Havana to catch a glimpse of what they perceive as the 'real Cuba.' They grab a few selfies of themselves beside an old car or at Hemingway's bar and then whoosh… it's back to la-la-land for dinner and drinks."

"Don't be so snotty. We're here aren't we?" Sara scolded. "Not everyone is adventurous. Case in point, the woman in the pool."

"I guess," Lars agreed. "By the way, did you happen to notice how many mobile bars there are between the stationary ones?"

"I wasn't really paying attention," Sara admitted.

"So like…are they there for emergencies in case people can't hold out in between the stationary ones?"

"I've no idea Lars,"Sara replied, her thoughts drifting. "Let's just enjoy it for what it is without critiquing everything. I can appreciate the modern features, but I won't be sad to leave. It's too far removed from reality for me… at least the Cuban reality. It's like we're in some antiseptic bubble."

"Yes, but one with with free drinks," Lars added with a smile.

Next day…

Despite the rising temperature, the water in the pool felt chilly when the two of them met the instructor there just after nine.

"Are we the only ones?" Sara asked.

"Si Señora," the deeply tanned man, with the nameplate Miguel answered. "That means more time to practice for you and your man," he added.

After confirming that neither of them had ever used scuba equipment before, they listened to what Lars considered a rather brief set instructions, before donning the gear and testing it out in the shallow waters. Right from the start however, it was obvious that Sara did not feel comfortable in this new environment, repeatedly standing up and removing the mouthpiece. Nonetheless, when the hour was up, they both signed on for a dive in the sea set for the next morning.

"You're sure you want to go through with this," Lars asked, as they sat in the shade, savouring a late morning coffee. "You didn't exactly look like you were having a good time."

"I couldn't get used to hearing my own breath. I sounded like Darth Vader. If I can feel so uncomfortable in the pool, I'll probably panic when I'm any deeper."

"Then why did you agree to the dive?" Lars asked.

"I guess I just want to jump over my own shadow," Sara confessed. "Snorkelling at the island was amazing so I'd like the chance to see things from another perspective. Besides, the instructor will be with us the whole time... right?"

"I presume so."

"Get a load of the Heidi Klum wannabes over there," Lars said with a grin, as he and Sara lounged on the grassy embankment just above the beach.

"What the heck are they doing?" Sara asked, holding her hand to shield her eyes from the sun.

"Either they're attempting to create a portfolio for a modelling agency or they're just goofing around and it will all end up on an Instagram account. Judging by how unnatural the blonde's poses are, I suspect it's the latter."

"As long as they're not hurting anybody, let them have their fun," Sara remarked, laying back down.

"I don't think I can stand so much excitement. I'm going for a swim, if you care to join me," Lars said.

"I'd rather just stay here and read a little. You go ahead. You brought your face mask. Why don't you try a little snorkelling?"

"Not a bad idea," Lars replied, pulling the mask from his day pack and heading off to the water. But it wasn't a good idea either. Not only was it less than refreshing to swim in water the temperature of a lukewarm bath, there was nothing to see on the sea bed but sand.

Adhering to the routine followed by all the guests, Lars and Sara sat down to dinner at the six o'clock serving. Retreating to one of the bars for a post-meal drink, they were able to grab the last table, where two male members of a foursome were deep in a heated conversation.

"If this political system is as great as you make it out to be," argued a balding man in a light blue leisure suit, waving his finger as if to emphasize his point. "Why don't they let people choose whether they want to stay or leave?"

"As far as I know people can apply to emigrate," answered the younger man, dressed more casually in slacks and a polo shirt.

"Pffff.. that's a laugh," the first man guffawed. "You can apply all you like. Good luck getting approval."

"Cubans get lifelong free medical care as well as the option of a free university education. It wouldn't be fair to educate them and see them all leave upon graduation."

"A fair point," the older man agreed. "But what they could do is require graduates to stay and work in their field for a specified number of years. That way they could repay their debt to the Cuban society, so to speak, while simultaneously supporting its economy. Then they could have the option of emigrating. Wouldn't that be fair?"

"I'm not sure how that would work... How would they determine the length of service required for example? But it's not a bad premise," the younger man admitted, glancing at the two women at their table who looked more interested in nursing their drinks than participating in the current discussion. "I know the political system here is oppressive, but I also know the previous regime was corrupt to the hilt, in bed with the Mafia raking millions if not billions from gambling and who knows what else. I don't imagine much, if any of those profits helped improve the lives of the local population."

"However the people may have been exploited before Castro… the Communists have made it worse. They have the power to make changes. Talk to them. I grant you the health system is an admirable achievement and free university is also a plus, but Castro and company have driven the economy into the dirt. Just look at the average Cuban's lifestyle. It's pretty pathetic."

"I'm not a political scientist nor a historian," the younger man argued. " so I can't really comment on what Castro's government has and hasn't done. What would be interesting to know is what he might have done if the belligerent policies instituted by their neighbour to the north had not resulted in an embargo. That crippled his chances of 'success' however you might want to define that. Oddly enough, the Americans seem to have no problem cozying up to other dictators when it's in their interests."

"Don't speculate on what Castro *might* have done," the older man said. "Look at what he *has* done. Allowing the Soviets to install those ballistic missiles for example."

"I don't know if he would have turned to the Soviets if the embargo wasn't in place. The US had been Cuba's main trading partner for decades before 1959. That could have continued."

"Come on now," the older man grunted. "Castro and the Soviets are two peas in a Communist pod."

"I don't know about you," Lars said quietly to Sara. "But I've had enough of Cuban History 101. This debate could go on for hours. We're supposed to meet the diving instructor in the lobby at 9:00 so finish your drink and let's get out of here"

"Fine with me Señor. Maybe we can grab one for the road and take it back to the room."

Next Day…

"So what you're telling me is that there will be twelve people on this dive, and you'll be the only one supervising?" Lars asked the instructor when the group met the next morning.

"Yes, sir," Miguel told him.

"How many of the twelve are inexperienced divers?"

"I believe about half."

"Half?" Lars repeated. "So the other half are first timers? Those don't sound like very good odds to me What happens if somebody runs into problems?"

"I don't think there will be any problems, sir. We will not be diving deeper than 8 to 10 meters."

"Eight to ten meters!" Sara blurted out with alarm. "Lars can I speak to you for a minute," she said, pulling him away, as Miguel turned to speak to other members of the group.

"I don't like this at all," Sara said. "Six out of twelve divers are beginners? A single instructor isn't going to be of much help if more than one of us gets into trouble at the same time."

"It's sounds risky to me as well," Lars agreed. "And old Miguel here pooh-poohs the possibility of trouble. Why don't we just blow it off. Who cares if we lose our deposit. It's only money. We don't have to be out of our room till noon so we have plenty of time to head back to the beach instead. Santa Clara is only a two hour drive so we can leave after a leisurely lunch."

Shortly after one, the Gee was gliding to a stop at the junction where the resort road met the main highway. Clustered in the shadow of the hotel's large identifying logo were a number of hitchhikers, some of whom were still dressed in their hotel uniforms.

"Up for a little company?" Lars asked Sara. "The ones from the hotel are bound to speak English. Might be interesting to pick his or her brains."

"But there's at least half a dozen of them there," Sara pointed out " How are you going to choose who to take?"

"How about the guy who's furthest from the sign? If they've been queueing, he's probably been here the longest."

"Muchos gracias, Señor," the young man in his early twenties said as he opened the rear door.

"Da nada," Lars told him. "Hop in... Do a couple of your colleagues also want a ride?"

"Si, si," the man said, as he turned and wolf-whistled to two young women a few metres away.

"Vamos, hay espacio para dos más," he shouted.

The two women wasted no time in responding and within seconds all three had squeezed into the back seat.

"So do any of you speak English?" Lars asked, once underway.

"Si, I speak English, Señor," the man answered, while the two women remained silent. "What do you want to know?"

"Actually I don't have a specific question," Lars told him, glancing back and forth between the road and the rear view mirror. "But I wouldn't mind asking you about your work in general."

"Si, no problem, sir," the man said, leaning forward to rest his arm on the back of Lars' seat.

"No need for the 'sir' bit," Lars told him. " We're not at the hotel anymore. My name is Lars, and this is Sara,"

"Buenos Dias, Lars... Sara," he said. "Me llamo Juan."

Whether they understood the conversation or not, the two women in the back made no attempt to introduce themselves, seemingly content to talk quietly with each other.

"How long have you worked at the resort?" Sara asked.

"Two years, Mamm," Juan answered.

"Sara," she insisted. "What is it you do?"

"I'm a waiter in one of the restaurants."

"But what exactly does a waiter do in a buffet-style restaurant?"

"I make sure all tables are cleaned and reset once guests are finished, and that food trays are re-filled before they are empty."

"With so many guests eating at the same time, that must get awfully stressful," Sara remarked.

"Si, but we have two shifts. Not all guests come at the same time."

"Who owns the resort?" Lars asked.

Juan paused slightly before answering. "The international corporation that runs the resort has an agreement with the government."

"With the government?" Lars echoed. "What sort of agreement?"

"The government owns 51% and the company 49%," Juan told him, a cautiousness noticeable in his tone. "The company pays the government so much a month per worker in dollars. The government converts that to National pesos and we receive a wage from the government."

"So I guess it's safe to assume the government takes a healthy chunk," Lars said, briefly recalling the previous evening's discussion at the bar.

"A big... chunk, as you say" Juan admitted, just as Lars glanced in the mirror to see one of the women elbow Juan in the ribs.

"Are there at least some other benefits to the job?" Lars wanted to know.

"Most people are just happy to have a job, even if there are strict rules we must follow," Juan told him.

"Such as?"

"For example, if cutlery is missing from the restaurant, or if other items are taken as souvenirs by guests, workers are docked."

"Really?" Sara replied. "But how can anyone keep track of things like that with so many guests?"

"They have people who check. Also workers are not allowed access to food leftover after a serving."

"You mean the food that's left in the trays?" Sara asked.

"Si,"

"So what happens to it then?"

"Most of the time it's thrown out."

"That's crazy," Sara muttered to herself.

"Officially, workers are also not allowed soft drinks during their shift, but that rule is often overlooked. Alcohol?

Never…" Juan added.

"But isn't it true that anyone can go to university for free?" Sara asked.

"Yes, Mamm… sorry, Sara," Juan corrected.

"Do you not want to go?"

"I did at one time, but I couldn't make up my mind what to study. When this job at the resort was offered, I took it."

Reluctant to probe what they sensed were Juan's limited prospects for the future involve, both Lars and Sara had no further questions. As a result conversation remained dormant for awhile.

"You are going to Santa Clara, yes?" Juan asked, as they were passing through a large plantation of palm trees bordering both sides of the highway.

"That's where we're headed," Lars confirmed.

"Santa Clara is my home town," Juan announced with a degree of pride.

"You mean live there and commute everyday?" Sara asked, somewhat astounded at the thought of his making the two hour journey daily.

"Si, sometimes I go with the bus. But they are not so reliable in Cuba, so often I hitchhike."

"Yeah, we've noticed," Lars said.

"But today is a special day. Today is the first time I ride with a foreigner," Juan revealed with a broad smile.

"The first time in two years?" Sara asked.

"Si. Outside of cities, not many Cubans have cars, especially up here. Those who do, pick up hitchhikers. Tourists not so much."

"A guy we were talking to in Havana told us it was illegal to pick up hitchhikers," Lars said. " A little late to be asking, but is that true?"

"It is not illegal for Cubans, but if a tourist does and gets in an accident, the insurance is cancelled," Juan explained. "Or so I have heard. I do not know this for sure."

"Hopefully not," Sara said. "But just in case, slow down a

bit Lars."

"Where do you stay in Santa Clara?" Juan asked, shortly after the two women had been let out at a bus stop in the middle of nowhere.

"Sara found a place in the guidebook," Lars explained. "We called to make a reservation… not that that will do us any good."

"I do not understand," Juan said.

"Not important," Lars assured him "Inside joke."

"A friend of mine has a pension just outside the city," Juan continued. " It is a very nice Casa and not expensive. That is where I am going today. I can ask him if a room is available."

"Thanks, but I think we'd prefer to stay in town. It'll be easier to get around."

"Then I must tell you places in Santa Clara that are worth seeing."

"Please do," Sara urged.

"Most important is the Che Guevara memorial," Juan declared. "He is buried there. That you must see."

"But I thought Che was buried in Bolivia," Lars asked.

"He was, but thirty years later his remains were transferred to Cuba. Even his hands," Juan said.

"What do you mean 'even his hands'?" Sara asked.

"The people who killed Che, cut off his hands and sent them to Argentina to make sure it was really him."

"How awful, " Sara said, shaking off a quiver.

"Nobody in Bolivia ever heard of finger printing?" Lars asked.

"That is a good question," Juan said. "But you can learn more about Che at the museum next to the gravesite. Do you know some of Che's sayings?"

"No, " Lars and Sara said in unison.

"I know many from memory… For example ' No podemos estar seguros de tener algo por lo que vivir, a menos que estemos dispuestos a morir por ello'. Or 'Por encima de todo, sé siempre capaz de sentir profundamente cualquier injusticia cometida contra cualquiera, en cualquier parte del mundo'."

"Sounds inspiring but what does it mean?" Lars asked.

"The first one is 'We cannot be sure of having something to live for, unless we are willing to die for it.'"

"And the second?" Sara wanted to know.

"'Above all, always be capable of feeling deeply any injustice committed against anyone, anywhere in the world,'" Juan said proudly.

Left to contemplate the quotes, they drove on in silence until Juan announced he wanted to be let off at the next junction.

"Muchos gracias, Señor Lars, Señora Sara," Juan told them, as he opened the back door. "I liked talking with you very much."

"As did we, Juan," Lars said, turning to extend his hand. "We wish you all the best. Before you go, can I ask one more question?"

"Si."

"It's a bit late, seeing as we've already been in a number of cities, but are there places in Santa Clara where it isn't safe to go at night? "

"That is a funny question," Juan answered.

"Funny?" Sara said.

"Tourism is Cuba's main industry which the government wants to protect as much as possible. The punishment for robbing or harming a tourist is very severe… probably more than for killing your neighbour," Juan added with a chuckle.

"Good to know," Lars said. "And I'm glad I'm not your neighbour."

"Adiós, amigos," Juan said, waving goodbye as he started down a dusty, gravel road.

"Wow," Lars mused aloud, as they pulled back on to the highway. "The things Juan had to say were really interesting, but I can't help feeling sorry for him. I know it was his choice not to go to university, and maybe someday he will. I sure hope he doesn't end up stuck in that resort for the rest of his life."

"That arrangement he talked about," Sara said. "Between the government and the corporation… It seems slightly ironic in view of Che's comment about not ignoring injustices. Makes me want to learn more about Señor Guevara."

"You are not going to believe this," Lars said, returning to where he'd parked on the crowded street in central Santa Clara.

"You have to speak louder," Sara told him. "Either that or get in the car. There's too much traffic noise to understand you."

"There was no record of our reservation," Lars explained, as he slumped down in the seat and slammed the tinny door shut. "I must be getting used to this because I didn't lose my cool. But at least the Casa owner was apologetic. He recommended a place right around the corner because they're fully booked."

"Well that's something, I guess," Sara answered. "We won't have to start searching for another place."

"And something else. I made us a reservation for dinner."

"At this Casa? Why that?"

"While I was waiting for the guy to check in his book, I got a glimpse of the restaurant on the terrace. It looked incredible. All the tables are separated by trees and bushes so not only do you have privacy, you must feel like you're being served in the middle of the jungle."

"So something to look forward to this evening," Sara said with a smile. "That is unless we show up and find someone else has taken our table."

A short, jovial woman of an indeterminate age, Elsa turned out to be the most welcoming Casa owner of all they'd encountered so far, insisting that Lars and Sara join her for afternoon tea and biscuits, before they'd even confirmed they would take the room.

"You can park car in garage… no cost extra," she

explained, as she guided them to a table in the courtyard. "You like peppermint tea?" she asked.

"That would be fine," Sara answered. "So what do you think?" she asked, once Ester had bustled off to the kitchen. "The room looked fine, and I almost feel guilty saying no to her. She's so friendly and bubbly."

"Then I say we take it. This place seems pretty central so we can probably walk to many of the sites, except maybe the Guevara memorial. And we already have a dinner date right around the corner."

"You hope," Sara told him, glancing around at all the private decorations amidst the lush greenery of the courtyard. "Then it's settled."

"Did you know that Santa Clara was the site of the final battle of the revolution?" Sara asked, looking over the top of her reading glasses as she skimmed the pages of the guidebook while they awaited their meal.

"Hum a few bars," Lars answered, lifting his freshly arrived mojito in a toast. "To Che and his comrades," he added, before taking a first sip. "Wow, now this is one decent mojito," he gushed. " Not like that stuff they were dishing out at the resort. So when exactly did this battle take place?"

"Late 1958, it says here," Sara told him. "Che and some guy named Camilo Cienfuegos Gorriarán, if I'm pronouncing that right, led their men to victory here, and 12 hours later Batista fled the country. Fidel and his army marched into Havana unopposed."

"Speaking of Batista, I read somewhere that he died in Marbella, not exactly the sleaziest part of Spain. Obviously he must have taken a few pesos out of the till before departing."

"It says that Che was appointed the head of the Bank of Cuba and later the Minister of Industry after Fidel took power," Sara continued.

"I thought he was a doctor."

"He studied medicine in Argentina, but I'm not sure he

finished. Either way, that must have been some adjustment."

"What do you mean?"

"One day you're a revolutionary living in the mountains, and the next day you're a staid government employee in a stuffy office somewhere."

"Well I guess we'll find out more about Che's adventures tomorrow," Lars said.

Lars had just finished making that remark, when suddenly, all the lights in the restaurant went out, leaving them in total darkness.

"You still there?" Lars asked.

"Still here," Sara answered.

"This must be one of the famous blackouts they're always talking about," Lars commented, as he caught sight of someone approaching with a lit candle. "Looks like they're used to it though. Too bad we hadn't eaten already. We could have skipped out before the power comes back on."

"Only you would think of something like that," Sara replied.

"I was joking," Lars said. "But assuming the lights do come back on at some point, and we're able to see what we're eating, how do you feel about checking out Santa Clara's night life afterwards?"

"To tell you the truth, I'm kind of tired. It doesn't seem real that it's the same day we were in Cayo Santa Maria. I think I'd rather go back to Ester's and maybe read up on what we can expect to see tomorrow."

"I'm okay with that too," Lars told her as the lights flickered back to life.

Next Day...

"Che Memorial is not far," Elsa told them next morning at breakfast. "Best you leave car and walk."

Despite Elsa's suggestion, Lars chose to drive. the two kilometres.

"Look at the size of this place," he exclaimed as they walked out on to an enormous parade grounds capable of holding thousands and thousands of comrades. At the far end of the complex, which was situated on the crest of a hill overlooking the city, stood a lengthy white wall five metres in height, its facade full of carved figures in a relief depicting a group of revolutionaries on the march. To the right of the wall was a tall rectangular pedestal, at the top of which stood a six meter bronze statue of Mr. Guevara toting a rifle while still in marching mode.

"What does *'Hasta la Victoria Siempre'* mean?" Lars asked, reading the quote on the face of the pedestal.

"Give me a second," Sara answered, flipping through the pages of the guidebook. "Until Victory Forever," she told him.

"Are you sure? That doesn't translate too well."

"That's what the guidebook says," Sara replied.

"Well Juan was right... the place is impressive, albeit a little overblown," Lars said, as he stared up at Che's imposing figure. "I mean look the size of everything... this statue, the wall and the parade grounds. Nothing subtle about this guy."

"Don't ask," Sara blurted out, as Lars approached yet another rectangular block the same height as the wall.

"Don't ask what?"

"Me to translate all of those Spanish words engraved on the surface of that cube," she told him snapping the guidebook shut.

"It would take me months."

Looking back out over the huge plaza, empty now save for a tourist or two, Lars could make out two large billboards emblazoned with quotes by Cuba's illustrious leader, Fidel. Oddly enough, both were written in English. The first was dedicated to Che, declaring "*It was a star that put you here and made you of this people*", while the second urged "*We want everyone to be like Che.*"

"Would get kind of boring if everyone was like Che, don't you think?" Lars pondered out loud.

"I don't think Señor Castro was suggesting people become clones of Che, just more aligned with his revolutionary philosophy. He was apparently a devout Marxist."

"Somebody's been doing a lot of reading," Lars quipped. "According to that sign over there, the Mausoleum must be right behind the statue. Let's go see."

Descending a short set of stairs at the rear of the wall, they entered the grounds housing the Mausoleum. All along a curved wall that faced Che's grave, a number of niches had been slotted in, each representing the burial plots of twenty nine of Che's colleagues from Bolivia and Cuba. Che's remains were entombed in front of a decorative wall relief illustrating various phases of his career.

"Do you want to check out the museum?" Sara asked, after they had stood in front of Che's eternal flame for several minutes. "By the way, apparently it was Fidel who lit this flame in 1997."

"I'll call the newspapers," Lars said. "All due resect to Che and his struggle for justice, but as far as the museum goes, I'm not terribly keen on visiting it if it's anything like the Revolution Museum in Havana. Who needs to know what kind of toothpaste Che used. I'd rather go back into town and just walk around."

"Then let's do that," Sara told him. "According to the guidebook, Santa Clara is unique in that it offers a more authentic depiction of everyday life for the average Cuban."

"I'm up for that," Lars said, as they left Che to rest in peace and retraced their steps to the parking lot.

"And thank you by the way," Sara said as they reached the car.

"For what?"

"For not saying anything inappropriate when we were at Che's grave. You didn't seem overly impressed so I was half expecting you to say something like, "Hey, that was quite the career. Let's give the man a hand.""

"I never thought of that, but that's not a bad line," Lars

told her. "You're learning."

After several hours spent exploring central Santa Clara, both Lars and Sara came to the same conclusion. Although the city may have provided a more genuine view of daily life for the average Cuban, it simply lacked the flair of Havana.

That night after dinner at the same restaurant, this time without a blackout, they decided to see what Santa Clara had to offer in the way of a night life, eventually ending up at a Salsa bar not far from their Casa.

"This is obviously a Cuban pastime," Lars commented, once they'd ordered drinks.

"What is?" Sara asked, straining to hear him over the din of music and conversation.

"Hauling unsuspecting tourists up on to the dance floor to try their luck at Salsa."

"When we were in Viñales," Sara began. "I seem to recall your claiming you could rise to the challenge. Why don't you give it a try here Señor? "she goaded.

"What? And show up all the locals with my fancy footwork?"

"I dare you," Sara added.

"Let me think about it while I enjoy my drink" Lars suggested , as he noticed their waiter weaving his way towards them through the tables.

"Phewie…" Sara groaned, a short while later, halfway through her second drink. "I don't know if they put something else in this besides rum, but I can sure feel the effects tonight."

"Then maybe you should be the one to get up and Salsa," Lars told her.

"Yeah sure… and fall right on my butt. I may do so anyway because I need to go to the ladies room badly. I'm not going to finish this so why don't you have it," she added, sliding her glass over to Lars.

"Fine… but once I'm done I'll wait for you outside. It's way too warm in here…not to mention loud."

Outside in the cooler evening air, Lars was standing by an open window, watching the continuing festivities on the dance floor, when he felt a tap his shoulder. The perpetrator , he discovered as he turned around, was a girl in her late teens, dressed in hot pants and a tank top.

"You like Chicas, Señor,?" she said with a half giggle, holding her hand up to her mouth as she glanced over at her partner, a girl of similar age and dress.

"Sorry, what did you say?" Lars answered, somewhat distracted by the music.

"You like Chicas?" the girl repeated.

Although fully aware as to what the two young girls were implying, Lars nonetheless decided to play dumb.

"I'm sorry I don't speak Spanish. What are Chicas?"

"You want Chicas? Much fun, Señor... Very cheap... one Euro."

"One Euro?" Lars answered with surprise, almost giving himself away. *'More likely to get a whack on the head in a dark alley than any fun for just one Euro,'* he thought to himself just as Sara emerged from the bar.

"Who are your friends?" she asked, smiling at the two girls.

"A couple of ladies selling Chicas... whatever they are," he told her as the two girls scurried off into the night without another word.

"What do you mean they were selling Chicas?" Sara said with a growl. "You know what a Chica is don't you?"

"Of course I do. It's not as if I thought they were pedalling Chiclets."

"They were just trying to appeal to your erotic fantasies."

"For a Euro?"

"A Euro? What the heck would you get for a Euro?"

"My thoughts precisely...other than a vanishing act of watch and wallet."

"So I saved the day...or should I say spoiled? Would you have been interested?"

"Well the taller one was kind of pretty," Lars admitted, playing along. "I might have been tempted if you hadn't suddenly appeared. To at least find out what I could expect for a Euro."

"You pervert you," Sara scolded in jest, as they left the bar, still able to hear its music for several blocks on the way back to Elsa's.

Next Day...

"So what's the plan for today" Sara asked, as she accepted a second cup of coffee from Elsa.

"Well, I've been thinking about whether we should change our plans," Lars said.

"How so?"

"The room at the National Hotel is booked for tomorrow night, It's almost a 300 kilometre drive back to Havana, which on these roads is a bit of a haul. My suggestion is we aim for some place in between. Somewhere along the northern coast where we could stay the night, and then cruise into Havana tomorrow in time to check in."

"Sounds better than doing it all in one day," Sara said. "Do you have a place in mind?"

"I was looking at the map when you were in the shower but I don't know any of these places. Best thing is to play it by ear. There's always people on the street offering places to stay so that shouldn't be a problem. After we say 'adiós' to Elsa, you can consult the guidebook for possible destinations. One thing for sure though... I definitely don't want to stay in Varadero. We should just look for a small town somewhere."

"I'll see what I can find... So let's get a move on. The sooner we leave, the sooner we get there."

Knowing that travelling smaller roads would lengthen their time in the car, Lars chose to stick to the main highway for the first leg of the journey.

"It isn't exactly the quaint Cuban village I would have preferred, but I guess it will do," Lars said, as they slowly cruised one of the main thoroughfares in the coastal city of Matanzas.

"This looks like the industrial area so why don't we drive towards the sea and try our luck finding a place there," Sara suggested, tossing the guidebook into the back seat.

Luck however, was not on their side that day. After fruitlessly searching for a suitable accommodation for well over an hour and no offers coming from any street merchants, a new plan was in order.

"We managed to come a lot further than I thought we would, and it's now less than 100 kms. to Havana," Lars told her, while they were parked on a residential street.

"And?" Sara asked.

"If we bite the bullet and drive back to Havana today, we should be able to get there before dark. Do you still have the card the Professor gave you? Maybe we can call from a pay phone and see if the flat would be free tonight."

From the look on Sara's face as she walked back from the gas station, Lars knew the answer.

"He told me that they wouldn't rent it for just one day, but he said in al likelihood we could probably stay at a friend's place not too far away," Sara told him, leaning down through the open window. "He promisd to call and reserve a room."

"Yeah… we know how that game works," Lars said with a snarl.

"How can he be so sure there's a room available?"

"I think we can trust the Professor. At least I hope so."

So back they went, arriving at the address the Professor had provided, just as dusk was falling.

"Okay… it's not the Ritz," Lars remarked to Sara, after the Casa owners, Alexandro and his wife, Louisa had shown them the room. "Yeah… it's also no big thrill to have to share the bathroom but it's only for one night. One plus is that it's not far from the La Viejo Greco so we could try and eat there one last time," Lars rationalized.

But lady luck continued to elude them. With a booked out

Greco, and no desire to seek out another venue, they decided to order a pizza from a takeaway and return to the Casa.

"Well that wasn't exactly the most exciting day of our trip," Sara said, as they settled into a sagging bed that night. "Tomorrow can only be an improvement."

"*Ahhh tomorrow, Señorita,*" Lars said, adopting a poor Spanish accent. "*Tomorrow we stay in Havana's most prestigious hotel, with a room overlooking the Malecon and the deep blue sea.* This place has an amazing history," he added, switching back to a normal voice.

"Tell me more," Sara said, curling up beside him. "I don't think I'm going to be able to get to sleep too easily on this mattress anyway. Plus I think there's a damm mosquito in here."

"'*The hotel was built by American investors on an outcrop above the coastal road.*'" Lars began reading aloud from the guidebook.

"They're referring to the the Malecon."

"That much I know," Sara said.

"'*The two towered structure, a mixture of Roman, Moorish and Art Deco, opened its doors in 1930, offering over 450 rooms. In the intervening decades it has been home to a countless number of celebrities and heads of state, too numerous to mention. In the 40's and 50s it was also the turf of the US mafia, including such notorious figures as Meyer Lansky, Lucky Luciano, Vito Genovese, and Albert Anastasia. Photos of other illustrious guests can be viewed in the hotel's hall of fame'.*"

"You think they included photos of those Mafia guys?" Sara asked in a drowsy voice.

"I doubt it," Lars answered. "But you never know. Anyways, as I was saying, '*The five-star hotel offers picturesque views, including the entrance to Havana's harbour, and remains a coveted location for travellers.*' So listening to all that, are you looking forward to it with bated breath? " Lars asked.

Fast asleep, Sara offered no reply.

Next Day...

"What the hell?" Lars shouted, loud enough to be heard in the adjacent rooms. "What happened to the water? " he asked, when he heard Alexandro's voice on the other side of the door. "I just shampooed my hair."

"I'm sorry Señor Kierey. The water will come back shortly," Alexandro assured him.

"How often does that happen?" Lars asked awhile later, as he and Sara joined Alexandro and Louisa at the breakfast table.

"This is Cuba, Señor Kierey," Alexandro told him.

"Please call me Lars."

"We are used to power outages and because the electricity runs the pumping stations, the water stops. I do apologize," he said.

"Not a major catastrophe," Lars said. "I just wish it had waited till I was done, because I had shampoo dripping into my eyes."

"We should have told you it is best not to shower in the morning, because that is when many people do it," Louisa told him.

"I guess there's a lot of things you have to get used to, what with the embargo and everything," Sara interjected, hoping to prevent Lars from droning on about the shower.

"Cuba is one big prison," Alexandro said abruptly, garnering an earnest stare from his wife. "It is true Louisa," he said. "We cannot do as we please. If we could, you two would be sitting here talking to someone else," he said to Lars.

"What sort of things do you have to deal with on a daily basis?" Sara asked, genuinely interested in subjects not found in the guidebook.

"Dios mío...where do I begin?" Alexandro said. "You know of course, there is political repression against those who harbour different views to that of the government. The media is heavily censored, so it is often difficult to determine what is really going on in the world. That has changed somewhat with the Internet but the government also controls that... plus the connection is extremely slow here in Havana. In the countryside, you can forget it."

"We know all about that," Lars told him. " We tried sending an email from one of the big hotels downtown and gave up after half hour. But having a functioning Internet isn't all it's cracked up to be," Lars argued.

"What do you mean," Alexandro asked.

"Oh oh, you've got him started," Sara mumbled.

"Social media for one thing. One of the biggest mistakes was allowing it to evolve into this anonymous forum where every amoeba can spew his or her vitriol without fear of having to be accountable."

"Lars, I'm quite sure Alexandro and Louisa don't want to hear your manifesto on social media," Sara said.

"No Miss Sara, I am very interested in what Lars has to say," Alexandro objected. "Please continue."

"The Internet may still be in its infancy here, so maybe, just maybe, Cuba has the chance to avoid such an irreversible debacle."

"But even if it improves, it will be heavily censored or controlled by the government."

"Obviously that's not great either, but at least they can make the people who use it accountable."

"You asked about other difficulties," Alexandro said, looking to Sara, apparently still eager to vent his frustrations. "There are restrictions on assembly to prevent people from protesting against things like food shortages, power outrages or wages. Those who do voice their objection are often arrested. The jails, where conditions are a crime in itself, are full of political prisoners. I was a lawyer so I know about such things."

"That's quite a list," Sara told him. "I am not a fan of Communism by any stretch, and have nothing but respect and admiration for the people of Cuba for having withstood such trying conditions for so long. I realize in many ways they've had no choice but still... how *do* people keep up their morale?"

"Alcohol and drugs are a big problem in Cuba, although the government will deny that," Alexandro answered.

"But this is such a beautiful country. It's really offensive that people have to suffer such indignities and hardships," Lars said.

"Not all people suffer," Alexandro told him. "We are relatively lucky. As a lawyer I earned a decent salary, so we can afford a house and car. Have you been to the western section of Havana?"

"You mean the neighbourhood with the huge villas?"

"Precisely," Alexandro grinned, as if having made his point.

"When we drove through it on the way to Viñales, I thought I'd taken a wrong turn and ended up in Beverly Hills."

"Most of those homes are owned by high officials and I assure you their water does not run out in the middle of a shower."

"Puts a different glow on things talking to someone like Alexandro, doesn't it?" Sara said, as they were packing up their belongings. "I'm kind of glad we didn't have such a discussion at the beginning of the trip."

"It does seem pretty unjust and I have the feeling things aren't going change anytime soon."

After saying goodbye to Alexandro and Louisa, the first item on the agenda was to return their rental car. As that was accomplished with little fanfare or last minute complications, they soon found themselves in line at the reception counter in the hotel's cavernous lobby. Although customers were being dealt with much more efficiently than at the pharmacy they had visited, when their turn finally came, Lars was not pleased to learn that the hotel was overbooked.

"We do apologize for the inconvenience, sir," a young dark-haired woman in a black uniform told him." But we intend to put you into another hotel that is of an equally high standard."

"Do you think there's a hidden camera somewhere," Lars asked Sara, briefly turning away from the reception desk.

"What are you talking about?" Sara answered impatiently.

"Somebody wants to capture me Gringo losing it and slamming his fist through the counter."

"Lars, please… don't make a scene," she pleaded.

"Look," Lars said calmly, turning his attention back on the receptionist. "I know it's not solely your fault that the hotel is overbooked. But I made this reservation and paid for it months ago. This is our last night in Cuba and I'm not about to be shunted off to spend it in another hotel. I paid for a room at the National, and I want a room at the National."

"I'm very sorry sir, but there's nothing I can do except offer you an alternative," the receptionist said, maintaining her decorum.

"Nothing personal, Ms…. Diego," Lars said, after straining to read her gold nameplate. "I believe there is nothing you can do about it, therefore I would like to speak to the manager… now," he added in a polite but convincing tone.

"I will see if I can speak with him, sir. If you wouldn't mind waiting in the lobby. I will be right back."

"Interesting to see all these other people," Lars remarked, as they observed the shifting crowd. "I wonder which one of them got our room."

"Easy, Kemo Sabe. Don't spoil our last day here," Sara said.

"I'm not going to spoil it, and I'm certainly not going to let anyone else spoil it either," Lars said firmly. " No matter what this manager has to say, we're not leaving here without a room. I'll sleep in the bloody lobby if I have to."

"Buenos Dias, Señora and Señor," a smartly dressed man in his 40's greeted them. "My name is Gonzales and I am the day manager here at the hotel. My assistant has explained the situation and I wish to extend my apologies for any inconvenience this may have caused you."

"It did rather come as a surprise," Sara told him, hoping

to deflect any rebuttal Lars was considering.

"I understand," the manager said. "Under such circumstances, we normally see to it that a customer obtains a room at another hotel. But seeing as you are only staying for one night, what I can do is offer you the Royal Suite."

"The Royal Suite?" Lars echoed, his simmering anger brought to a standstill.

"It is a three room suite on the 7th floor. It usually costs considerably more, but because of this unfortunate error on the hotel's part, we will charge the same rate you paid for your room."

"That's very kind of you," Sara said, grabbing hold of Lars's arm just to make sure he stayed calm.

"Unfortunately, because the suite was occupied last night, it will not be ready until 3:00 this afternoon."

"Can we at least leave our luggage here until then?" Lars asked.

"Of course, sir. Once we have you checked in, Ms. Diego will see to it that your luggage is delivered to the suite.

"Great," Lars said, extending his hand. "Thank you every much. Your generosity is very much appreciated."

"That means we can head back into old Havana for a last look around," Lars told Sara, after the manager had left to arrange for their luggage to be stored. "Hard to believe. Here I was ready to defend the Alamo at all costs, and they turn around and offer us the Royal suite. Sort of makes up for all those cancellations."

"It does sound pretty luxurious... The Royal Suite," Sara mused aloud.

"Look," Lars said, glancing at his watch. "We still have over three hours until we can get into the room."

"Suite," Sara corrected.

"Suite... Why don't we go somewhere for lunch and then make a final loop through the streets?"

"Sounds good to me," Sara replied with a smile, hooking arm in arm with Lars as they walked out of the lobby into brilliant sunshine.

"What is it about this country... especially Havana," Sara pondered, as they sauntered down a familiar avenue, "that makes you feel like life absolutely throbs here? I mean just look around. There's so much going on. It's absolutely intoxicating."

"It is a tad more lively than dull old, not to mention cold, Canada," Lars answered.

"I'm not comparing the two," Sara told him. "I like our life at home... it's just that this place is so... different."

"People in southern countries in general are more outgoing. That's probably because they never have to deal with the prospect of -40."

"True, but then they have other things to worry about, like hurricanes."

"Or living under a Communist government," Lars added. "But you have to remember, a certain percentage of the people on the streets are tourists, who are by and large in a good mood because they're on vacation.

"Just humour me, Lars. I'm on a bit of a high right now, what with all we've seen and done. And now being treated to the Royal Suite... what else could you ask for?" Sara said, letting her thoughts trail off. "I'm so happy I could almost cry."

"Save that for when we go back to the National and find out the the suite has been given to someone else."

"Oh you dream wrecker, you," she said, swatting him on the arm. You always know the wrong thing to say. Let's go eat. I'm starving."

Following lunch at a cubby hole of a restaurant, where they were the only occupants at one of three tables, they made their way back to the Capitol for a last, longing look at the vintage cars.

"Where else can you visit a car museum like this?" Lars raved, as he gazed upon a sleek 1960 Cadillac Coupe de Ville with tail fins that resembled those of a shark. "So many old cars in mint condition give or take a wheel or two," he added, recalling the episode with the Oldsmobile. "In the last ten minutes alone, I've come across a 52 Buick, a 57 Rambler, a Plymouth whose year I wasn't sure of. They even have a bloody Corvair. It's crazy."

"I must admit they are impressive," Sara agreed. "Unlike today's box like cars, they really do have a distinctiveness about them. And I'm not even a car buff."

After Lars had had his fill of the old cars, they retreated to the park adjacent the Capitol, perched on a bench for well over an hour, quietly absorbing the energy and exoticness of the city.

Fortunately for all concerned, the track record of cancelled reservations proved to be history. Handed their key cards at 3:00 on the dot, they couldn't help feeling a sense of expectation as they ascended to the 7th floor.

"What a strange design," Lars said, upon opening the door to discover a tiny foyer with two opposing doors leading off of it.

"Any preferences?" Lars asked.

"Why don't we each take one and see where we end up?" Sara replied.

Sara's door led to a luxurious bedroom and a large bathroom outfitted with bath, shower and bidet. A second door led back to a mutually shared, living room, complete with a deep-piled carpet, overstuffed chesterfield, large flat screen television and a floor to ceiling picture window offering a spectacular view of the sea and coastline.

"So this is how the other half lives," Sara remarked when Lars joined her in the living room. "I presume your room is as fancy as mine. Curious who else may have stayed here."

"Or were garrotted here," Lars quipped.

"Ugghh! What a terrible thought," Sara said, shaking off a shudder.

"Well this was a Mafia hangout," he reminded her. "Who knows what may have taken place in this suite. Think of all the famous couples who may have frequented it over the decades."

"Wow. Look at this view," Sara marvelled, having moved to the window. "And look at those dark clouds on the horizon. We're lucky we went to town when we did because it looks like a storm may be coming. Is it true that Florida is really only 90 miles away?"

"So they say," Lars answered, flopping down on the sofa and putting his feet up on a matching hassock. "What does it say on that plaque above the tv?" he asked, folding his hands behind his head.

"Apparently Geraldine Chaplin wants to let everyone know she stayed in this room at one time," Sara informed him.

"Why would someone leave a signed photo of themselves to announce that?"

"No idea… Maybe we should replace it with a selfie of us," Sara joked.

"Think the suite comes with complimentary room service?" Lars asked.

"I think that would be pushing it. I wouldn't risk it unless you're in the mood for being handed a bill where a drink costs $20."

So instead of indulging themselves, the next couple of hours were spent entranced by the sea view, while trading highlights and low points of the last two weeks.

Shortly before six, having had the hotel concierge make a reservation, they made their way to the El Vieja Greco for a final meal. Declining the owner's offer to call them a taxi, they chose to walk back to the National, free of any sense of foreboding on the darkened streets, Juan's comment about 'killing neighbours,' still fresh in their minds.

Final day …

Whether it was the churning memories of the last two weeks or the mild melancholy of knowing the trip was coming to an end, something woke Lars around 4:30. Slipping quietly out of bed so as not to wake Sara, he made his way to the living room and opened the door to the balcony. Dawn was still a good hour away as he stared out at the city lights, the distant dome of the Capitol rising above the surrounding buildings. Listening to the waves hitting the break wall on the Malecon far below, he pulled a chair up to the open window and sat there watching the sun slowly erase the lingering remnants of the night.

"How long have you been up?" Sara asked groggily, as she came into the living room to find him still at the window.

"What time is it now?"

"Just after seven," she told him.

"A couple of hours I guess. Something woke me and I couldn't get back to sleep. Rather than just lay there, I figured I'd come out and take advantage of the view. I can sleep on the plane. This is so crazy when you think about it," he continued."To have done and seen everything we have, and then have it end like this. How lucky can you get?"

"I know," Sara said, resting her hands on his shoulders as she stared out at the calm sea. "All the same, I'm glad we didn't stay here at the beginning of the trip."

"Why's that?" he said, turning to face her.

"I don't know... it might have spoiled us in some ways. As nice as this place is, it's almost as far removed from reality as the all-exclusive resorts. But seeing as we're here, what say we be decadent and take a long shower in each of our bathrooms... get dressed and head on down for breakfast."

"I guess the big names ordered breakfast in their suites," Sara said, as she followed Lars back to their table in the crowded breakfast room. "I don't see anyone famous."

"No... but there's two dubious looking characters over by the door that look a little out their element and could pass for you know what," Lars told her.

Throughout their meal, the two could hardly keep from gawking at their fellow guests, hoping to recognize at least one famous face.

"I'm afraid it's just a mix of old monied matrons and nouveau riche showboaters," Lars said, finishing up his coffee.

"And which category do you suppose other guests think we fit into?" Sara asked.

"No idea but it's nonetheless interesting to see who you're rubbing elbows with. Enjoy it while it lasts."

With their flight not scheduled to leave until six, the pair returned to the suite, content in doing a whole lot of nothing other than staring out at the now tempestuous sea. As a parting gesture, of goodwill, the hotel arranged and paid for a taxi to the airport. Whether by choice or accident, Lars was thrilled to discover their means of transportation would be a 1955 Chevy convertible. After a drive was all too short, they halted briefly on the departure level of the terminal, taking a long last look at the cluster of palm trees wavering below a darkening sky. Two hours later, after an exit infinitely smoother than their entry had been, the plane was hurtling down the last stretch of Cuban soil. Staring out the window as the countryside disappeared beneath a layer of thick cloud, the two tired travellers were struck by the same unspoken thought, *'It's going to take awhile to be back home'*.

✻

THE ROAD STARTS SOMEWHERE

Early that spring morning, Karin Davison and her husband, Carsten were huddled over their kitchen table, discussing what for both of them was a painful subject, her upcoming court appearance.

"Are you nervous?" Carsten asked, reaching across to refill Karin's cup.

"No, no… not at all," she answered sarcastically, waving both hands to decline his offer. "What a silly question, Carsten. Of course I'm nervous. And having more coffee certainly won't help. How would *you* feel knowing you were about to put yourself on the chopping block, so some arrogant lawyer can feel free to try and cast dispersions on your reputation? Were you sleeping during the whole process of jury selection?"

"Of course not."

"Well then, that should have given you some inkling of what we may be up against."

"But *you* did nothing wrong. It was Nelson who assaulted *you*."

"That's not going to stop his lawyer from attempting to convince the jury otherwise… to twist the facts and make it look like I enticed him, or that somehow his actions were simply those of an overly affectionate goofball, and there was nothing sinister about them."

"But *you* know that's not true. His actions were simply part of a treacherous plot. The phone call proves that. And if he denies having made it, phone records don't lie."

"I'm not sure how much that will help us," Karin said, her voice rising in frustration. "It may just come down to his word against mine."

"Hey I'm on your side remember. It's critical that you stay calm and focused, so the lawyer can't rattle you. You were the victim."

"Sorry," Karin replied. "I know you're just trying to help. I'm somewhat tightly wound."

At that same moment, not far from the Davison's fifth floor apartment, Gerald Nelson and his wife, Arlene were seated on the patio behind their large two-storey house.

"I still can't get past this," Arlene said, setting her empty mug down on the placemat. "What were you thinking?"

"Arlene," Gerald moaned with impatience. "You've asked me that a hundred times since Ms. Davison filed the charges."

"Maybe if I'd received an honest answer I could have saved myself ninety-nine questions."

"As I've told you... I was just trying to show..."

"Not that same old line again," Arlene fumed. "What you did is not a sign of mere appreciation in my book. I can't help wondering what it was you were hoping to achieve?"

"God help me," Gerald replied, his anger flaring. "It's a good thing they're not putting you on the bloody witness stand today."

It was a few minutes before ten a.m., when the lawyers and their clients entered the wood-panelled chamber, taking their seats behind their respective tables at the front of the room. Almost immediately the clerk of the court requested the murmuring crowd to rise for the judge's entrance, as all eyes turned to see a middle-aged, balding man with a tinge of grey in the hair fate had allowed him to keep, emerging through a side door. He quickly ascended to the raised bench and called the court into session with a bang of his gavel. After the clerk had delivered an opening remark indicating which case was about to commence, the judge asked both parties if they were ready to present their cases. When the answers came in the affirmative and several more formalities dispensed with, he called for the jury to be shown in. Entering through a door on the opposite side from where the judge had come in, a group of six women and six men, a balance fiercely fought over during jury selection, shuffled in like members of a chain gang.

"The prosecution may proceed," the judge announced, once the jury was seated.

"Thank you, your honour," said Maurice Shaw, a man in his late fifties, with a full head of premature white hair. Rising slowly from his chair, he purposely brushed a speck of fluff from the lapel of his suit, a sly gesture meant to illustrate his intentions to make his presentation flawless. Inhaling deeply, he turned to face the jury.

"Ladies and gentlemen of the jury, as you will see from the evidence presented, this case is a prime example of assault, one that if condoned, can easily set a precedent, ultimately offering an open invitation to commit more heinous crimes. The road has to start somewhere. I urge you to listen carefully to all of the testimony of the witnesses called. Once you have heard all the evidence, I am convinced you will find the arguments brought forward by the defence invalid. There is only one verdict you can reach. Guilty as charged. Thank you."

"Thank you, Mr. Shaw," the judge said, once the prosecutor had re-taken his seat. "Mr. Hatcher, are you ready to deliver your opening remarks?" he asked, directing his attention to Mr. Nelson's lawyer.

"I am, your honour."

"Proceed."

Considerably younger than his counterpart, Lawrence Hatcher was clad in a patently expensive, three-piece, anthracite suit, with carefully groomed hair and manicured nails. Even his manner of approaching the jury fit the image of that of a high-powered attorney.

"Ladies and gentlemen, as peculiar as this may sound, I agree with my honoured colleague. I too believe this to be a clear cut case, one where when all the facts have been presented, it will be easy to reach a verdict. Where I differ from Mr. Shaw is that this is not a matter of assault, but merely a case of over exuberance; a gesture meant to convey appreciation and regret. As you will hear from my client himself, his actions did not cross any boundary of decency. He has the utmost respect for Ms. Davison. Once you have heard his testimony, I have no doubt you will find my client, Gerald Nelson, innocent of the charges.

"You may call your first witness, Mr. Shaw," the judge advised, once Hatcher had thanked the jury and returned to his place at the defence table.

"I call Ms. Karin Davison, your honour."

Dressed in a light blue blouse, dark suit jacket and matching slacks, her hair pulled back and tied at the rear, Karin took the stand and repeated the oath as required. Her nervousness was apparent to all in the crowded courtroom, as she waited for her lawyer to approach. Unlike similar cases, the courtroom that morning was filled to capacity, partly because of friends and colleagues who had come to support Karin, and partly because of the interest generated by the fact Gerald Nelson was a well-known professor in the community. The decision to have the plaintiff take the stand had by no means been a given. In the weeks prior to the proceedings, heated discussions had taken place between Karin and her lawyer about the wisdom and risks of letting her testify.

"I think it's crucial that you do," Shaw had argued. "Jurors are more likely to be empathetic to a person like yourself, than they will be to Mr. Nelson, who in my opinion oozes arrogance. During my preliminary discussions with his lawyer, Nelson acted disinterested, almost cocky. If he behaves like that in the courtroom, it will not go unnoticed by the jurors. The benefits of your testifying definitely outweigh the risks."

"But what about the cross examination?" Karin had asked, while sitting with Carsten in Shaw's plush office. "Won't his lawyer try to distort the facts and tear my story apart?"

"He will no doubt try to cast dispersions on your

character, but it's my job to see that he fails. In my experience, aggressive tactics, no matter which side employs them, tend to backfire with jurors. All *you* need to do is to calmly deliver the facts. If you simply explain Nelson's actions and how violated you felt by them, Mr. Hatcher's attempts to discredit you will fail."

"Good morning, Ms. Davison," Shaw began, standing so that the jurors' view of his client was not blocked.

"Good morning."

"Ms. Davison, There's no need to be nervous," Shaw advised.

"You and I have discussed the facts of this case at length, as well as the testimony you are about to give. All you need to do today is to tell the jury what you've told me. First of all, can you tell the court what it is you do for a living?"

"I'm a physiotherapist."

"A physiotherapist," her lawyer repeated. "And how long have you worked in that profession?"

"Almost twenty years."

"A considerable length of time wouldn't you say?"

"I suppose so," Karin answered, her tension visibly easing.

"And during those twenty years, have you ever been confronted with a situation that forced you initiate legal action?"

"Never."

"Not once in twenty years," Shaw repeated for emphasis, turning to face the jury. "And in reverse? Have customers ever filed any serious complaints about your work?"

"There have been instances where a customer has not been satisfied, but never anything serious enough that led to legal action, if that's what you mean," Karin explained, her tone gaining confidence with each passing minute.

"Have you ever experienced what in your opinion was inappropriate behaviour from a customer?"

"Objection, your honour. Calls for the witness to speculate on what is considered inappropriate," Mr. Hatcher called out.

"It is not speculation your honour, for my client to relate experiences she considered inappropriate."

"Overruled," the judge declared. "You may answer the question."

"I've had patients make comments I thought were improper; innuendos...come ons if you will. You meet all kinds in this business."

"And what did you do in such situations?"

"I just ignored them, and things went no further."

"Ms. Davison. I'd like to focus on the events of the morning of June 12th, specifically in regards to the patient, Gerald Nelson."

"Yes."

"What treatment was he seeking that day at your Practice?"

"Mr. Nelson had been coming for treatment on a wrenched shoulder."

"So this was not Mr. Nelson's first appointment?"

"No. In fact it was the last of a series of six treatments prescribed by his doctor."

"The last in a series of six treatments?" Shaw repeated.

"That's correct."

"And how had the treatments been going up to that point?"

"There's was a definite improvement."

"In your opinion as a qualified physiotherapist, was it unlikely he would need further treatments?"

"I think that's a fair assessment. Mr. Nelson seemed to be satisfied and did not indicate he intended to seek a follow-up prescription."

"Had Mr. Nelson ever come to your Practice for other treatments, prior to this series for his shoulder?"

"Mr. Nelson had been a client for sometime. I would have to consult my files to give you a precise answer," Karen explained.

"I see. How many years would you say Mr. Nelson had been a patient? Would you prefer I refer to him as a patient or client?"

"Patient is fine," Karin told him? "I'm not sure. Perhaps four or five."

"So Mr. Nelson had been a patient… for various ailments for a number of years," Shaw restated. "So it is safe to say you knew him."

"I don't know if I can say I knew him. Mr. Nelson was a patient I was familiar with."

"Was there anything different or unusual about this last series of treatments, in comparison to others over the years?"

"Not that I can recall."

"Can you please describe what happened on the day of the last treatment."

"After the treatment was finished, I went to the reception desk to prepare the prescription for Mr. Nelson's signature."

"And what was Nelson dong during this time."

"He was putting on his shirt."

"Could you see him doing so?"

"No, he was behind the curtain."

"And then?"

"He came over to the desk to sign the prescription. Once he had done so he told me that he was sad that I was closing the Practice."

"I think now is the time to inform the jury that after almost twenty years in the same location, you had decided to close the Practice and move to another part of the city?" Shaw announced. "Why did you want to do that Ms. Davison?"

"The Practice was located in a building that was being converted into condominiums. I had no choice."

"And when were you scheduled to leave?"

"At the end of the month… the end of June."

"At the end of June," Shaw repeated. "In other words, approximately two weeks after Mr. Nelson's last visit."

"That's correct."

"Were all your patients aware the Practice was closing?"

"Most probably were. I had been informing the regulars and there was a sign posted at reception as well. I had stopped taking new patients the month before."

"I see. Had any patients expressed their feelings to you about the closure?"

"A number had, yes. Plus I had started receiving cards."

"So Mr. Nelson would have known, prior to his last visit, that the Practice was closing"

"I believe so."

"Had Mr. Nelson expressed any thoughts about the closing?"

"Not until that morning."

"And what precisely did he say to you that morning?"

"As I said, he told me that he was sad to see me go; that my work had helped him over the years, and that it would be hard to find someone else as good."

"And what did you say in return?"

"I simply thanked him."

"Where were you in relation to Mr.Nelson when he told you this?"

"I'm not sure what you mean?"

"Was he standing beside you? On the other side of the desk? Where was he exactly?"

"As far as I recall he was standing at the side of the desk."

"And then what happened?"

"After he signed the prescription, he stepped closer to me, leaned forward and embraced me in a hug before placing a kiss on each cheek, like the French do."

"And how did you feel when he did that?"

"It surprised me. He had never done anything like that before. He'd often compliment me and said he felt better etc. but never anything physical."

"And then what happened?"

"Once he had pulled back from my cheek, and still had his arms around me, he planted a kiss directly on my lips."

"And did that surprise you?"

"It most certainly did.´"

"And what did you do?"

"Well… to be honest," Karin answered hesitatingly. " I think I was in shock."

"But what did you do?"

"Nothing, I'm afraid."

"Did you say anything to him?"

"No," Karin said, her head drooping slightly.

"Were you okay with what he did?"

"No, not at all."

"Then why didn't you react? Tell him what you thought of his behaviour."

"As I said, I was shocked."

"And then what happened?"

"He let me go, picked up his jacket, said good bye, and left."

"And what did you do after that?"

"I went to the bathroom and rinsed out my mouth. I felt violated."

"Yet you did not say anything to Mr. Nelson."

"If it hadn't come as such a shock , I think I would have said something. I didn't have much time to think about what had just happened because there was another patient in the waiting room."

"Was this other patient witness to what had just taken place between you and Mr. Nelson?"

"No. The reception desk is around the corner from the waiting room."

"So there was no witness to this encounter?"

"There were just the two of us in the room," Karin told him, putting her hand to her mouth to clear her throat.

"And later, when you did have time to reflect … what did you think or do then?"

"I deeply regretted not having told him that I felt what he did was not okay, or perhaps even slapped his face. But it all happened so fast, I was in shock."

"Let me get this straight. According to your testimony, Mr. Nelson kissed you on the lips without your permission."

"That's correct."

"And you were so shocked by his unexpected behaviour that you didn't say or do anything."

"Again… correct."

"Did you feel flattered?"

"Certainly not."

"Did you kiss him back?"

"No."

"Did you do anything to encourage his behaviour?"

"No. I did no such thing."

"Did you feel threatened or frightened?"

"Not at that precise moment. It was only later that I thought about what might have happened."

"Can you tell the court what you mean by that?!

"If he had decided to take it any further. Groping me or whatever."

"So he didn't grope you or anything else of that nature?"

"No."

"Ms. Davison, several weeks passed between the time this incident took place and your decision to press charges against Mr. Nelson. Can you explain what caused that delay?"

"On the day it occurred, I spoke about it with my husband and several friends when I got home. One of them said she wasn't surprised at all by Mr. Nelson's behaviour, or for that matter by my lack of response. She told me many men have been brought up to believe that they can treat women as they see fit without any consequences. She also said that going into shock is common for women who are unexpectedly assaulted."

"How did your husband react when you told him?"

"He was very angry and wanted to go over and confront Mr. Nelson that very evening. But I talked him out of it."

"Who decided that you should press charges?"

"We discussed the possibility of doing so the next day, but after weighing the odds of whether we could win such a case , we decided against it. We felt it might ultimately come down to a 'he said, she said' scenario. I probably wouldn't have gone ahead with the complaint if it hadn't been for the phone call."

"The phone call?" Shaw repeated, attempting to sound as if this was the first he'd heard of it. "Please explain what you mean."

"This incident with Mr. Nelson took place on a Friday. On the following Tuesday, I was at my desk when the phone rang. When I answered, someone said hello, but I didn't recognize the voice. I asked who was on the line and a man said, 'it's Gerald'."

"Gerald..." Shaw repeated. " And who was this Gerald?"

"That was my first reaction. I asked, 'Gerald who?' and he answered, 'Gerald Nelson.'"

"And what did you say?"

"I asked him 'since when are we on a first name basis?'"

"Had you ever called him Gerald before?"

"Never."

"And what did you do then?

"I let him know in no uncertain terms what I thought about his actions the previous Friday. I told him that I found his behaviour totally inappropriate and unacceptable, and who the hell did he think he was taking liberties like that. Suffice to say I tore a strip off him."

"And what was 'Gerald's'response?" Shaw asked.

"I guess he hadn't expected that kind of response because at first he didn't say anything. Then he started to mumble some sort of feeble apology."

"And what did you do?"

"I told him I had a patient waiting and wasn't interested in anything he had to say. I said goodbye and hung up."

"So, Gerald... or Mr. Nelson apologized *after* you had given him a piece of your mind?"

"That's correct."

"Is it possible that was why he was calling?"

"Objection," Hatcher said. "Counsel is leading the witness."

"I will rephrase the question your honour," Shaw said before the judge had ruled on it. "In your opinion, is it possible he was calling to apologize?"

"The fact that he only did so after I had told him what I thought of him, makes me believe it was not the reason he was calling."

"But you can't be sure whether that might have been Mr. Nelson's original intention. To apologize."

"No."

"Far be it from me to steal Mr. Hatcher's thunder, but I'm sure he's going to press you on this point and claim that apologizing had in fact been foremost in Mr. Nelson's mind that day, arguing that he didn't have the opportunity to do so because you were so quick to chastize him."

"I don't know what was in Mr. Nelson's mind. What his motivation had been for calling. It was only when I got home and told my husband about the call, that I began to suspect he'd been 'fishing.'"

"Fishing?" Shaw echoed.

"It was my husband who used that term. He figured Mr. Nelson had interpreted my passive response to his having kissed me on the lips as a sign that there might be mutual interest. He believed Mr. Nelson was simply 'testing the waters' with the call."

"And what did you think about your husband's assessment?"

"Well it certainly seemed like a feasible explanation, supported by the fact he'd suddenly switched to using 'Gerald'. If he trully wanted to apologize, why did he wait four days to do so?All the pieces seemed to fit."

"Thank you Ms. Davison. No further questions at this time, your honour."

"You may cross exam the witness, Mr. Hatcher," the judge

declared.

After briefing conferring with his client, Hatcher rose and slowly apporached the witness stand, posturing there for a moment as if to imply he was about to say something momentous.

"Ms. Davison," he began, looking directly at a visibly tensed Karin. "I imagine this an uncomfortable situation to find yourself in."

"Not as uncomfortable as the morning in question."

Slightly stung by her unexpected reply, Hatcher took a few seconds to regain his composure.

"Well, Ms. Davison," he said, turning to face the jury. "I will try my best to avoid making matters more uncomfortable for you this morning. But I'm sure you must realize that in my quest for the truth, I will be forced to ask a series of rather personal questions."

"I expected no less, Mr. Hatcher. But I came prepared," Karin assured him firmly.

"I'm sure you did, Ms. Davison. I'm sure you did," he said, glancing to where Shaw was seated. "Tell me Ms. Davison, do you like your work?"

"Yes, I do… for the most part."

"For the most part?"

"It's like any job. It can get boring at times, especially when you treat the same person for months or years on end and there doesn't appear to be any visible improvement."

"Was Mr. Nelson one of those patients you found boring?"

"I wouldn't say so. He was not a patient I saw every week for months on end."

"I see. You did not consider Mr. Nelson to be boring.

"I didn't say my patients were boring. I said the work was often repetitive, which sometimes made it somewhat dull."

"As a physiotherapist, what kind of treatments do you offer?"

"We offer a fairly wide variety of treatments, dependant on the patient's situation."

"I don't think it's necessary to get into too much detail, Ms. Davison. What I *would* like the court to know is whether your work includes giving massages?"

"Yes, it does."

"Am I right in assuming that would include a full body massage?"

"It doesn't happen very often, but once in awhile, yes."

"And for such massages, is the patient required to be naked?"

"No. Patients, both men and women, are requested to retain their undergarments. At least that's how it is in my Practice."

"I see. Do you enjoy giving massages, Ms. Davison?"

"I wouldn't use the word *enjoy*."

"What word would you use?"

"Massages are intended to help patients relax. It is gratifying when they do so, but I wouldn't necessarily say it was enjoyable."

"Of the limited number of massages you give, is there a difference between treating a young, muscular man as opposed to an older, perhaps overweight specimen?"

"Objection, your honour," Shaw said. "The question is not only irrelevant, counsel is also leading the witness."

"Your honour, I am merely trying to establish how Ms. Davison might feel when treating a specific client," Hatcher shot back.

"Mr. Nelson was not there for a massage," Shaw replied.

"Overruled," the judge ordered. "You may answer Ms. Davison."

"I suppose there is a difference."

"And what would that difference be?"

"It is more aesthetically pleasing to treat someone who has taken care of their body."

"Would you say Mr. Nelson has taken care of himself?"

"Objection," Shaw called out. "Mr. Nelson was there for a shoulder treatment, not a massage."

"Sustained," the judge ordered.

"Let me put it another way," Hatcher replied. "Would you describe certain elements of your work as being sensual?"

"Obviously there is physical contact, but I wouldn't say it was sensual."

"Never?"

Karin paused before answering. "As I said, it is sometimes aesthetically pleasing to treat someone who is fit, but it is not sensual."

"Do patients enjoy your treatments?"

"Again, I don't think enjoy is the right word. They appreciate the work if it helps them. In reverse, people will tell me if I am applying too much pressure or causing them any undo pain."

"Could you describe the nature of Mr. Nelson's treatment on the day of the alleged offence?"

"He came for physiotherapy to treat an injured shoulder."

"So he wasn't naked."

"Of course not."

"But you told the court he had removed his shirt."

"I told the court he had put his shirt back on when the treatment was finished, so I assume people would understand that he had taken it off beforehand," Karin replied, causing a ripple of snickering in the gallery."

"You also testified that Mr. Nelson had been to see you on previous occasions," Hatcher said, after the judge had reprimanded the crowd. "What were the nature of those treatments?"

"I don't recall them all. I would have to look in his file."

"But we *have* established that Mr. Nelson had been a patient for some time."

"Yes."

"Despite Mr. Nelson's having been a patient for years, you told the court that you didn't really feel you know him,… that you were merely familiar with him. Do you not talk with patients during a treatment?"

"Of course I do."

"About what?" Hatcher asked.

"It depends. Sometimes I need to know the background of how an injury occurred. Or what kind of activities they may have been doing that could possibly aggravate the problem. Some patients tend to talk about subjects unrelated to the treatment. In some cases if it is too much, I suggest it is better to remain quiet and concentrate on the treatment."

"Do you ever talk about personal subjects?"

"Sometimes."

"Did you have personal conversations with Mr. Nelson?"

"I may have talked about various subjects with him. I don't recall every conversation I've had with patients."

"Do you share your own thoughts with patients?"

"It is usually a dialogue, Mr. Hatcher, not a monologue… although that's not the case with all patients… unfortunately," Karin said, prompting another round of chuckling.

"So you cannot recall any of the dialogues you may have had with Mr. Nelson?"

"Not in any great detail. I do know he's a Professor and that he and his wife have travelled a lot. We've talked about things like that."

"So you *do* know a bit about him. Tell me Ms. Davison, during these discussions with patients… or dialogues as you call them, do you show any interest that could be interpreted as beyond a professional level?"

"Objection," Shaw interrupted, before his client could answer.

"My client does not know what delusions may exist in the mind of her patients."

"Sustained."

"I withdraw the question your honour. Ms. Davison, do you ever flirt with patients?"

"Objection," Shaw repeated.

"Your honour, I am merely trying to establish the kind of rapport Ms. Davison has with her patients."

"Overruled," the judge said.

"No, I do not.," Karin answered.

"Never?" Hatcher pushed.

"Not intentionally, but I suppose some people may interpret friendliness as flirting."

"Did you ever flirt with Mr. Nelson?"

"I would not describe our conversations as flirting."

"But you admit you don't recall all of those conversations. What do you do if a patient flirts with you?"

"I either don't respond or I discourage it."

"And how do you do that?"

"Usually by changing the subject."

"Did Mr. Nelson ever flirt with you?"

"If he did, he couldn't have been very good at it because I didn't notice anything. That's what made his behaviour that day so unexpected," she said, resulting in another burst of laughter from the gallery.

"Ms. Davison, I would like to shift gears here if I may, and have you repeat what took place after the treatment with Mr. Nelson had finished that morning."

"I went to my desk to arrange for Mr. Nelson to sign the prescription."

"And then?"

"He came and signed it."

"And where were you?"

"I was standing behind my desk."

"And Mr. Nelson?"

"He was standing at the side of the counter."

"Did he say anything to you as he was signing?"

"Not that I can recall."

"And then what happened."

"After he signed the receipt he told me that he thought it was a shame that I was leaving."

"And what did you do?"

"I told him that I didn't want to leave but that I'd had no choice given that the building was being converted into condos."

"And what did he say?"

"I think he made reference to having appreciated my work and that he would miss me."

"Please continue," Hatcher urged.

"I thanked him and extended my hand."

"So you made the initial gesture."

"Such a gesture, as you call it, is nothing out of the ordinary. It's normal to shake hands with a patient when a prescription has been completed."

"And then what happened."

"Instead of accepting my hand, Mr. Nelson stepped forward and took me into a hug."

"Did you hug him back?"

"I may have. I found it somewhat surprising, seeing he had never done anything like that before."

"And what did you think when he did that?"

"Initially I figured maybe that was just his way."

"That was just his way," Hatcher repeated, with a trace of sarcasm. "Did you say anything when he was hugging you?"

"No."

"Did you tell him you found it inappropriate?"

"No. I didn't like it, but as I said, I thought maybe that's just him. He had always been nothing more than a professional acquaintance, so it came as a surprise."

"So, where were we?" Hatcher interjected. "Ah yes... Mr. Nelson and you were hugging."

"He was hugging me," Karin quickly replied.

"But you said you hugged him back and you weren't objecting," Hatcher countered. "How long did the hug last?"

"I didn't time it," Karin answered, noticeably irked by the question.

"Was it simply a perfunctory, short hug or something a bit more personal?"

"Objection, your honour. Ms. Davison cannot be expected to analyse the motives behind a hug."

"Overruled, Mr. Shaw," the judge answered. "The witness will answer the question."

"I'm sorry, but I don't know where the line is between the two. I can only repeat what I said. It came as a surprise and and I didn't like it."

"But you didn't tell him so."

"No."

"Why not?"

"I guess I saw little point. I thought it was a one time gesture. I felt it was disrespectful of my privacy but I could live with it."

"And then what happened?"

"And then he kissed me on both cheeks... not really kissing, more like the French do... one after the other."

"And how did you find that?"

"I also did not appreciate it, but it all happened so fast, there was virtually no time to respond."

"Was he still holding you in a hug when he kissed your cheeks?"

"I believe he still had his hands on my arms."

"So the hug was long enough for him to have kissed you. Could you have stepped back from him if you'd wanted to? As an expression of your... shall we say dissatisfaction?"

"Objection, the witness has already stated that Mr. Nelson was still holding her arms, making it difficult for her to have stepped back from him."

"Sustained."

"So you didn't step back as he was kissing your cheeks?"

"No. As I've explained this all took place so fast."

"Go on."

"And then he kissed me on the lips."

"And what did you do?"

"Nothing."

"Did you kiss him back?"

"No."

"Ms. Davison... An 'acquaintance' kisses you on the

mouth without your consent and you do not object."

"At that point I was completely shocked and just froze. I didn't say or do anything. I just stood there."

"Did Mr. Nelson have his mouth open during this kiss?"

"No."

"And then what happened?"

"He released me, said goodbye and left."

"And what did you do after he left?"

"I felt dazed. I couldn't believe what had just happened."

"Dazed in what sense? Did you feel flattered?"

"No, of course not. He had no right to do what he did. I felt violated."

"And yet you didn't object."

"I cannot explain it any other way than to say I felt stunned into silence. I've read that momentary paralysis is common amongst assault victims."

"Do you honestly believe it was Mr. Nelson's intention to assault you?"

"I don't know what Mr. Nelson was thinking."

"My client has maintained that his actions that morning were merely his way of expressing his appreciation for your good work."

"A handshake would have sufficed," Karin retorted.

"Perhaps," Hatcher agreed, "but a hug and kisses on the cheeks were, as you yourself described it, 'just his way'."

"That was my assumption in the moment and it might have passed for a reasonable gesture had it not been for the kiss on the mouth and then the phone call," Karin said.

"Ah yes… the phone call. I was just getting to that Ms. Davison.. You said that you hadn't initially recognized the caller to be Mr. Nelson."

"That's correct."

"What did Mr. Nelson say when you asked who was calling?"

"His exact words were, 'it's Gerald.'"

"And that's when you recognized who was on the line?"

"No, not exactly. I said 'Gerald who?', and that's when he said 'Gerald Nelson'. I've explained all this before," Karin said, clearly irritated.

"Yes. I know, Ms. Davison. I just wanted to refresh the jury's memory. And what did Mr. Nelson then say to you?"

"He didn't say anything. When I realized who it was, I let him have a piece of my mind in regards to his behaviour."

"Yes, yes, Ms. Davison, so you have testified. In that testimony you told the court that you thought Mr. Nelson had been 'fishing' because he'd apologized after you had criticized his actions. How can you be so sure he wasn't in fact calling to apologize, but never had the chance before you, as you put it, 'tore into him?'"

"Then why did he wait four..." Karin began.

"No further questions at this time, your honour," Hatcher said, interrupting Karin before she could complete her answer.

Having acknowledged the time, the judge announced that court would adjourn for lunch and reconvene at 2:00 p.m.

Karin was absent-mindedly picking at her food in the courthouse cafeteria, when she felt herself slipping back to the day she had told Carsten about the events at the Practice. To say the least, his initial reaction had not been what she might have hoped.

"So this creep has the gall to kiss you on the mouth without your permission," Carsten had said, his anger and disgust clearly apparent. "I just don't understand why you didn't just slap him or better yet, knee him in the groin?"

"Carsten, the last thing I need is for you to badger me about what I should have done. I've tried to explain. I went into temporary shock. I felt frozen."

"Okay...I'm sorry," Carsten apologized. "It's just that I feel so bloody angry. If I knew where this guy lived I'd drive over and either punch in the nose or inform his loving wife about what kind cretin she has for a husband."

"I understand you feel angry, but it almost feels like a part of you is angry with me," Karin told him.

"No… I'm not. Even if I don't fully understand."

Karin had been able to calm Carsten that day, only to see his fury flare up again when she informed him about the subsequent phone call.

"What kills me is that not only does this guy kiss you without your consent, he has the audacity to call you several days later. You do realize he could have misinterpreted your passivity as interest."

"Carsten, please… I did nothing wrong."

"That phone call is evidence of his treachery. We can't let him just walk. Who knows what else he's capable of. I think we need to take legal action."

Just as the afternoon session was about to get underway, Hatcher asked the judge whether both counsels could approach the bench. In the following discussion between the threesome, Hatcher voiced his intention to call his client to the stand. He then made the unusual request that Mr. Shaw be allowed to question his client first. Although somewhat suspicious of the irregular tactic, Shaw agreed, provided he be allowed a followup after Hatcher had completed his round of questioning.

"Mr. Nelson," Shaw began, after the defendant had taken the stand and been sworn in. "Please bear with me if some of my questions sound somewhat repetitive. I feel that repetition is essential for the jury to fully comprehend the context of this case. This morning we heard Ms. Davison describe the events on the morning of your last treatment. I would like you to relate those events as you saw them, as well as the motivations behind your behaviour that day."

"I understand," Nelson replied calmly, having apparently been coached to make his responses sound less arrogant. "On the morning of my last visit, I was aware that Ms. Davison was going to be closing her Practice. I was sorry to see her leaving and wanted to express my appreciation for all the good work she had done for me over the years.”

“Ms. Davison told the court that you had been a patient for a number of years. Had you ever expressed your appreciation for her work before?”

“On several occasions I told her that her treatments had helped me and that I was grateful for that.”

“It’s my understanding that some patients bring flowers or a bottle of wine as a means of expressing their appreciation. You never did that?”

“No.”

“So perhaps you can explain what was it that was different this time?”

“I knew she was leaving. I felt it would be a loss not only for me, but the entire neighbourhood as well.”

“Mr. Nelson,” Shaw drawled, moving to retrieve a folder from his table. “Before I continue,” he said, as he removed a sheet from the file. “Are you aware of the law in this country regarding what constitutes sexual assault?”

“I can’t say that I am.”

“Well let me inform you, as well as members of the jury. As odd as it may sound, the law in this country does not consider it a crime for unwanted kissing or touching. What do you think of such a law?”

“I wasn’t aware of that law and therefore have never given it much thought.”

“Quite… Well let me put it another way. Is your wife here in the courtroom today?”

“Yes, she is.”

“Fine… I would like to ask you how you might feel if, theoretically of course, I were to walk over to her right now, thank her for coming to support her husband and then kiss her on the lips as a sign of my appreciation.”

“Objection,” Hatcher called out.

“Your honour,” Shaw began. “If Mr. Nelson feels his behaviour was as innocent as he claims, then theoretically, he should have no objection to someone else expressing their appreciation in a similar manner."

"Overruled. You will answer the question."

"I suppose I would not like it."

"You suppose?"

"I would not like it."

"Why would that be?"

"Because she does not know you."

"She does not know me," Shaw repeated. "Now let's suppose this case were to drag on through the courts for several months... and during that time..."

"Objection," Hatcher interrupted. "Where is this going?"

"Mr. Shaw?" the judge asked.

"I wish to ask Mr. Nelson, to clarify whether he sees a difference between a relative stranger kissing someone on the lips without permission, and a professional acquaintance doing the same."

"Overruled. Continue, Mr. Shaw."

"You have heard Ms. Davison refer to you as an acquaintance. Did that status somehow grant you permission to violate her private sphere?"

"I did not consider expressing my appreciation as a violation."

"That sir, was not your assessment to make."

"Objection," Hatcher repeated.

"Mr. Shaw. I think you have made your point. Let's not belabour it."

"I'm sorry, your honour," Shaw said, turning back to Nelson. "Let us move on to the phone call," Shaw announced. "You have maintained that your behaviour was merely one of appreciation.

"That's correct."

"It has been testified that you made the phone call to Ms. Davison several days after the incident we've been discussing. Is that correct?"

"Correct."

"What prompted you to make that call ? And remember Mr. Nelson... you are under oath."

"I felt I owed her an apology."

"And why did you feel you owed her an apology?"

"I thought she may have misinterpreted my gesture."

"And just when did you come to this conclusion?"

"It wasn't a conclusion... it was a suspicion," Nelson answered.

"At some point it was enough of a suspicion that you concluded you should make the call," Shaw countered.

"It had been nagging at me that perhaps she had taken it in the wrong way."

"And what way was that?"

"That there was something else behind it other than a simple gesture of..."

"Yes, Mr. Nelson. We know... a simple gesture of appreciation."

If it was as you say... nagging at you, why did you wait four days before calling?"

"I wasn't sure what I should do. A part of me thought that if she hadn't misinterpreted it, calling her would make me look like a fool."

"What made you think she may have misinterpreted a simple gesture of appreciation?"

"People tend to define boundaries differently."

"And what boundary would that be, Mr. Nelson?"

"One's private sphere, I suppose."

"There's that word again... suppose. Let me ask you directly, Mr. Nelson, do you believe that kissing someone on the mouth without consent is violating someone's private sphere?"

Nelson remained silent, glancing at his lawyer.

"Mr. Nelson, I ask you again. Do you consider kissing someone on the mouth without their consent a violation of someone's private sphere.?"

"I guess it depends on the situation."

"Mr. Nelson, a short while ago you told the court that if I

were to approach your wife and express my appreciation in the manner in which you apparently felt it was okay to do with Ms. Davison, you would not have liked it. Correct?"

"Correct."

"So, let's leave the subject of defining boundaries aside for the moment. You claim that after much tossing and turning, you decided to call and issue an apology. Is that correct?"

"Yes."

"In her testimony this morning, Ms. Davison reported that when you called and she did not initially recognize your voice, you told her it was 'Gerald'. Is that your recollection as well?"

"I may have."

"Ms. Davison stated you had never used your first name on any previous occasion. Why would you have done so this time... assuming for the moment that you did."

"I don't recall if I had ever used it previously."

"Well Ms. Davison seems pretty sure that it was a first. In any event, when Ms. Davison realized who was calling, she told the court she let you know what she thought about your 'gesture of appreciation.' Is that a fair statement Mr. Nelson?"

"She told me she thought it had been highly inappropriate."

"So that must have confirmed your suspicion that she had 'misinterpreted' the gesture, did it not?"

"Yes, I suppose so," Nelson said with some hesitation.

"And that was when you claim you proceeded to deliver your apology... *after* she had told you what she thought about your behaviour?"

"I didn't have the opportunity to do so beforehand. It was only after she chastized me."

"Mr. Nelson...it has been suggested that your phone call, rather than having been motivated by the desire to issue an apology, had in fact been part of a fishing expedition."

"Objection," Hatcher said, rising from his seat.

"That because Ms. Davison did not physically or audibly object to your 'gesture'," Shaw pushed on, ignoring Hatcher's complaint. "You wanted to see if there might be a sliver of mutual interest."

"Objection, your honour," Hatcher repeated more vociferously.

"'That's quite enough, Mr. Shaw," the judge said. "Sustained."

"I apologize, your honour. I retract the statement. Mr. Nelson, do you like Ms. Davison?" Shaw continued.

"Yes, I suppose… I mean yes. She's always struck me as a very friendly person," Nelson answered. "And she's very good at what she does."

"She's very good at what she does," Shaw repeated slowly. "Besides treatments for your shoulder, have you ever had any massages at Ms. Davison's Practice?"

"Yes. I believe one or two."

"Would you say you enjoyed them?"

"They were pleasurable and helped me relax. "

"When you were relaxing during a 'pleasurable' massage, did your mind ever wander?"

"Objection, your honour. Counsel is leading the witness."

"Your honour, I am merely trying to establish how Mr. Nelson viewed Ms. Davison and her work. "

"Overruled. You may answer the question, Mr. Nelson.

"I think every man, if he's honest, would tell you that his thoughts tend to wander when he is being massaged. But if you are insinuating I had fantasies… I can assure you I did not," Nelson said firmly, casting an accusatory glance at his lawyer.

"I wasn't insinuating anything, Mr. Nelson, but thank you for clarifying that. If, as you claim, men's minds are prone to wandering, it would seem that most have the moral decency to control themselves and not try acting upon any fantasies or delusions they may be harbouring."

"Objection, your honour," Hatcher moaned, again rising

to his feet. "Why is counsel so persistent on pursuing this line of questioning? It's already been established that Mr. Nelson was not there for a massage in this instance. "

"Sustained. I agree with Mr. Hatcher, Mr. Shaw," the judge replied. "I will give you the benefit of the doubt that this is leading somewhere beyond what's already been covered. Don't disappoint me."

"Thank you, your honour."

Sensing he was trying the judge's patience, Shaw changed tactics. "Mr. Nelson. We've already touched briefly on the law here in this country," Shaw said, picking up the sheet of paper he had referred to earlier. "Allow me to paraphrase... it says here that it is perfectly legal to kiss someone on the mouth or grope them without their consent, as long as it is in a public place and he or she doesn't object or fight back. I repeat, perfectly legal. You stated that you weren't aware that such a law exists."

"Not in such detail. no."

"Do you find it a just law?"

"In the wording you gave, it sounds excessive," Nelson conceded. "I find it hard to believe that is truly the intent of the law. But I don't feel it applies in this case."

"I find it excessively lenient, Mr. Nelson. As it now stands, it suggests that a man can kiss or grope a woman until she 'objects or fights back'. It's only if he persists in his actions that he is liable for prosecution. In other words, he is legally allowed a "freebie," if you will."

"Objection, your honour. The jury doesn't need a lecture in legal..."

"That's precisely what it needs, as does Mr. Nelson," Shaw interrupted.

"The jury has heard what you had to say, Mr. Shaw," the judge warned. "Let's call it a draw, shall we, gentlemen? You may proceed."

"It just so happens, Mr. Nelson," Shaw began again. "That in some countries, any non-consensual physical act, and that includes kissing someone on the mouth, can be considered a crime."

"Objection, your honour. What bearing does jurisprudence in other countries have on a case being tried here?"

"Your honour, I was merely trying to illustrate how certain 'gestures' are viewed differently."

"I'll allow that, Mr. Shaw. Continue."

"Mr. Nelson, would you be so kind as to tell the court what your wife's reaction was in regards to the allegations made against you."

"Objection, Mr. Nelson's wife is not on trial here."

"Your honour, Mr. Nelson admitted that people tend to define boundaries differently. I am trying to establish how Mr. Nelson's behaviour may have been viewed by others more familiar with him to determine whether this was an isolated incident or a pattern practiced on other occasions."

"Overruled."

"She believes me."

"What does she believe?"

"That it was a gesture of appreciation."

"So in other words, she's used to your expressing yourself with acquaintances in such a manner... because that's 'just you'."

"Objection," Hatcher called out. "Counsel is taunting the witness ... again."

"Sustained. Mr. Shaw, my patience is not endless. I suggest you try another tack."

"I withdraw the statement, your honour. Mr. Nelson, have you ever been accused of overstepping boundaries before?"

"In what sense?" Nelson asked.

"Let's say the boundary of what might be considered decent behaviour."

"As I have said, boundaries are open to interpretation. But no, nobody has ever objected to anything I've said or done... at least to my face."

"Do you believe you overstepped a boundary with Ms. Davison?"

"No, I do not."

"But you did suspect she may have misinterpreted your gesture?"

"Yes, but…"

"No further questions, your honour," Shaw concluded and returned to his seat.

Accepting he may have erred in allowing his client to take the stand, Hatcher requested a brief recess to discuss future strategy.Retreating to an anteroom off the main courtroom, Hatcher and the Nelsons proceeded to review the day's events so far.

"I wouldn't exactly call that a stellar performance," Arlene snarled at Hatcher, once they'd seated themselves around a large conference table.

"Arlene," Gerald warned. "Don't make it worse."

"Worse?" Arlene snapped at her husband. "How could it be any worse. After her lawyer got finished with you I'm surprised they didn't haul you away in cuffs," she said, nervously tapping her fingers on the table.

"A part of me feels what Arlene says is true," Nelson told his lawyer. "I was getting mauled out there. Why didn't you come to my defence more often?"

"I was constantly objecting, but often overruled," Hatcher said in his defence. "I admit it was a mistake to let you testify. I thought hearing from you directly was the best way to counteract Ms. Davison's empathy factor. Obviously it wasn't."

"So what happens now?" Arlene asked. "I was watching the jury during parts of Gerald's dissection and some members didn't look like they were overly impressed with his arguments."

"That's something we have to try and overcome."

"And what are we going to do about this phone call?" she

added, turning to her husband. "Her lawyer certainly raised doubts about whether it was really your intention to apologize. Why the hell didn't you just send her a bloody 'thank you card' in the first place?" Arlene seethed. "We would have avoided all this chaos."

"All I can tell you is I called to apologize," Nelson said.

"I would like to believe you, Gerald. I truly would. But I can't overlook the fact that for as long as we've known each other, you've had the capacity to be an incorrigible flirt."

"Oh God," Hatcher groaned. "That's just the kind of thing the jury needs to hear. You can be thankful that Shaw hasn't called her as a witness," he told Nelson. "But your wife is right about the timing of the apology. I think our best way to discredit the 'fishing' aspect is…"

"Oh we know how reliable your ideas are of 'the best way'," Arlene interrupted.

"Let him finish," Nelson said to his wife.

"Thank you," Hatcher acknowledged. "The best way is for you to admit in hindsight that the kiss on the mouth, however well intentioned, was misguided. That you honestly didn't have any ulterior motives, and now see it as having been a mistake that you have already apologized for. But I don't want to put you back on the stand and have you open for more cross examination. Instead I will tell the judge I have no further questions and read out your statement. Any additional points will have to be made in my closing arguments."

"If I was a member of that jury," Arlene said. "I'd prefer to hear Gerald repent himself, rather than through his lawyer."

"Let's just be glad you're not on the jury," Hatcher said, gathering up his papers. "I'm not putting him back on the stand if I can help it."

Following through on his promise, once court resumed, Hatcher stunned the assembled audience by telling the judge he had no further questions.

"My client wishes to make a statement but I will reserve

that for my closing remarks," he added. Upon hearing Hatcher's announcement, Shaw told the judge he would base his decision on whether to forgo his right to any follow-up, on the contents of Nelson's statement. Rather than have counsels begin their final arguments , the judge announced that court would adjourn until ten a.m. the next morning.

That night in a downtown restaurant not far from the courthouse, Karin, Carsten and Shaw met to discuss their perceptions of the day's proceedings.

"I have my suspicions why Hatcher allowed Nelson to testify," Shaw admitted after they had ordered. "But talk about a plan backfiring."

"I was observing the faces of the jurors when he was on the stand," Carsten began. "I had the feeling not many were buying Nelson's story. Especially the women. What's he facing if he's found guilty?"

"It's a first offence so there will likely just be a fine. But it *will* go on his record. He will likely appeal a guilty verdict for that reason alone."

"I don't wish the man jail time, but I hope if it's a fine, it will at least smart," Karin said. "He's not suffering from too little money."

"You heard me detail the law. A fine is probably the most we can hope for. But we shouldn't assume the jury will find him guilty. A couple members looked uncertain and it will only take one vote to have a hung jury. If that were to occur, I doubt if it would be worth it to go for a retrial. So let's hope for the best," he added, raising bis glass in a toast."

Court was gavelled into session at precisely ten a.m.

"So, gentlemen," the judge addressed the two lawyers. "I presume you are prepared to present your closing arguments?"

"We are, your honour," the two replied in near unison.

"Mr Shaw, as you know, you're entitled to go first."

"Thank you, your honour," Shaw replied, moving to a position close to the jury box. "Ladies and gentlemen, you have heard the testimony of the witnesses. You've learned that Ms. Davison is a friendly person who engages with her patients. One can assume that for two people to feel comfortable sharing thoughts on various subjects, a certain degree of trust must be established. Up to the day in question, Ms. Davison had never had any reason to question Mr. Nelson's behaviour, which makes his actions that day all that more alarming, coming as unexpectedly as they did. She had trusted him and he violated that trust by an unprovoked assault. Mr. Nelson would have you believe that his hug and kisses were simply a spontaneous act. That he was sad the Practice was closing and merely wanted to express his gratitude for all the treatments he had received. That the 'gestures' were just 'his way' of doing so. One might have been inclined to accept such a story, had it not been for the subsequent phone call," Shaw said, pausing for effect. "As jurors you must ask yourselves several questions. First, what was the true motivation behind Mr. Nelson's actions at the Practice that morning. Second, why did he choose to adopt the more informal greeting of 'Gerald' when he placed the call, and third, why did he wait four days to, as he claimed, issue an apology? The answers to these questions are pretty clear. I'm sure some jurors have questioned why Ms. Davison failed to respond to Mr.Nelson's inappropriate kiss. She has told the court she had been shocked by what was happening and felt momentarily paralyzed. Psychologists will concur that the inability to react is a common reaction amongst many assault victims... Ladies and gentlemen, I submit that Mr. Nelson's actions were nothing less than part of a calculated plan. The phone call all but confirms that. Had Ms. Davison not foiled his plan by reading him the riot act, I'm fully convinced he would not have apologized, but in all likelihood, have issued a casual invitation for coffee or dinner. The man was indeed 'fishing'. It was only once he realized the jig was up, that he found it prudent to deliver a facsimile of an apology. What else could he do? It is your duty to not let Mr. Nelson's behaviour go unpunished. If you choose to find him innocent, he and others will have no reason to alter their behaviour. Think of the other women who might have to face the actions of a man like Mr. Nelson someday. Send a signal. Express your indignation. Find him guilty. The law as it stands, may not provide for a just sentence, but a guilty verdict will be a warning to him and others. It will also go a long way to convince lawmakers the law needs to be changed. Thank you."

As Shaw returned to the prosecution's table, he made sure to deliver a smile of confidence to Karin before sitting down.

Told the floor was now his, Hatcher wasted no time in walking to jury box, resting one hand on the railing.

"Ladies and gentlemen of the jury, once again in this somewhat tumultuous trial, I find myself agreeing with my honoured colleague. Not that Mr. Nelson deserves to be found guilty and punished for his alleged actions, but rather that the current law as it stands, needs to be altered. But ladies and gentlemen, this trial is not being conducted to determine a future law. This trial is about 'misinterpretation'. If one accepts the premise that friendliness can be interpreted in different ways, then one must also accept that friendly gestures of appreciation can also be interpreted differently," Hatcher said, moving away from the jury box. "Nobody has the right to invade another person's private sphere without their permission. Some of you may feel that Mr. Nelson needs to be rebuked for his behaviour. Such behaviour however, as disrespectful as some may view it, does not constitute a crime. Members of the jury, I could take the time to rehash elements of the testimony, and rebut arguments presented by my colleague. But rather than doing so, I wish to issue a formal statement on behalf of my client."

"Mr. Nelson, are you in agreement with Mr. Hatcher?" the judge asked the defendant. "Do you wish to issue a formal statement to this court?

"I do, your honour," Nelson answered firmly.

"Then please continue, Mr. Hatcher."

After removing a sheet of paper from the defence table, Hatcher turned to face the jury and began reading.

'*In light of all that has taken place, I now see that what was meant as a well-intentioned gesture may have been misguided. I deeply regret that my actions may have been taken the wrong way and would like to use this opportunity to issue a formal apologize, not only to Ms.Davison, but to this court as well. I swear I did not have any motives beyond expressing my appreciation.*' signed Gerald Nelson."

"Order," the judge demanded as a murmuring rattled around the courtroom. "Is that the extent of your closing remarks, Mr. Hatcher?"

"Your honour, as I said, I do not wish to prolong the proceedings, but there are a few points I would still like to make."

"The floor remains yours, Mr. Hatcher."

"Thank you your honour. Ladies and gentlemen of the jury, while some of you may consider Mr. Nelson guilty of moral turpitude, he is not a criminal. He has shown the courage to admit that he made a mistake. When considering your verdict, I urge you to take into account that Mr. Nelson has already been tried in the court of public opinion. Merely being accused of what some view as distasteful behaviour, has tarnished his reputation. If this case has taught him anything, it is to use one's judgement more carefully. I ask you to find my client, not guilty. Thank you."

Within seconds, Shaw was on his feet, moving directly to the jury box.

"Ladies and gentlemen, I have to give it to him. Mr. Nelson certainly has a knack for issuing timely apologies. Have you ever witnessed a more transparent ploy for sympathy and hence acquittal? I can't help but wonder whether Mr. Nelson and Mr. Hatcher might have saved us all a lot of time and trouble had they issued this so called 'apology' before this even came to trial. But don't be swayed by such a blatant tactic. Focus on the facts as they've been presented. When retiring to reach a verdict, you must ask yourself, why in this day and age does a woman have to come to court to defend her dignity and right to privacy? Who do these perpetrators think they are that they feel free to behave in such a manner and not be held to account? Women have the right to decide what is permissible with or without a supporting law. That moral stance needs to be upheld and finding the defendant guilty will go a long way to achieving that goal. I thank you."

Later that afternoon, after several hours of deliberation, the jury marched back into the courtroom and quietly took their respective seats. Asked by the judge if they had reached a verdict, the foreman stood and answered in the affirmative. Both Nelson and Karin sat with no expressions. The court clerk accepted the verdict from the foreman and dutifully handed it up to the judge. Donning a pair of reading glasses, he quickly scanned its contents before asking the defendant to stand before the foreman announced the jury's decision.

"We the jury find the defendant, Gerald Nelson, guilty as charged," he stated, to the sound of several muffled cheers and applause from the gallery.

"Order," the judge said. "Before I pass sentence, I would like to thank members of the jury for their patience and judgement. Given that this is a first offence," he continued, turning to the defendant. "And the fact you have expressed remorse and regret over your actions, I hereby levy a token fine of $50. In recognition however, that a boundary of decency was indeed overstepped, you will be required to issue a public apology. The case is now closed. Court is adjourned."

Once the judge had banged his gavel, Carsten rushed forward from the gallery to congratulate Karin, who then briefly embraced Shaw in a display of gratitude.

"What constitutes a public apology exactly?" she wanted

to know, as the courtroom slowly cleared. "Getting down on one knee in the public square?"

"Not quite," Shaw answered with a grin. "I suppose we could request that if they choose to appeal. But Mr. Nelson should be glad we don't live in 13th century England. Under the reign of Edward II, those found guilty of serious crimes such as rape, had their eyes gouged out and their testicles crushed."

"Ouch," Carsten groaned in jest. "I don't think we need to go quite that far. Why the eyes?"

"Because the eyes were seen as how desire entered. The testicles are self-explanatory. At any rate, seeing as the judge didn't specify anything, it will be up to the two parties to determine an acceptable method of apology. It's often in the form of a letter published in the newspaper. But as I said previously, I half suspect Hatcher will appeal that part of the sentence, arguing that Nelson's reputation has already been sullied by the charges and innuendo surrounding them. "

"Oh God," Karin sighed. "I do not want to go through all this again. It was gratifying enough to see him exposed before the community so I don't really need a public apology. The point has been made and hopefully a lesson learned. I don't know about you two, but I'm all up for a drink. We've earned it."

❋

Acknowledgements

My sincere thanks to Ingeborg & Ina Schmitt, and Janice Smith for taking the time and effort to review the stories and suggest changes. In their diligence they didn't go as far as revoking my poetic licence, but at least made me earn it, and for that I am grateful

Other books by the same author

Shards

A collection of six short stories.

An ill-fated Friendship

The Law and the Limo

The Bonds of a Breed

Falcon Summers

Karmaleon

Cairo

Life in the Raw Lane:
Nepal
The Gifts of a Glimpse

There are countries in the world
you may never get the chance to see. For
the longest time, Nepal was one such land.
Fascinating yet bewildering, frenetic as well as
soul-soothing, inspiring grandeur matched with
challenging misfortune are just a few of the paradoxes
of a country whose name immediately conjures up images
of Himalayan peaks, pagoda-style temples and the mysterious
city of Kathmandu. Less familiar perhaps, but nonetheless
applicable are encounters with wild rhinos, elephants and
crocodiles co-existing amidst tropical heat. Add in
Stupas, shrines, trekking tours with a slew of
foreign women, and a session with a
Shaman, and you have a few of the
adventures savoured during a
month long glimpse of the
mystical country.

Welcome to Nepal.

Loose Cargo

A collection of stories that couldn't have less to do with one another.

America Calling

It's 1969. Two dudes. Two trips. Too much, man.
The lure of the open road, the bright lights of Vegas &
LA, the beauty of southwest America, a glimpse of
Mexico and several brushes with the law, are just a few
of the adventures that make for a fortnight of fun and
furor, south of the border.

Meeting Lisa

After a gap of twenty years, Chris and Lisa run into each
other at a garage sale; a brief encounter that results in
an unexpectedly candid journey down memory lane
brimming with "what if's and if only's." A funny,
poignant, and painful tale, that reveals how both men
and women can be predatory, conniving, fun-loving
creatures.

The Future of Death

Despite decades of disinterest, denial and dread, an
encounter with one's own mortality is inevitable. The
question at hand is whether it is desirable or feasible to
encourage people to be more genuine about their
mortality, before they are abruptly confronted with
what is fundamentally already a "fait d'accompli."

Careening thru Cambodia

The difference between a vacation and an adventure

For no particular reason, Cambodia had never made it on to my list of potential travel destinations. That all changed in late 2010 when as part of a film crew, I spent two intense weeks in the country, filming the exploits of a man involved in the removal of land mines. Despite my limited exposure to people and places, it was enough to enthral me; so much so that once back home, it was impossible to dismiss the idea of returning. Six weeks later, I was back for a three-week tour, solo.

For those who've had the pleasure, a twisted tour down memory lane. For those who've yet to venture to Cambodia, a fascinating and frenzied run through a culture so foreign, you can hardly imagine it exists.

Episodes from a 20 Year Vacation

"Why squander your life away in your own hometown, when you can do it in London, Paris and Rome?"

Eight months after landing what many had considered to be a plum job with the Federal government, Fred Z. suddenly realizes that his safe and secure position is rapidly luring him towards an insufficient destiny. Abandoning his home and native land, Fred heads for Europe, only to be faced with the even greater challenges of a new language, new culture and a new life. After six months spent exploring the continent and a year-long respite in Cornwall, he returns to Germany and is immediately thrust into an array of lurid, sublime and downright ridiculous situations in the on-going struggle to establish himself as a freelance cameraman. Plagued by uncertainty whether he's made the right decision, it's through a chance meeting with a fellow North American that the doors to real opportunity fling wide open. From that point on, whether it's dog sledding in the Yukon, getting mugged in Naples, removing land mines in Cambodia, tracking Dracula in Romania, interviewing Hitler's telephone operator in Berlin, chasing cheetahs in Vienna, flying in a Black Hawk over Bosnia, or replacing a cancerous esophagus in Hamburg, to name just a few, all play a part in providing for eclectic glimpses of just how the world works, laying the groundwork for what would become a twenty year vacation.

Höttlland Part II

A Life after Deaths

"He was a very dangerous person… He only looked out for his own advantage. He was very crafty and impenetrable. You couldn't pin anything on him. But he was a swindler nonetheless." Edith Frischmuth (former member of the Austrian Resistance)

Unlike many Nazi colleagues whose careers finished at the end of a rope or in exile, the former Austrian SS officer and SD operative returns to Austria in late 1947, ready to embark on a series of equally opaque activities. Taking advantage of the rivalry created by the growing Cold War, Höttl resumes plying his wares, initially with the American Counter Intelligence Agency (CIC), and German based Organization Gehlen, and later with whomever happened to show interest. Eventually outed as a dubious source and cast back into the cold, he returns to his academic roots, founding a school and assuming its directorship, while managing to publish three stylized versions of his wartime recollections. Despite suspected involvement in the 'Ratlines', a mechanism set up to aid Nazi fugitives flee to safer havens, entanglement in a Soviet-American spy scandal, a death sentence handed down by a Hungarian court, and numerous demands to testify at the trials of former colleagues, including that of Adolf Eichmann, Höttl nevertheless slithers through the jaws of justice to emerge as a 'qualified Zeitzeuge', catering to an enduring media circus willing to pay for his flawed reflections right up until his final breath.

Höttlland

How and why an educated man became and remained a Nazi

Why them? Why there? What caused a nation of 'Dichter und Denker' to be transformed into one of 'Richter und Henker'?

Höttlland attempts to answer those questions by examining the life and times of Wilhelm Georg Höttl, a former high-ranking member of the Austrian SS. The trail begins in Vienna in 1915, moving up through a culture of envy, past people and events that influenced a young man to make a fateful leap aboard the Nazi bandwagon at the age of 19. Tracing his rapid advance within the 'seething ranks' of the SS, which saw him emerge as a heeded advisor in the SD intelligence apparatus at 24, Höttlland documents Höttl's involvement in various wartime intrigues that included everything from a counterfeiting operation, the kidnapping of Mussolini, the rescue of Hitler's art treasure, and the occupation of Hungary, to name just a few. With priorities shifting in late 1944, the book follows Höttl as he dons the mantel of peacemaker to confer with American officials about a separate peace and the sabotaging of the much feared 'Alpenfestung'. Arrested at war's end, Höttl diligently polishes his past to salvage a future, evading post-war justice by supplying interrogators at Nuremberg with detailed information on the inner workings of the Nazi intelligence apparatus, portions of which later help incriminate such former colleagues as Ernst Kaltenbrunner and Adolf Eichmann. Part I concludes as Höttl resurfaces in Austria in late 1947, ready to resume plying his wares with various agencies clamouring for intelligence under the gathering clouds of the Cold War.